The White Boy Confessions

The Explosive Story of
Marcus Valdespino
& San Antonio's Hood

Marcus Valdespino

13-digit ISBN 978-1-939521-09-5
10-digit ISBN 1-9395210-9-2

This book is dedicated to all the homies I met in the cause of human struggle and freedom, not freedom from bondage, but freedom of their minds to do the right thing. This book is also dedicated to the people of San AntonioTexas. This is the greatest city in the United States to settle down and have a family. San Antonians are the most hospitable people. They will give you the shirt off their backs, no matter your race, color, or creed.

And finally, this book is dedicated in loving memory of the following people: Vincent James Valdespino,Henry Valdespino, Mary E. Nious Wilson,Alice Hayes (Aunt Doll), Otilia Lucia, Frazer Canestaro (Aunt Tillie), Edward "ED" Frazer,Raul Tomas Cervantes Jr., Rose Marie Bailey,

Ronald Rene Green, Andrew Ashwood (Gorilla), John F. McClendon, David Johnson, WillieHeights, Della Kyle (Mama), MeshionMathis - Larry Williams (son) and Adrian Hilliard (R.I.P).

CHAPTER ONE

PARENTS?

I AM ABOUT to tell you a story of crime, drugs, poverty, interracial violence, and the nightmares of ghetto life, and give you an inside look at the life of young gang members in a small, unsuspected neighborhood of Texas. Most of the characters are now in the penitentiary, dead or their whereabouts are unknown. A few, but very few, remain free men, and I number among this very small group. How I made it out alive, I still question to this day, and how I kept out of the penitentiary is due in part to my family, my own wits, and a good bit of luck. I lived through twelve years of the most harrowing existence, dodging Feds, beating people down that crossed us and running a small drug empire that nearly got me killed more times than I can remember, but to understand this story, you must first understand where I began.

I was born December 17, 1972, to Patricia Amick and Joseph Mark Valdespino. My mother is Caucasian and my father is Hispanic. Because of my light complexion, most people identified me as white. I was not my mother's first child. She had a daughter a few years before me. She was too young and not ready for a child, so she had to give her up for adoption. My understanding is that she is with a nice family in Corpus Christi, Texas. I almost died of spinal meningitis when I was 3 months old. It was so serious that my grandmother gave me my last rights from the Bible. That was the first of many life and death situations I was to survive. I knew at an early age that my mother loved me very much. A child can sense when he or she is not loved, and usually feels neglected in these instances. This was not the case with me. I felt the love of my parents in our household.

The problem with my mother is that she was easily influenced and still exhibited a great deal of child-like behavior. My parents were not very mature when I was born. I don't know why they had me or what intentions they had about my future or about raising a child, in general. At an extremely young age, I had a warped view of the world. My father sold marijuana and cocaine, and worked with the Mexican Mafia. This crazy lifestyle garnered my father lots of cash, and he slept with lots of women. My mother, who was not the sharpest tool in the shed, slept with lots of men. What an existence for me, to be brought into this world under these terms. It didn't seem like it could get much worse until my father brought these two guys into our house in 1975, named Buck and Nick.

These two men were destitute, and my father's thinking was, hey, I'll bring them in and put them to work in my growing operation. They were a father and son team. Buck was in his fifties and Nick was his seventeen year-old son. After a few weeks of staying with us, Buck and Nick saw how lucrative this situation was to them. They were making decent money, got free meals and a place to stay. They say that money is the root of all evil, but usually, it is greed and the temptation to steal money that is the root.

Nick and Buck started by skimming money from my father on different drug deals. When people see easy money from drugs, their minds wander from being grateful to being greedy in a hurry, and sometimes they figure that that money that comes easily or is gained illegally doesn't rightfully belong to anyone really. Whatever their motivation was, it began to happen. When lots of money flows in, you have situations like, "Hey, Mark. Here's $18,000 we made today. No, maybe we made $14,000.", and they'd pocket the other four that wasn't theirs. To make matters worse, my mother made a conscious decision to get sexually involved with the seventeen year-old, Nick.

Before my father could put two and two together and figure out the missing money and sexual liaison my mother was having with a teenager, Buck and Nick and my mother took off together. My father figured out that these two idiots stole thousands of dollars from him, and worst of all, his wife. My father, at this point, should have just cut his losses and let them go, but that's not what men do when they're in love and have been hurt in their heart. Also, from what I've heard, my father was a pretty bad hothead. He wasn't about to let this happen.

So there is my father, after he figures where they're at, off to the Southside to retrieve my mother. These two guys know how my father is, and he has connections with the Mexican Mafia and he's always packing a gun. They know my father doesn't play around. As my father gets to the door, Buck comes out with a shotgun and without any warning or hesitation, shoots my father right in the stomach. Buck left my father to die right there, holding his guts together. I asked my father in later years, "What does it feel like to be shot?" He said, "If you fry up a load of grease for a while til it gets real hot and boils, then you splash that hot grease on your mid-section. Then, turn the pan over, press it hard on your stomach to let the burning and the pain set in. That's what it was like."

I thought to myself, wow, that would suck, and all for what, to get back this mindless woman, but she was the mother of his first born child. Buck disappeared a few days later. We never heard from Nick again, and my mother returned home. My father never told me that he had anything done to them, but he had friends that were good at those kinds of things.

I didn't have a very good depiction of women growing up. My parents let me watch Stanley Kubrick's "A Clockwork Orange" when I was four years old. I remember thinking, wow, that's how you get a girl? You have to snatch her, and lay on top of her until she quits fighting you. Then, you can do whatever you want?

My father and mother were heavily into the drug trade, and this must have been one night my father was away on business. I went to the drive-in with my mother and some guy I didn't know. I watched him kiss my mother, and they told me to just watch the movie. After the movie, we went back to some apartment complex, where I guess he lived. I pretended to be asleep because I was very intrigued about what my mother was doing and what she was going to do. When we parked, their conversation was about what to do with me. Do we carry him up or leave him in the car? They chose the latter. That's one of the worst feelings in the world, knowing your mother, who is supposed to be with your father, is going up to some strange man's apartment. Your mother, your rock and foundation, is cheating on your dad and neglecting you at the same time.

Anything could have happened to me in or out of that car, parked outside of that apartment complex. My mother chose her pleasure over my safety. After about maybe thirty minutes, I started to cry and try to get out. I knew it was real late at night because I looked out the window and noticed it was very dark and all the cars were in the parking lot, in for the night. They wouldn't be turned on again until the morning. That was the perspective of a four year-old. Even I knew that most people were already in bed with their families, getting rest so they could go to work or school the next day, but not my family. My mom was in an apartment having sex with some strange man.

My father was not around and here I was, a four year-old sitting in a car, crying, in the middle of the night, hoping that someone would come and help me. I don't remember if it was a security guard or a regular guy just walking around the area, but when I saw him pass by, I started banging on the window to get his attention. At the time, that was a risky proposition, but I didn't know that because I was just four years old. I didn't know the guy at all.

I could have ended up like John Gosch, Etan Patz, or Adam Walsh. I hope those children are playing in heaven somewhere. As bad as my childhood was, they weren't as fortunate as I was. I unlocked the door for him, and he said, "Hey, little guy. Are you okay? Where are your parents?" I started to cry, and he bent down and took my hand and said, "It's gonna be alright." Just then, my mother came running up and said, "Oh, my baby, are you alright?"

I embraced my mother. I was glad to see her, even though she left me. The guy started having words with my mother and the guy that my mother went to the apartment with. He let them know that this could have been a bad situation, and he could call the police. My mother and her friend convinced him not to call the police, and he left. In today's society, the police would have come out and Child Protective Services would have been called, and I might have ended up in a foster home even if my grandparents tried to come get me, but this was 1977. People still left houses and cars unlocked. I could have told my Dad what happened when I saw him, but like any four year-old, I wanted my parents to stay together, and besides, it would have made the situation worse. He would have just beat the hell outta her, and they still would have stayed together, so how would it have helped?

CHAPTER TWO

STRIPPERS AND ALIENS

A **FEW DAYS** later, my mother and father and I got into my father's brand new, blue Mercury Cougar and went for a ride. I remember crossing over the New Braunfels Bridge on the Eastside of San Antonio listening to Boz Skaggs, "Dirty Lowdown". The Eastside of San Antonio is predominately a black side of town. My father took a right on Hays St. (I know this now because I have travelled down these streets many times as an adult and I know them like the back of my hand) and pulled up into a driveway. When we pulled into the driveway, my father got out of the car and said, "I'll be right back" and my mother and I started looking around. My mom said, "Look, Marcus. They're looking at us like we're aliens." When she said that, I looked out the window and noticed people had stopped mowing their lawns, and then I looked on the other side and they were just staring at us. I said, "Yeah, Mom, they're looking at us like we're aliens." My mother started laughing, and said, "They're looking at us like we don't belong here," and as soon as she said that, I saw a couple of ladies get off their front porches to have a better look at us. Within a few minutes, my father got back in the car. My mother told him they were staring at us. My father said, "What did you expect? It's not too often a white family comes in the neighborhood in a brand new car. Let's get the fuck out of here," as he was laughing.

About fifteen minutes later, my parents were arguing about something I didn't understand. My father pulled up to a Wendy's and gave me five dollars and said, "Get yourself something to eat. We'll be here waiting." I was real sharp with money at such a young age, and I was very happy my dad gave me the responsibility to go in and get my own food. I came back with my kid's meal, and I noticed my mother with her head down and she was sobbing. When she looked up, I saw blood running down her nose, and figured out pretty quickly that my dad just hit her. I said to my father right away, "Daddy, why did you hit Mommy?" My mother answered, "Because he is an asshole!" He replied, "Shut up! Because she is fuckin stupid! That's why!" That was an eye opener, but at the same time, I wasn't disturbed by it. I thought that's what men did. They have full control of their woman. I started eating my french fries, as we drove away.

A few weeks later, I woke up in the middle of the night to the sounds of loud music being played. I got out of my bed and opened my door, and saw a party going on. There were people everywhere having a good time, laughing and dancing. I also noticed something no 5 year-old should know. I saw some of the people holding bongs. I knew it was a device to help get yourself high since I had watched some Cheech and Chong movies. As I started walking around, a couple of cute, white girls came to me as if I was in need of aid. "Oh, honey. What are you doing awake? Let's get you back to bed." The other one said, "Get Patty. Tell her we're gonna take her son back to bed." They took me to my room and tucked me in. My mother came running in there and said, "You alright, my baby?" I told her, "Yeah, Mom. I'm okay." She said, "Go back to bed, honey." She asked her two friends, "Isn't he cute?" They both responded, "He is so adorable." They left my room, and I remember thinking, "What they were doing out there wasn't good." I didn't know it was against the law, but I knew it wasn't normal. Along with watching"A Clockwork Orange" and Cheech and Chong movies, I mixed in a few episodes of Brady Bunch and Leave it To Beaver, but I knew this kind of stuff wasn't happening at our house. My parents could have written a "How To" book on "How Not To... Raise a Child". Instead of Roger Staubach and Tony Dorsett on my wall, I had a huge poster of the Dallas Cowboy Cheerleaders, blondes, brunettes, redheads, long legs, huge tits, short shorts and small tops. I'm four, maybe five years old. What the fuck is a kid my age doing with a poster of the Dallas Cowboy Cheerleaders on his wall.

My father ran a business called A TrippleA Building and Maintenance as a cover for his drug trade. One of the main places Tripple A serviced was the Wet and Wild Strip Club on Main St. Some guy named Scott was the owner of the Wet and Wild. My dad took me there all the time. Two of the strippers named Debbie and Donna took a real liking to me. I used to see girls with their tops off all the time. It was normal. One night after everyone left, Debbie and Donna took me on stage and let me dance with them. I learned that women were just sexual objects. They were there for men's pleasure, and nothing more. The shit that I was exposed to was simply mind-boggling, but it was all about to come to a "screeching halt" as they say, and come crashing down on my parents. None of us would ever fully recover.

CHAPTER THREE

THE INEVITABLE

TOMMY AMICK WAS my mom's brother, a college kid who liked to hang around my parents and do what a lot of people did in 1977, get high. Tommy and my mother had a mutual friend named Jack from Uvalde who would score cocaine and marijuana from my dad. The San Antonio Police Department were trying as hard as they could to get to my father. They figured Jack was a likely candidate to infiltrate my father's operation. SAPD followed Jack one day, cornered him, then took him in for questioning. To Jack's credit, he didn't say shit to the police at first, but when you start to get your ass whooped, your mind begins to change. The cop's plan was to send Jack back in to get some hard evidence on my mother and father. The next day, my mother heard loud knocks, lots of banging on the front door. My father was in his room watching a game. I was in my room playing. My mother answered the door. What do you know? It's Jack from Uvalde and some girl nobody has ever seen before. Patty says, "Hey Jack. How are you doing? Come on in. And who's this lovely lady?"

My mom greets them gleefully. To her, everything is a good time. She's a joyful soul. To her, this is just another party. Jack said quickly, "Hey, Patty. This is Stacey. She's my new girlfriend. I didn't wanna tell y'all about her until it was official. No more foolin' around for me." Patty smiled. "You must be special to tame Jack. I've never heard him say that." Stacey extended her hand to Patty. "Well, Patty, it's nice to meet you. I've heard so much about you and your husband and your son, from Jack. I feel like I'm part of the family." "Well, let me take your coats. Make yourself at home." "That's okay, Patty. I get a little cold sometimes," said Stacey. "Jack?" Jack handed Patty his coat. Patty said, "I was just about to light up. Y'all want some? Jack knows how we get down over here. Ha, ha, ha." Jack said, "Now there's a lady who knows how to greet company

As my mom lights up, Jack, looking a bit nervous, begins to look at my Mom, waiting his turn to take a hit. Stacey says, "You're not afraid of your son walking in, Patty?" "No, he's in his room. Plus, he's seen all this before. And he wouldn't know what's going on." Jack takes a puff, then passes it to Stacey. Still looking nervous, without great surprise, my mother is oblivious to the fact that one of Jack's eyes is darker than the other. He is developing a black eye, and has a cut on his lip. There is silence for about a minute as the marijuana begins to set in, and their systems begin to absorb the smoke and the THC. Then Jack bursts out, "Hey, Patty. Where's the blow? I need a little something to tickle the nose," as he brushed his thumb across his nose. Stacey says, "Jack, you're so crazy. Don't tell Patty like that." Patty said, "It's ok, honey. I've got just the cure to help Jack out."

My mom leaves the room. As she turns her back, Stacey and Jack look at each other like, holy shit! We're doing this. My mother came out with a bag of cocaine and poured it onto a metal tray. Jack started getting lines ready and proceeded to snort one of them. My father comes out of the bedroom with a puzzled look on his face, and notices the injuries to Jack's face. More important than that, he notices the new girl, Stacey, in his living room. Jack looks up after doing a line and says, "Hey, Mark. Have a seat. We were just getting acquainted with my new girlfriend, Stacey."

My father quickly responds, "If she is your girlfriend, why are you just getting acquainted with her?" Jack nervously replies, "Oh, well, Mark. You know what I mean. I meant that…" Stacey cuts him off and jumps in, saying, "Hi, Mark. I'm Stacey." Mark said, "Yeah, I've heard, Patty. Can I talk to you for a minute?" Patty says, "Sure, honey. I'll be in there in a second." Mark replied, "No. I mean now," he answered back impatiently and with a slight tone of anger brewing within him.

As my mom and dad go in the back room, Stacey looks at Jack, annoyed and says, "Jesus Christ! You sure aren't getting an Academy Award any time soon." Jack looked at her and said, "You think he noticed?" Ignoring his rhetorical question, she says "Oh, my god. Your eye looks worse than it did before we came in here," with a worried and agitated look on her face. My father and mother are still in the other room, and my father tells her, "Why the fuck would you let someone in our house that we've never seen before, and on top of that, give 'em coke? She looks like a goddamned banker! Or a fuckin' narc." Patty said, "Oh, Mark. It's okay. It's Jack. You know, Jack. And it's just his new girlfriend, Stacey. She seems nice. Don't be a big party pooper."

My dad just glares at her, completely astonished. "I don't think he even knows if that's his fucking girlfriend. Did you hear what he said when I asked him why they would be getting acquainted if that's his fuckin' girlfriend? You don't think there's anything suspicious about her, or about the fucking black eye on Jack. Looks like somebody worked him over. You gotta be fucking kidding. That's why I don't ever trust you with a goddamn thing. You're a fucking idiot! Get them the fuck out of my house, because if I have to do it, it's not gonna be nice." Patty said "Ok, ok, honey. I'll get it." As my Mom comes back in the living room, Jack has already found his coat and they are standing in the living room, waiting for Patty. Patty enters and begins. "I'm sorry. Mark is in a pissy mood, as usual. We'll have to do this another time."

Stacey quickly replies, "That's ok, Patty. I understand. We need to go visit my mom, anyway. Thanks for your hospitality. Sorry I didn't get a chance to meet your son, but we will definitely do this again. Tell Mark I said bye. I'll see him tomorrow." "Thanks," said Jack. "See y'all later," my mom replied. As she escorted them to the door and closed it, she turned to face the wrath of my father from whom she never knew what to expect. He might forget about it cause he was watching sports, or she might get her ass beat. She couldn't be sure. When coke and money and the prospect of getting busted catch up with you and fuck with your mind, no telling what you will do. I would understand this eventually.

The funny thing about this whole exchange with Jack and Stacey and my mother was that all that, "We'll see you tomorrow" crap and "We'll get together soon and do this again soon" bullshit is just that. Bullshit. And everyone in the room knew it, except my mother. She just thought she made a new friend, someone to hang out with, that she could talk to and get high with. That was her in a nutshell, serving cocaine to some woman whom she had never met before in her life like it was fucking cookies and milk, at her own house where her son would sleep in his little room with his comic books and his toys, and his huge poster of the

Dallas Cowboy Cheerleaders that his parents had plastered on his wall. Un-fuckin-believable!

The next day, Jack gave up my mom and dad and my mom's brother, Tommy. The undercover(aka, Stacey, Jack's "girlfriend") saw everything she needed to see. That day, our door was kicked in and police were everywhere throughout my house, turning over tables and going through kitchen cabinets. I'm sure even my toy box was under suspicion. I remember hearing yelling and screaming. I came out of my room and saw my mom and dad in handcuffs, being dragged out of the house. My mom was handcuffed in the front. They don't do that procedure anymore.

Today, everyone is handcuffed in the back, but you have to remember that this was 1977. They took us all downtown to book my parents. I was taken in a separate vehicle. I knew my parents were doing something wrong, but I didn't know it was criminal. When my parents were being booked, there were some female officers there who were trying to cheer me up by playing with me. They were also telling me how cute I was, and I remember thinking, "You just took my parents away from me! Don't talk to me about being cute!" but in actuality, it was my parents who took themselves away.

My father thought that he had gotten all the drugs out of the house, but once again, my mom still had a stash of marijuana and cocaine with her, and the cops found that. The best thing she did for him was to take the rap for that bust. He claims that it was her stash anyway, and that it was no great noble gesture on her part, but I was told recently by a relative who looked at the arrest record from that day on July the 5th, 1977, that my father was charged with cocaine possession(and when I looked at the archived record from the San Antonio Light newspaper from that day, I discovered that my father had a whole stash of drugs of his own that got seized that day. My mother might have taken the rap for that bust, but it was not for her small, personal stash of drugs only.

The cops discovered more than $8000 worth of marijuana—adjust that for inflation from 1977 to today, and a large bag of cocaine and cash, enough to put my father behind bars for some time, but if it was my mother's first offense, it would make sense that she would take the rap).

`About an hour later, I finally saw a familiar face, and I was very happy about that. My uncle, Edward Valdespino, better known as Uncle Spunk, came to get me. I remember asking him, "Is my Daddy a bad man?" And he said, "Sometimes good people can do the wrong thing." He and his girlfriend, Diane, took me to see what would become one of my favorite movies, "Sinbad and the Eye of the Tiger". I felt much better. It was probably the first time in my life that I realized that movies could make you feel better, that they could transport you away from the reality from which you wanted to escape.

A few days later, I was reunited with my parents, but it would only be for two more years. I woke up one night and saw my father yelling at my mother and wrapping the telephone cord around her throat because she was saying she was gonna call the cops, to which he responded, "If I go down, you go down with me!" They yelled at me to go back to bed.

In 1980, I was adopted by my grandparents, Joe and Gloria Valdespino, my father's parents. They were in their 50s, quickly approaching 60, and they did their best to raise a child at this age after raising ten children already. My dad was born in 1948, and my grandparents had nine more children from then until 1967.

My uncles and aunts, who legally became my brothers and sisters were very intelligent and successful people. There are three attorneys, an Air Force Colonel, a columnist for the Orange County Register, a real estate broker, and a teacher. They have attended schools like Stanford, Michigan, NYU, Wellesley, Tulane, Boston College, SMU, the University of Texas at Austin and other distinguished institutions of higher learning. They each have bachelor's degrees, and among them are more than half a dozen master's degrees and three law degrees. I got most of my intelligence from my grandmother who is, to this day, the best woman I've ever known in my life.

I never blamed or will ever blame my grandparents for anything that happened to me. They are, to this day, good-hearted, generous hard-working people who raised eleven children and sacrificed much of themselves to do so. I ended up making my own choices, many of which I regret. If anyone had an impact on me from my childhood, it was my real(biological) father and mother. Despite my wonderful grandparents, my path was very different from the rest of my family. In the early years, I went to private Catholic schools like they did, but as my education progressed, I went to various public schools and lost interest in school in general. Much of what I have learned in life after my years in high school has stemmed from a process of self-education in which I have read books, magazines, and newspapers. I am a newspaper, political and sports television and radio junkie. I read newspapers avidly and am extremely interested in non-fiction. This has been my education.

When I was eight years old, something happened to me. I was molested a couple of times by someone I thought was one of my friends. He was a neighbor named Johnny Holguin, who was a few years older than me and my friends. He preyed upon my interest in girls and my naivete about how to be with them. Me and a couple of the other neighborhood kids, including his little brother, Chris Holguin, used to talk about what women we wish we could fuck. I loved Thelma from the TV show Good Times and Daisy Duke from Dukes of Hazzard.

It's hard to understand that eight year old boys would already be obsessed with sex and talking about the women we fantasized about, but for me, especially, this was something very real. I had grown up with the pictures of the Dallas Cowboy Cheerleaders on my wall, going into strip clubs with my father when I was four or five years old and seeing topless women everywhere, watching women being raped and brutalized in Stanley Kubrick's "A Clockwork Orange", but not really understanding sex at all cause I was really too young to understand it. Johnny Holguin was a young predator who understood this about me and his little brother and the other neighborhood kids he might molest. He would get away with it by telling us that if we didn't practice sex, girls wouldn't like us, and we would never be able to have sex with them. When he got me by myself, he used to take me to the back of my grandparent's house, outside in a secluded area, bend me over and put his penis inside me. He did this with the other kids too. He used our innocence and naivete and our fascination with girls to convince us, and we bought it, hook, line and sinker. Many years later, my brother, Martin, who was a real estate agent, was doing research on a particular area of San Antonio and came across information about Johnny Holguin. He told me Johnny Holguin was on the sexual predator list. He was very surprised. I told him I wasn't surprised at all and for the first time, I finally told someone in my family the real story.

My father went on to turn his life around, and got a degree from St. Mary's University. He went into the hotel business and became a General Manager. To this day, I don't have a true relationship with my mother. She went on to start a new family and had three sons. Good luck with that, Mom! Maybe you will do better this time.

I can never know for certain how my life could have been different. If my parents had been different, if they hadn't been dealing drugs or getting busted, or letting me see twisted, violent films at an early age, or cheating on each other and indulging in sex and drugs right in front of me, I'm not sure how my life would have turned out. I know my life has been altered. The question is for better or for worse. Sometimes, children don't recover from shit like this.

CHAPTER FOUR

SEAN ELLIOTT (NBA ALL-STAR)

WHEN I WAS about 16 years old, my favorite sport turned from football to basketball even though I loved them both. My favorite college basketball player was Sean Elliott, from about 1987, when he was a sophomore at Arizona. I tried to watch all the Arizona games. Some of my favorite Sean Elliott games were when he went up against Duke and Danny Ferry. By the end of the game, Ferry ended up with 24 points and 10 rebounds and Elliott had 21 points and 8 rebounds. I thought after that game, clearly the better player was Sean Elliott. The Greatest player ever to lace 'em up, Michael Jordan said, "If I had to pay to watch a college player it would be Sean Elliott". Another one of my favorite games is when Sean destroyed Stacey Augmon and UNLV and Dick Vitale said, "Sean is the best player since Jordan." My favorite Sean Elliott game, however, is an Arizona loss. When Sean was a Junior in 1988, he took his team to the Final Four and lost to Oklahoma. Sean was unstoppable and had 31 points. One of the reasons

Arizona lost? Look at the box score and see Steve Kerr's stat line. His shooting was horrible.

So when my favorite team, the San Antonio Spurs, drafted Sean Elliott with the 3rd overall pick in the June 1989 NBA Draft, I was overjoyed. I had to go meet my favorite player. I found out the next day when he was going to make an appearance. It was at Blossom Athletic Center. There wasn't that much fanfare back then. You could never do this today, but I walked right up to him and started talking to him. I told him how he was my favorite player. I told him that I could shoot the ball really well and part of that was from watching him shoot. I told him about specific games I watched. I even told him about shaving his head before the big UCLA game. He looked at me and said," Man you know a lot about me. You are one of my biggest fans." I was scared to bring the subject up to him about being one of the last ones cut from the Olympic Team in 1988. I was still pissed off about his dismissal from that team.

That was a sore subject with me. I couldn't imagine how much it probably bothered Sean. We developed a friendship right off the bat. A few weeks later, I was at Blossom Athletic Center. Sean and I were shooting around. I think he was surprised about how well I could shoot the basketball. I'm sure people tell him all the time that they can do this and do that and really can't do any of it. I'm glad he found out that I'm not a phony.

I asked Sean if we could play my favorite game, Horse. It's a shooting game where you make a basket from a certain spot on the court and then your opponent has to make the same shot or he or she gets a letter. If you end up with 5 letters that spell Horse you lose. Sean agreed to play me. You would think a 16 year-old would be nervous to shoot it out with an NBA player, his favorite player no less. But I wasn't. I was overflowing with confidence in my ability to shoot the basketball.

After about twenty minutes, Sean had H-O-R and I had H-O. Just then, a rookie trying out for the Spurs passed by, named Jens Gordon. He started shooting where we were playing and Sean motioned for him to move. Jens had a look on his face like, "Oh Lord Sean, you're playing a kid." Then Vernon Maxwell, another rookie passed by and yelled out loud, "UH! OH! Sean, you can't lose to no kid!" Sean didn't want to hear it. He didn't respond and kept shooting. The funny thing is, listening to Vernon, I got more confident and started to talk while Sean was in the motion of shooting.

I yelled, "Sean you can't lose to me. You're my idol," as he missed. I know that pissed him off a little. I finally won, I had H-O-R, and he had H-O-R-S-E. About 5 minutes after that, I asked him to play me a game of one-on-one up to 15. I knew I would lose. I just wanted to see where I was at, in terms of my game. As he started to guard me I told him," Don't take it easy on me. Play me like I'm John Stockton." He said, "Okay." After about five minutes, I realized it was the hardest game of one-on-one I have ever played in my life and that includes any game that I have ever played since. I got destroyed 15 to1, and the only one basket I made was the proudest basket I ever made in my life, a step back jumper after I faked a drive.

A couple of weeks later, Sean was doing a radio show appearance for WOAI with the voice of the Spurs Jay Howard at Tony Roma's, A Place for Ribs. After the event, I introduced my homeboy Lester Kyle (Puka) to Sean and he gave us 20 dollars to eat at Fuddrucker's next door. He asked Elva Barnett, his girlfriend at the time, "Elva give me that 20 that's down there on the floor." Elva reached down and she pulled out a twenty dollar bill from the passenger floor of the car and handed it to Sean and he gave it to me. I would go watch some Spurs practices at the Convention Center, and especially the shootarounds on game day. It was a joy to watch the coach of the Spurs, Larry Brown, teach. Sometimes he would frustrate the players because he would stop the flow of practice to critique everything he saw that he thought was wrong. During shootarounds on game day, it was fun to watch Coach tell the players where to go on the court. I saw him get frustrated with a few players more than once. I thought that one of them would be traded before tip-off.

I learned a lot of basketball, watching Coach Larry Brown. I learned a lot by watching coach R.C. Buford show NBA players, Pete Myers and Vernon Maxwell, how to set up, coming off screens and using the correct foot work. Regular fans would be amazed at the detail of doing the little things to give yourself the best chance to win or be successful individually. Vernon was extremely confident. You would have thought he was an All-Star already. I also made a friend in the media, Tom Orsborn, who was covering the Spurs for the Express News, along with Glen Rogers. Tom introduced me to Kevin O'Keefe who wrote columns for the San Antonio Light. I would also see Buck Harvey, a writer for the San Antonio Light stand and watch shootarounds with a very serious look. I never got introduced to Buck Harvey and I'm sad for that. Buck was the best writer then, and flash forward today, he is still the best. You hear that great minds think alike. I would see things that happened in the Spurs and Cowboys games, and I would put deep thought into what I just witnessed and there have been about a hundred times where Buck would write about the same thing I had been thinking and had told one of my friends or my brother.

It was uncanny. I've never had that kind of coincidence happen to me on a consistent basis, especially regarding someone I did not know. I may have disagreed with Buck Harvey maybe 5 times in the 25 years on his column for the Light and the Express News. Tom Orsborn was the best though, out of all the media, coaches and players I met. He was a very humble, personable man who is still going strong, covering the dysfunctional Dallas Cowboys today. He taught me that this business is not as glamorous as it looks, getting to cover the teams.

The Spurs players were allowed two tickets to each game. I would sometimes sit with Elva, Sean's girlfriend for a couple of home games. One time Elva wasn't there and I sat with Sean's older brother Noel. I once told Noel Elliott that Sean's skill set is such that if he were 6'4 instead of 6'8 ½ he would still make it in the NBA as a two-guard, because he does everything very well. Noel looked at me and said, "Wow pretty good insight, you know your stuff." Sean dropped me off at my home after some practices and home games. One time, he dropped me off at my basketball practice at Edison High School and my teammates were amazed. Nobody could tell me shit at school after that. We talked about a lot of stuff, about how I got into fights sometimes at school and Sean replied "Yeah I got into my fair share of fights as well. Sometimes you can't just walk away. You have to stand up for yourself and fight."

We got along really well because I was not an awestruck fan. I acted like I'd been there before. I never asked him for an autograph .I think he respected that, especially because I was a little kid. I could have told Sean all about my dad selling drugs to __________, and that a couple of professional Basketball players used to argue about whose cocaine was better, my dad's or the other player's connection, or that my dad used to attend parties in

Alamo Heights and a couple of the white guys on a Professional Basketball team would get high from his marijuana, but I was worried if I said that, that would be an end to our friendship. I was thinking if I mentioned it, he would think I don't need to be around this kid anymore He might be trouble. I told Sean a lot of things about myself, but I didn't feel comfortable telling him about this. Even though it's not my fault my father sold drugs to

__________,

I didn't want to take that chance that he would no longer want to hang out with me. I had developed some small relationships with other Spurs as well. Greg (Cadillac) Anderson used to let me sit in his two allowed seats, as did the late Dallas Commegys. I sat with Dallas's friend Rhonda, who was really cool. Also, another Spurs player, Scott Roth, dropped me off at my house once. Scott Roth was a 6'7 small forward who could shoot lights out and who is currently an assistant coach with the Toronto Raptors. Once, Johnny Dawkins gave me his shoes and I gave them to my brother, Martin Valdespino. They were a size 10. They fit him perfectly and he wore them out.

The game right before the All-Star break was against the Indiana Pacers. I was sitting in Sean's seats as I had many times before and Sean had a bad game, especially at the free throw line where he missed 3 in a row. The Spurs lost the game. After the game, when he was driving me home I said," I have never seen you miss that many free throws in a game before." He replied with a surprised look on his face and said, "You know what? I can't remember missing that many free throws in a game before either." I said, "Don't worry about it, the next few days just get in the gym and practice." He replied very quickly, "Oh no. I'm not going to pick up a basketball for 5 days. I'm tired of basketball. I eat drink and sleep basketball. Sometimes it's good not to think about it." I thought, "Wow, ok let's change the subject." He dropped me off and I said,"Alright Sean, See you in a week." He responded, "Alright Marcus, take care."

Later on in the year, I took my friend from school, Tullie, to meet Sean and I asked Sean if he could help Tullie with his game. Sean responded," I'll see what I can do." It didn't seem like he wanted to. I wasn't mad at him for not doing it. Like I said before, he was a busy NBA player and we were just kids. Sean and I maintained a cordial relationship until he was traded to Detroit in 1993. After that I only talked to him 3 times, once in 1996, 1997 and 1999. Sean Elliott will always be my favorite basketball player.

CHAPTER FIVE

A THUG IS BORN

THE ANTICIPATION WAS brewing that day. All Tullie(Tool-ee) and I could talk about that day was either basketball, which was our most common interest, or the club. The club, what a place. It was magical in my eyes. I had not been to too many clubs, but I knew the two main objectives. One was to see beautiful women and two, was to get phone numbers. This was the end of 1989. We had pagers, not cell phones. We had to actually get the girl to take the time out to write her number down. I had only known Tullie(pronounced Tool-ee), whose real name is Lawrence Bailey) for about 4 months up to this point. He was the coolest fourteen year-old I've ever met in my life because he acted above his age. He had an old soul, as did I.

We clicked right away, for our love of basketball and football. We played a lot of 2 on 2 basketball at Kenwood or around San Antonio, in which, we won most of those games. Tullie, at the time, was a freshman at Edison High School. He had just turned 15 years old. He was 6 foot 4 and 190 pounds. I was 16 years old,

5'10" and a sophomore at Edison H.S. and about 170 pounds, and I could shoot the lights out in basketball! I used to sell programs at Spurs games at the Hemisfair Arena. About three hours after every game, the place would clear out except for the cleaning crew and there I was shooting 3 pointer after 3 pointer at the same spot where I had seen Danny Ainge, Byron Scott, and Jon Sundvold shoot their 3 pointers, night after night.

Tullie and I were trying to figure out how we were going to get to the club. Earlier that day, I had Lester Kyle, aka Puka, but he declined because he was going to a party. Four other girls were going to the club from school: Latonya Kyle, Tarsha Kyle, Jackee Coleman, and Gloria Shelton, aka Shawn. Latonya is Lester's little sister, who is fine as she wants to be. She had a beautiful shape. Tarsha is Lester's cousin, who was tall, dark and thick. Jackee was short in stature, but real thick. Shawn's main attraction was that she had a big chest and Tullie was infatuated with her. He would always tell me, "Shawn has some big titties. I can't wait to suck on them hoes."

I was kind of talking to Jackee, but it was nothing serious, just some phone conversations and notes at school. I am sitting in Tullie's living room, waiting on him to get ready, he comes out with everything on but his shirt, he was splashing baby powder on his chest and Tullie says, "Lester said he couldn't take us, right?" and I said, "Naw, he going to a football party with John Hodge and dem."Tullie responded, "Well, shit! You better call your brother, Rob. We need to get there. So, can he drop us off?" I said, "I'm finna call him right now." As I got up to use the phone, I said, "What about Edie (LaTonya's nickname) and dem."Tullie said, "Fuck them. How the fuck they gonna get there? Hoes never have trouble getting rides to the club. Any nigga is gonna be happy to take them up there."

I said, "You are right about that one." Tullie said, "You know them East Terrace niggaz will be up there and probably Wheatley Courts, Sutton Homes, which is really Sudden Death. Shit, nigga, don't go in there unless you're strapped, cuz it has the right name. Your death will be sudden. Most of those niggaz will be strapped tonight. I heard that nigga Blue from the East Terrace be holding niggaz for ransom. I said, "Ain't nobody worried about that." I played it off pretty well, but in my mind, "I'm thinking everybody is going to have guns in their rides? What the fuck am I getting myself into?

My love for seeing fine black women was taking over my brain and my instinct for self-preservation. But that was me being naïve. I didn't care. I didn't grasp the potential of what could be a serious situation. Tullie's Mom, Rose Marie Bailey, was very strict. He couldn't leave the house at 8 or 9 o'clock and come home at 3 o'clock in the morning. He had to say that he was staying the night at my house in order to go to the club. I said, "You told your Mom that you were stayin the night at my house?" Tullie said, "Hell, yeah, but if we get some hoes, we can just go through my window. My mama will be asleep at that time." I said, "Shit, that's what I'm talking about. Let's hope that happens."

My brother Rob dropped us off around the corner, and not in front of the club because that does not look good for the image. Girls can get dropped off. That's okay. Guy's getting dropped off. That doesn't look good. When you are a guy, you are supposed to come to the club with your ride, no matter how it looks. At least, you have a car. Tullie and I were broke as a joke; we couldn't afford one. As we were walking closer to the club, you could hear the bass from the vehicles outside. I could see some of the guys with their cars were not meant to be played with. It looked like they were thugs to the heart. I knew all of them had straps in the trunk of their cars. So, we were standing in line to get in. We see a bunch of fine girls bypass the line to talk to the bouncer, and they went straight into the club.

One of the girls that went straight into the line was Felicia Thomas, a gorgeous 6 foot 2 black girl that went to our school. She was real good in sports. I said to Tullie, "There goes Felicia fine ass." Tullie said, "Hell yeah, niggaz will break their neck tryin to fuck her." I said, "I think Lester told me he already did." And Tullie said, "Well, lucky him." When we finally walked into the club, I could feel the energy of everyone in there. I would say there were about 300 to 400 people inside and outside the club, and I noticed right away, that I was only the non-black person there, except I saw two Hispanic girls there. The music was blaring to the song, "Shake It" by McShy D. Most of the women looked perfect and gorgeous. Their bodies were off the chain. A lot of them were wearing tight little skirts and high heels. I thought I was in black heaven.

It's amazing how so many black women look; they have a small mid-section and a big ass. It looks as if the food they eat bypasses their stomach and goes to their ass and muscle. That's a freak of nature. Their hair was perfect as if they just got out of the beauty shop. I was a sucker for braids. If a black woman I talked to had braids, I pretty much had to have her. Their nails were all done. Some had tattoos and gold necklaces on, and they were shaking their booties to the music. This was the biggest turn on in my life. If that wasn't enticing enough for me, it was what was inside most black women. They have a fighting spirit that is unmatched. They don't take any shit, and they don't play. That probably comes from 300-400 years of oppression in which they were the backbone of American civilization. In the first couple of hundred years, she had to bow down and submit to the white man through rape, and then simultaneously had to raise the white children which her slave master made with his wife.

That's a heavy burden to carry, for a race of women who, when they came to America, had their own children ripped away from them through the brutality of chattel slavery. What an existence black women had to endure, to live in a world of despair and death. No other race of woman would have been strong enough to survive that ordeal, and still be alive and kicking today. Knowing the history of black women as well as their outer beauty, attracted me to them even more. It's crazy how America has done a 180, when it comes to black women. For 200 years plus, white men couldn't get enough of black women. They would have sex with black women whenever they wanted and still have sex with their white wives.

Needless to say, these men were oversexed, while the black man could barely touch the black woman because she was over-worked raising white children and raising children of her own, children who they didn't know sometimes if they would be black or white until the baby was born. While white men could have sex with any black woman, and black men couldn't even look in the direction of any white woman. So, here is the 180. Black men in today's society can't get enough of white women because most white women were locked away for 300 years. And today if you see a black man with a white woman, it's normal. If you see a white man with a black female that is rare. I think most Hispanic and white men are put off by black women because they perceive them as being either arrogant or mean. The perception of them being mean is what I'm drawn to. I understand why they're mean and sometimes mad at the world. I have to admit I take full advantage of that. I was amazed to watch the aggressive nature at the club of the black man pursuing the black woman - ultimate objective: get them out of their panties by any means necessary.

Tullie caught onto this as well. He grabbed a girl as she walked by and said, "Hey girl, what's your name?" She responded and said, "Jasmine." She was looking as though she was mad at him for grabbing her but once she looked up and saw how tall he was, her guard went down. That's the advantage Tullie had over me. Most girls want to be with him because he is tall. Tullie said, "Where your man at?" Jasmine said, "Don't have one. You think if I had a good man, I'd be up here? Besides they too possessive, always wanting to know where you going, who you going with? Fuck that shit, I don't need that. You are probably the same way?" Tullie said, "Naw, I just want to be your friend. Give me your number so we can get into something when you have time." She said okay, and I handed Tullie a pen. She wrote it down, and handed Tullie the paper, and simultaneously looked at Tullie and said, "Who is the white boy?"

I jumped in to answer for myself and said, "My name is Marcus. Nice to meet you, Jasmine." As I grabbed her hand and shook it she said, "Marcus? Whatever." She walked away, and I looked at Tullie and said, "That was good. You definitely need to call her tomorrow." I had to remind myself that he just turned 15 years old. Right about that time a song came on with a real good beat and all of a sudden about 100 girls joined in unison and chanted "Where the Big Dicks At! Where the Big Dicks At! Where They At! Where They At! Where They At!" Then about thirty seconds later in the same song, a chant rang out from about half the girls in the club, "Ain't No pussy like the Wheatley Courts pussy cause the East Terrace pussy ain't shit!" Right after that, a role reversal with, “Ain’t no pussy like the East Terrace pussy cause the Wheatley Courts pussy ain’t shit!”

Tullie whispered in my ear and said, “I would like to see for myself which one is better.” I said, “Yeah, me and you both.” A couple minutes later a little fight broke out by the door, but it quickly stopped after some security got over there. I had seen Latonya, Tarsha, Shawn and Jackee talking to guys all night. It didn’t bother me that I saw Jackee talkin to guys, even though we were supposed to be talking. It wasn’t really shit.

About five minutes later, a hail of gunfire rang out in the club and everybody started charging to the exits, mostly towards the front door. It was no joke. I saw girls get trampled. I lost everybody I was with. I just started running to the front door. As I got to the front door, I saw long legs underneath the table where you get stamped, before you get in. I looked under the table and there I saw Felicia Thomas, who I had seen earlier going into the club. I had never spoken to Felicia once at school, but she knew who I was and I definitely knew who she was. I looked at her and said, “Felicia, what are you doing down there?” She said, “Boy, you betta go on, they shootin!” So, I ran outside with everybody else.

People were scrambling, trying to get to their cars. Cars were driving out very fast. I saw a group of men arguing with each other. I didn’t have a car to go to, so I quickly went to the side of the building. Then, I saw Tullie, Latonya, Tarsha, Shawn and Jackee and they came towards me. Tullie said, “These niggaz ain’t playin, let’s get the fuck up outta here.” I looked to them and said, “That fight from earlier probably had something to do with it. Did you guys see Felicia, her ass was under the table as you walk out.” And they all started laughing. Then, we all quickly started walking to the Diamond Shamrock gas station.

Jackee starts walking with me and I'm thinking, "Wow, maybe I can get her to Tullie's house and go through the window." As we approached the store, I noticed everyone kind of step away from me. It felt for a minute like I was alone, in a wilderness. As I stepped onto the Diamond Shamrock parking lot, I heard someone from the crowd say, "Aw shit, Joe Rick about to go off on the white boy" Suddenly, this little, black guy, older than me, maybe about twenty, jumped in front of me and said, "Say nigga, you fuckin' wit my fuckin' girl, nigga." I said, "Your girl? Who's your girl?" He said, "Her, right there, nigga!" as he pointed to Jackee. I said, "Naw, I go to school with her. She's my friend."

As my stomach is racing up and down, I'm thinking, what did I get myself into? I felt I was alone in the world right there like if nobody wants me there. I was being surrounded like I was the prey and they were the vultures about to devour me. I said, "We just talk a little, but it ain't nothing serious. He said, "Naw nigga you ain't talking to shit!" I had fought all throughout school for the last sixyears. I was somewhat of a hothead, but for thefirst time in my life, I was scared to fight.

I was not prepared mentally for this situation. He started to swing on me and I backed, away but one of his punches grazed me. So I defended myself and got into a fighting stance, and started to swing on him. My heart was not all the way into it but I connected on him and he started backing up. I started getting the upper hand a little bit and out of the corner of my eye I could see a Cadillac that had pulled up and guys jumping over their cars to get at me. The next thing I knew I got hit in the back of my neck really hard and someone hit me on the side of my face with full force. At that point I knew I was being rushed from all angles. I lost sight of Joe Rick, when a new person got to the party and hit me and I went to the ground. When I was on the ground I glanced up and saw Joe Rick kicking me in my back. I started to get back up and got hit again by somebody else and went back down.

At that point, I made a business decision and played possum. They quit kicking me. I overheard one of them say, "Say nigga, should we kill him?" and the other one replied, "Naw he ain't shit," and at that point of my life I was glad I wasn't shit. So, if I was somebody big time in their eyes, I would have been killed. I could hear Latonya Kyle tell Jackee in anger, "Why you let that boy get beat up like that? That wasn't even right." Jackee responded, "I didn't let them do shit. Joe Rick crazy." Latonya said, "They wrong for this. Marcus, you alright baby, get up."

There was blood on my shirt but I didn't know what part of my body it came from because I was hit from all angles. I was just some white boy who happened to be trying to date a black girl, and almost paid the ultimate price. I started to become very angry. A rage was growing inside me that I had never felt before. The hell with being scared anymore. Even though my body was hurting, my mind was ready to take on the world. As I got to my feet, I could see a disgusted and embarrassed look on Tullie's face because he didn't help me. At that moment, it dawned on me. I just took on one of the most notorious gangs in San Antonio, East Terrace Gangsters aka ETGs. They were crips. They rocked that blue.

I had heard of some of the names before, Joe Rick, who I just had a confrontation with, and there was Tweedy, Skull or Shooter is what they called him, Michael Dorn known as Blue and Derek Asberry. I was very lucky to still be breathing. I was not mad at Tullie for not jumping in. Had he jumped in he would have gotten beat too because there were too many of them and, worst of all, he probably would have gotten shot. They would have made an example of him. Who's this black boy sticking up for this white boy? Kill his ass Fa sho. I could just picture it. What would that accomplish? Nothing.

As I went into the store I told Latonya, "I just want to be left alone," and she said, "Okay, we'll be right here." I went into the restroom, visibly angry. I punched a hole in the bathroom wall. I looked in the mirror and saw that my lip was bloodied and my upper back was bruised. I stared into the mirror and made a promise to myself and said, "I will never be a victim again." Some people might have gone the other way, and thought the hell with this. I'm completely out of my element. Not me. At that point I made a conscious decision, I want to have my own crew. I will decide if someone gets beat up or killed or not, and I was going to rock that red and be a blood. I would like to thank the ETG crips for what they did. They made a monster that night. A thug to the heart was born.

CHAPTER SIX

BLACK LOVE

ABOUT TWO DAYS or about thirty-six hours after the club incident, I showed my face back in Kenwood. I still had visible cuts and bruises, but I wanted to show my homeboys in the hood that I ain't no punk. I was not going to run and hide. I earned respect that way. You get beat, so what, as long as you don't back down. Take your ass-whoopin like a man. I was back at Tullie's house playing with Tullie's nephew Peter, aka Phat Cheez, and Tony. They were 9 and 10 years old. Their mother, Bonnie Kaye, was a hard-working single mom of two. She also didn't have no playing bone in her body. If you are going to start a conversation with her, you betta come correct and ask the right question, or you will be shut down. Tullie's older brother also lived there. His name was Ronald Green. He was 6'2" and gay, and one of the funniest human beings you'd ever want to meet. He was Madea before there was a Madea, but on crack.

You could make a comedy film just by following Ronald's daily life. Bexar County jail had released him with an ankle monitor.

They also gave him what looked like a speaker. This was monitored as well. After 10 pm, the Bexar County authorities would call him from downtown through this device, and he would have a few minutes to answer accordingly. If he did not respond, the police would be on their way to pick him up. A few times in the middle of the night, that crazy device would wake me up when it was calling him. Sometimes he wasn't there, and me and Tullie would have to scramble and find him. We probably woke up neighbors with our yelling for Ronald, but Rose Bailey, Tullie's Mom, was adamant about making sure that her son didn't end up in jail just for not answering a call. When Ronald would hear us yelling for him, he would come out of nowhere, running fast to make it to the monitor. A couple of times, we saw where he was at. You see, Ronald had a major problem. His dependency on smoking crack cocaine was more important than anything or anyone, even responding when the authorities were trying to locate him, and even if a misstep could land him back in jail.

I also walked over to Lester's house quite a bit. I always felt real good at Lester's house. It was a very homey atmosphere. What always drew me to Lester's house was his grandmother, Della Kyle. Everybody called her Mama, so I joined in, offering that same respect. She always made me feel at home, like there was no place else I'd rather be than 311 Odell. I had been to other friend's houses, but there was a line or boundary they drew, a line that said that this is the parent or grandparent's house, you're the guest, remember your place, and don't step out of line. Not Mrs. Kyle(Mama)! She made me feel like I was part of the family. I'd go over after school, and I could smell the aroma of good food in the air, and I'd say, "Hey, Mama. What you cookin'?" She'd say, "I makin' pork chops, baby. You get you two pieces of bread. I'ma get you one right now." She showed me that you love someone, and they don't have to be a family member. I said, "Ok, Mama. Thank you!"

As I was pouring myself some Kool Aid I said, "What about Lester? I don't want to take his." She said, "Baby, look in there. I made plenty. He know to come in here and get his own." I remember thinking, "Damn. I'm never leaving here." I stayed the night on school nights, sometimes on the couch, and went to the refrigerator whenever I wanted to. They had a few roaches in the house, but so what. I had roaches at my house too. I didn't care. Mrs. Della Kyle (Mama), besides my grandmother, who became my mother, was the best woman I'd ever met. She passed away in 1996. Rest In Peace, Mama. I will always be thinking of you.

Another attraction of being at Lester's house was Latonya and Tarsha Kyle. They were both real fine, and I liked their company. I had a little crush on Tarsha, and it was fun just talking to them and watchin' TV. That same day I was eating pork chops, Lester came walking in, looking at me and laughing and said, "How the fuck did you get here so fast?" As I was eating my pork chop on the couch, watchin' TV with Latonya and Tarsha, I said, "Lenton dropped me off. We was looking for you, but Lenton was in a hurry." Lenton Collins was a mutual friend of ours at Edison. Lester went straight to the restroom, and then went to get his pork chop. Lester sat down and said, "Say, Marcus. We was driving the other day, and we got pulled over and you know ain't nobody got ID or license and insurance, so when the cop asked me my name, I said 'Lawrence Bailey'." Everyone in the room started laughing but me. I gave a little smile and said, "You need to quit doing that, dawg. That boy gonna have a bad record before he eighteen." Tarsha said, "You wrong for that shit." and Latonya said, "That's fucked up." I said, "You crazy, dawg." Lester said,

"I can't get no record. I'm trying to get a football scholarship." I said, "I know, but Ga-damn. Pick somebody besides Tullie, though." Lester said, "Hey, you see that new boy that across the street from Tullie? Tarsha said, "He a Mexican boy. He cute.His name is Henry Toscano." Latonya said, "He suppose to be from the Eastside I think." I said "I was just over there the other day. I didn't see shit." "I hope he don't come over here with all that 'I from the Eastside shit, and get whooped," said Lester. We all started laughing. What I didn't realize at the time is that Henry Toscano would help change my life forever.

CHAPTER SEVEN

I AIN'T NO HOE!

A COUPLE OF days later, I had gotten a gun from someone in Kenwood who shall remain nameless. It was a .380 caliber, and I thought it was the shit. A .380 is a step below a 9mm handgun. I was over at Tullie's and I showed it to him and he said, "Damn, that's tight." It was fully loaded, locked and ready to go. I said, "You met that new fool, Henry?" Tullie said, "Yeah, he coola than a mutha fucka. Let's go over there." Just then, Henry stepped outside, "What's up, Tullie?" Tullie said, "What's up? This is my boy, Marcus." We both shook hands and said, "What's up? "Why you move here from the Eastside?" I said. He said, "Nigga, I don't pay no bills. I don't make those decisions. I guess my dad needed a change of scenery." I said, "I guess." We were chillin' for a while and I told him about my nightclub ordeal, and Henry got amped up. He said, "I know all them East Terrace fools. I can't believe they let you make it." I responded, "Fuck them. I ain't even worried about that shit anymore."

As I clutched my gun, Henry said, "I hope you don't have any crazy-ass intention of paying them back because you won't be able to. They go 50 to 100 deep, and everybody crazy and strapped." I said, "I'm not out for revenge. I'm just gonna be a lot better prepared if that kinda shit happens again." Henry said, "I like the way you think. I feel you on that. Say, I'm going to the East Terrace tomorrow to see my boy, David Johnson. Oh, shit. But I gotta stop off and get Dembo and Kendrick first, if y'all wanna come." Me and Tullie looked at each other and said, "Hell, yeah." Tullie said, "We talkin' to a few hoes in there now. I'm talking to Diane Johnson and I think Marcus is talking to Kimberly Johnson and Juaneeda. Fuck them East Terrace niggaz. I'm tryin' to pay some pussy back." We started laughing. Henry said, "I didn't know you knew all them." "Yeah," I said. "Let's go to McDonald's. I'm hungry." As we walked to McDonald's, I had my gun on me. I never went anywhere without my gun. "Well, shit. Then it's on tomorrow. I thought y'all be scared to go in there. I replied, "Say, Henry, Dawg, you got us fucked up. I ain't no hoe."

The next day, Tullie, Henry and I met up and caught the bus to the Eastside. We went to Kendrick's house on J Street. You talk about somebody that's not all there. That description fits Kendrick perfect. He was real dark-skinned with a jheri-curl. Within a few minutes, we were all talking about fucking hoes, and he started fucking his door. He made absolutely no sense. Damon Wayan's character in the movie "Colors" would look like Einstein compared to this fool.

Then, there was Alvin Dembo who was the cousin or nephew of the famous Fennis Dembo, who starred at Fox Tech HS and then Wyoming, and then won a ring with the 1988 Detroit Pistons. He appeared on the cover of Sports Illustrated, when he played for the University of Wyoming(see March 1987 issue). We didn't call him Alvin. He just wanted to be called Dembo. He was 6' 4" and could play basketball very well. I was thinking that with me, him and Tullie together, it would be hard for anyone to beat us in a 3-on-3 game. When we got to the East Terrace, we met up with David Johnson. Henry said, "Sometimes they call him Donkey Dick Dave." You can use your imagination, or you probably don't need to, as to why he was called that.

Incidentally, his cousin, Skull or Shooter was one of the ones that got a lick in on me at the club. I didn't see any of the main participants from my beating that night. I thought for sure that any minute one of them would pull up, and it would be on. I didn't give a fuck anymore. I had my gun on me. I knew I wouldn't be able to shoot all of them, but I didn't care. I knew before they took me out, I would surprise them and at least get one or two of them before I died.

David was pretty cool, down to earth, and loved basketball. Tullie and I left to go to Kimberly and Diane Johnson's house. When I walked inside Kimberly's house, it was a mess. What I didn't know at the time was that she had 6 or 7 children. One of her sons let me in. He was about 7 years old. I said, "Where your Mama at?" He replied, "You a friend of my Mama's?" I said, "Yeah, I told her I was coming to see her today." He responded, "She in the hospital." I said, "For what?" He said, "I don't even know." The house looked like it had just been raided by the police. Clothes were everywhere. Toys were thrown all over the place. Couches looked real bad.

I went to the refrigerator, and opened it. Her son said, "I'ma bounce." I said, "When you see your Momma, tell her Marcus came by." He said, "A'ight." I didn't even get his name. I opened the refrigerator, and all I saw was an old ketchup bottle. The freezer was empty as well. I thought, "Wow, this is fucked up." After seeing their situation, I felt really bad for her son. I wished I would have given him some money, ten dollars or anything, but he was already gone. I wanted to go find him, but I didn't know where to start looking. As I said before, he was probably only about 7 years old.

As I left, I could see Tullie talkin' to Diane a few units down. I told him I was going back up to David's. He said, "A'ight." I yelled, "Don't do anything I wouldn't do." He stuck the finger back at me in fun. I walked back up to David's house. When I got to the street by his house, I saw two SAPD cars coming right towards me. I had my gun on me, so I panicked and threw it in the Cadillac that was parked in front of David's. Luckily for me, the windows were down. The two SAPD cars stopped in front of me, and stared for a few seconds, then pulled away.

They were probably thinking, "What's this white boy doing in the East Terrace? He looks suspicious as hell." While they were looking, I started to walk away from the Cadillac I just threw the gun in. I waited until I didn't see them anymore, then started walking back to retrieve my gun out of the Cadillac. I was about two steps away from the car, when I heard, "Say, nigga. Give me your jacket before I blow your mutha fuckin' head off!" I said, "Shit, I got you."

I started to take my Dallas Cowboy bomber jacket off, and I turned to glance at his face for a half-second. As I saw his face, I noticed he was holding a black gun that looked like a big-ass piece from Dirty Harry. I didn't want to look at him directly because he might blow me away just cause I would be able to identify him one day. As I gave him my jacket without looking at him, he said, "Now turn toward the street and walk your bitch ass straight that way." I started to walk and I heard him start to run away.

I quickly turned around and got my gun out of the front seat of the car, clicked it back and pointed it at him. He was in my sight line, and I have real good vision. I was about to pull the trigger, when I heard a voice yell, "Don't do it!" I turned around, and it was David Johnson. He said, "Look across the street." I looked across the street, and there was a lady watering her grass, looking at me and shaking her head, looking like the Mama from "Good Times."

And I'm thinking, why is she shaking her head at me? Did she not see this fool rob me at gun point? I guess it didn't matter. I would have shot someone in the back, running away. Either way, I would have been in trouble. David said, "You was gonna shoot him? What that nigga do?" I replied, "He just robbed me with this big-ass gun. Fuck!" David said, "Shit, I feel you dawg, but that lady would have told that you shot him in the back." I said, "I know. Thanks for telling me not to do it." Just then, Henry came out. "What happened?" I was too pissed off to say anything, but David said, "Your boy just got robbed." Henry laughed and said, "Man, trouble follows you everywhere you go." I looked at him and I said, "I guess the fuck so."

I liked David from that moment on. David Johnson probably saved me from killing someone that day, and possibly going to the penitentiary for who knows how many years. Whether it would been manslaughter or murder, either way, it would have drastically changed my life. David went on to excel in basketball at Highlands HS. He died a few years later from complications from AIDS. It's crazy how you know somebody for a while, and bond with him and then the next minute, he's gone, but in life in general, that happens all the time. Especially in the ghetto.

CHAPTER EIGHT

ERICKA

A **FEW MONTHS** went by and me and Tullie and Henry were always together. We would be at either Henry's house or Lester's house. Henry and I had already dropped out of high school, and Tullie was still going because of basketball. It was late 1990, and when I met him in 1989, he was 6'4". Now, he was 6'6". We all thought Tullie would get a college scholarship, and then eventually end up in the NBA. Lester was a great high school football player, but his dreams ended with an injury, I think. Tullie and I got arrested at Brackenridge High School when we went to see some girls we were talking to. Tullie and I were charged with criminal trespassing. Henry was actually smart enough to stay outside the high school, so he wasn't arrested.

At the time, I had a girlfriend named Nikki Lawhorne. She was a year older than me. I thought she was a beautiful, black woman. She was brown-skinned, very petite, had big tits and had an even bigger mouth. She was always talking loud and about somebody. I met her at Ingram Park Mall. She told me, "I got a boyfriend." I replied that whenever I could, I would catch the bus to her sister's house and have sex with her. That's what teenagers do when there is no adult supervision and there is nothing to do. They sit around and talk, then have sex. Even though I thought I was in love, this relationship didn't last very long. It was too long of a commute just to have sex. Tullie, Henry and I didn't have to go that far to have sex. There were girls in the neighborhood, and girls that would catch the bus to come to us.

One day, Henry was talking about this petite, black girl he fucked a year earlier. Her name was Ericka Wilson. The story goes, she walked to his house on the Eastside, and Dembo, Kendrick and this boy named Rodney from Edna Street hid in the closet in Henry's room while Ericka and Henry had sex. Then, they arose from behind the bed when Henry finished. They were just standing there. They were watching the whole time. When Ericka saw them, she felt humiliated, put on her clothes and walked home. Henry loved telling that story, but the downside to it for him was that Ericka wasn't going to sleep with him again, knowing that he would do that to her. He called her up after he told the story. I was a little surprised he would still be able to call her.

You would think she would hang up on him after all that. I remember thinking, "Damn, if she thought Henry looked alright to fuck, I know she will give me some pussy." I was a little conceited. I thought I looked good by comparison. After their three-minute phone conversation, I said, "You may as well let me and Tullie have the number. She ain't gonna fuck you no more." Tullie didn't seem too interested. I think he was fucking about five girls at the time. Henry had been fucking Tarsha Kyle, who I fucked later on. It had been about two weeks since fucking Nikki, and that's desperate time in the ghetto. In other words, if you live in the ghetto and you haven't had sex in two weeks, people start thinking you might be gay or something's wrong with you.

People were fucking all the time. Henry called Ericka, and said, "I'm giving my boy Marcus your number." She said, "Who is that?" Henry responded, "He ain't black. He Mexican and Italian, I think." She said, "How you know I ain't gotta man?" Henry replied "Girl what do that matter? I wouldn't be telling you about him if he wasn't legit." She said, "Alright, whateva." and hung up. Henry told me, "Her number is 333-0938." I said, "I will call her tomorrow. If I call her tonight, that sounds desperate, right?" Tullie and Henry looked at me and said, "Yeah, that's a good idea."

I called Ericka the next day. I found out her full name was Ericka Deshawn Wilson. We talked for about a week non-stop. After a week went by, I set up a date for her to come by my house. I was real excited that day, and I knew she was also, from our phone conversations. I told her, "When you get off bus Number 8 on N. St. Mary's, just pass Hwy 281. You take a right, and start walking and my house is straight down. You can't miss it." She said, "Why you not gonna be at the bus stop waiting for me?" I said, "I'll be there, but I wanted you to know which direction my house is, in case the bus gets there before I do." She said, "Ok." What she didn't know was that I was going to scare her, to see how she would react.

I saw the bus approaching, and I went behind the bushes on the side street. I watched her get off the bus, and take a right, just how I told her. She looked just as I thought. She had a nice figure. She was very small and dark. I let her walk about twenty steps, then got behind her and grabbed her. She got scared for a second as I jolted her, and said, "Guess who?" Then I put my face in front of hers and said, "It's me, Marcus." She knew it was me.

She laughed for a second, then said, "You wrong for that." We vibed real good, and ended up watching movies and having sex. I rode the bus back downtown with her and watched her get on the bus back to her house, and then I caught the bus back home. I was a happy young man. I thought, I found the mother of my children.

A few weeks later, a bombshell was dropped on me. I found out Ericka was already pregnant from a guy named Walter Perry. It was a one- night stand. Ericka started having pain in her stomach, so I went to the hospital with her, and her mom, Mary Wilson, and Mary's friend, Suzette Thomas. I remember Suzette telling Ericka's Mom, "You got to respect Marcus because he is on the way to the hospital with your daughter, and that's not even his baby. He don't have to be here." Mary responded, "I know." I think I scored some pretty big points from Ericka's Mom from that day forward. But that wasn't why I was there. I wanted to make sure she was okay. The doctor said she was anywhere between five to seven weeks pregnant. That was a little tough on me. I don't think I could have raised another man's child.

I wanted a child of my own flesh and blood. But I'm glad I never had to face that decision. Ericka ended up having a spontaneous miscarriage a few days later. I was not happy for the loss of life but I wanted to be with this girl and start my own family. Walter Perry ended up, a few years later, spending time in the penitentiary for statutory rape. He had a baby by a girl named Neonesha, who was thirteen at the time. Truth be told, I ended up having sex with Argee, Neonesha's sister about ten or twelve years later. Phat Cheez ended up fucking with Neonesha. It seems like in the black community in San Antonio, everybody ends up fucking everybody.

Ericka and I, from that point on, were with each other every day. After a few months of that, Ericka's mother was kind of fed up with it because she never saw her daughter anymore. One day Ericka and I went back to Ericka's house to get some of her things and as we were about to leave, Ericka's mother Mary yelled, "There you go again leaving the house. I don't know whether y'all are coming or going or what. Y'all just up here ripping and running in these streets! Y'all need to just sit down somewhere and watch a movie or something." Upon hearing that, Ericka and I sat back down and watched television for about an hour then left. I cannot blame her for getting upset. She felt like she was losing her little girl. I don't know how she felt about me but over time I grew to love that woman. She is like most strong black women I know. She don't play around but she has a big heart.

A few days later, me and Henry, Tullie, Dembo, Tarsha, and Ericka decided to go to this club, across the street on Commerce from where they were building the Alamodome. The parking lot was too crowded, so we had to park at the Marriott, a few blocks away. When we got into the club, we found a table that could accommodate all of us. It's funny how shit works. Ericka is my woman who Henry fucked, and Tarsha is his woman, who I fucked, and it didn't seem to bother anybody. It was just life at the time. Tarsha and Ericka went to dance. Henry noticed all of the East Terrace gang was inside the club. He said, "I hope they don't recognize Marcus. And all that bullshit is squashed. Ima go holla at dem for a minute." Dembo went to go talk to some females. I told him, "Make sure you talk to the right girl, and her man ain't here, or we gonna be some fightin' niggaz up in here." Dembo replied, "Marcus, you ain't got to worry about that shit. I got mines."

Me and Tullie just stayed there listening to the music, watching all the girls in the club dance. Tullie said, "I see Derek Asberry(an ETG member). I said, "You want an award for seeing Derek Asberry?" "Naw fool, I fucked his woman". "Ga-Dam Tullie, you starting to fuck everybody. Now you fucked a bitch that could get us killed." Tullie said, "Man, fuck Derek Asberry. I'll whoop his ass." I replied, "Yeah, I know you can. But this ain't Kenwood though, where you can fight him one on one, beat his ass, and then everybody goes inside. These niggaz will kill us tonight. I got my gun in the car, but it's three blocks away, and they chasing us with guns. It may as well be three miles away. Fuck man! Just sit tight. Don't go the restroom. Don't do shit. You don't need any new phone numbers. You got plenty of hoes." "There is always room for new girls on my team," Tullie said. I said, "Yeah, that's true, but not tonight. When Dembo, Henry, and the girls get back, we'll leave quietly." About two minutes later, Henry and Dembo got back to the table. Henry said, "You're not very popular with them." I replied, "Funny, I thought they would give us a ride home." Henry laughed. "Yeah, did you know about Tullie and Derek Asberry's girl?"

I responded, "Yeah, Tullie just told me the good news." Henry said, "Yeah, that ain't cute. Oh, and I can't believe this shit. A couple of them remember you, Marcus. I'm taking a big chance with my life, just being around you two." "Thanks," I replied. "I gotch you later. How the fuck do we get out of here?" "I don't know," Henry said. "The car is too fucking far". Henry thought for a second, then said, "I got it." I said "What?" He said, "There are two SAPD officers outside the door, right?" "Yeah," I said. Henry said, "I'll be right back."

Just as Henry left, a frightening thought occurred in my head. Henry had said that about a week ago, Anthony Holmes, (who later came to be known as Priest Holmes) of the Texas Longhorns and Baltimore Ravens, an All-City football player for Marshall high school was at the club with his friend when a mess of the East Terrace gang was at the club. Michael Dorn, AKA Blue, their leader, wanted to kill Anthony Holmes and his friends cuz they were wearing maroon jackets and they were acting like they were big time, but somebody told Blue, "Naw, don't do it . That brother gonna be in the NFL someday. Let him make it, Blue." And Blue said, "Ok." I knew we wouldn't get such a luxury. They would kill us like we wasn't shit.

Henry came back in about three minutes. The girls got to the table right before that. Henry said, "Let's go now." Tarsha wanted to know why and said Ericka and her wanted to stay. Henry told them loudly, "Let's go!" Tarsha had an angry look on her face. I told them as well, "Henry's right, Tarsha. We gotta go, now. I'll tell you what happened in about five minutes." Right at that time, Dembo and Tullie got up from their chairs, and at the exact same time, as if they were watching our every move, the whole East Terrace Gang stood up, which seemed like half the club, and stared at us. I was thinking, "Shit. We're gonna die outside this club."

As we started to walk toward the front door, I could see some of the ETGs follow us. I quickly opened the door, and held it open so we could all get through. Then I heard Henry tell the cop, "That's it right here. This is our group. If you let them outside, it's gonna be on." The SAPD officer saw the ETGs about to come out and said, "No, you're gonna have to wait a few minutes before you can come outside."

I thought that was pretty clever. Henry let the two officers in on what could possibly happen, so the officers let us through and stopped the ETGs from coming out. I guess they didn't want a riot on their watch, or a possible blood bath. We got to the end of the street and Henry said, "Fuck that. Let's start jogging. They might let them out. Shit!" Tarsha said, "Will somebody tell me what the hell is going on?" I said, "It hasn't been five minutes, Tarsha." As we were running for our lives as if they might catch up to us, I asked Henry. "You think they'll notice us?" Henry said," Naw, how could they notice us? We got two black girls, two Mexicans, and two seven footers. They'll never notice us."

I started laughing. It's crazy how we could be shot at any minute and something was still funny. We made it to my car and back to Kenwood, and it was all good. Dembo went to Tullie's, and me and the girls went to Henry's. We had a good rest of the night, having sex, and watching TV, but I was about to be thrown into something for which I was not prepared.

CHAPTER NINE

CRACK

ABOUT A MONTH passed by and Tullie introduced me to Vidal Sauls, aka Sugar Bear. He was from the Northeast side of San Antonio by the Glen and Camelot housing projects. His mother stayed on Tuxford St. The reason Tullie met him was that his grandmother stayed real close to him on Melrose St. Vidal was fun to hang with. He was really funny. He had a love for basketball and football like we all did. Me, Tullie, Henry and Vidal and sometimes Carlton would all play basketball, sometimes til 4 or 5 in the morning. Carlton Wilson was a big time basketball player at Edison in the mid 80s. He was 6'5"and 230 pounds of muscle. He was left-handed and when his mind was totally into it, he could dominate games. Tullie used to say it's hard to guard Carlton because of the left-handed shit, plus he got some ups. But Carlton, a lot of times, didn't want to go with us because he had done all that already He played college ball and had been a star. Me, Tullie, Henry, and Vidal were inseparable from the get go.

We did everything together. We went to Lester's house one day and were talking, and Tullie was on Lester's house phone. After he hung up, he interrupted our conversation, and said "Say, this girl says I'm cute." Vidal said, "I know who you are talking about and that girl ain't even seen you yet." Everybody breaks out into laughter. Tullie responded, "Yes she has. She's seen me at the club where we all went the other night. She said I look like Johnny Gill." With everybody laughing, Lester said, "Tullie, quit lying. Y'all know that song by Johnny Gill? When she see Tullie, instead of singing that song, 'My, my, my, my'...she gonna tell Tullie 'Bye, bye, bye, bye'..." imitating the Johnny Gill song. We all started laughing. Vidal said, "I got to get back to Tullie's, my little brother gonna be at Tullie's house in a little while." We all got up and walked back to Tullie's. We were all there about five minutes. Then, a blue Impala pulled up with Vidal's brother, Chris Kelly, and his friend Melvin.

Chris and Vidal kinda looked alike. Chris was dark-skinned, big and kinda swoll. Melvin was light-skinned with a jheri curl. They were the two main parts of Big Tyme Playas gang, which were Bloods. I think Vidal said Chris lived in Kirby, but they'd usually be in Wheatley Courts, which is Blood territory, or Camelot and the Glen. Vidal went to greet them as they got out of the car. When they came inside the gate, Vidal said, "Say y'all, this my little brother Chris and my home boy, Melvin." We all said what's up. Then Vidal, Chris and Melvin went away from everybody to the side of Tullie's house.

Henry went back to his house. Me and Tullie were sitting on the bench inside the yard. Tullie and I were gonna get our money together and walk to the store. We had a total of five or six dollars. That could buy each of us chips and soda. Then, we saw something that blew our minds. We saw Chris and Vidal counting a bunch of twenties. They each had a stack of money in their pockets. Tullie blurted out to Vidal, "Damn, nigga. How you get all that?" I said, "Hell, yeah. Where'd you work at? Shit, I'm gonna get me an application, and apply there." Vidal said, "Shit, this ain't no job application that you can go apply. You wanna get this (while he's showing us his money)? You gotta apply YO SELF full time and hustle." I said, "What are you talking about?" Vidal pulled out a plastic baggie and there were about 6 or 7 little white rocks in there. He said, "This is about a 150 right here." I remember looking at those rocks and thinking, "Damn. That's about a hundred fifty-dollars?!"Vidal continued. "I'm gonna take five of these to Tony Ray's(as he pulled 5 of the rocks from the baggie) and he gonna give me a hundred."Then it just hit me like a ton of bricks, that that was crack cocaine. I had just seen New Jack City the other day with Ericka, Henry, and Tarsha, but I was just surprised it was in front of me. Vidal said, "Take this down there to Tony Ray. He walkin' down here right now."Tullie said, "I'll go down there wit you. Mildred might trip if she see your ass. You know Tony Ray ain't fin to take all that dope back to Mildred. He gonna keep some for himself." Tony Ray, 6'4", used to be a big time basketball star in high school. I watched him and Carlton play in Kenwood about 1 ½ years ago. Tony Ray was unstoppable. And now, he's smoking this shit. As we were walking down there, Tullie was calling Mildred, Mildew. I thought that was funny. Tony Ray and Mildred had a daughter and few years later. She was a real good basketball player at Edison. I remember telling her, "Keep it up. Stay in school. And keep playing basketball." Her boyfriend was a good football player at Fox Tech, and I remember thinking, "I hope she doesn't end up pregnant."Tullie and I sold the five pieces of crack cocaine for a hundred dollars to Tony Ray to give to Mildred and pretty much forgot about the store. We were thinking of this new trade we learned. We weren't thinking about becoming Nino Brown from New Jack City, but we wanted a couple of hundred dollars in our pockets. I had just learned that Ericka was pregnant with my child, and that made me go out and get a job. I got hired at Pizza Hut the day before, so I was happy about that. When we got back, Chris and Melvin were leaving and Melvin said, "Come by Camelot tonight. We're gonna have a little party." Vidal said, "Hell yeah. I need to holla at Charlie." As they drove off, I asked Vidal, "Who is Charlie?" Vidal said, "Oh, my home boy. He a half-breed, half-Mexican, half-Black. He cool than a mutha-fucka." I told Vidal, "Say, I just got hired at Pizza Hut. So tell Chris, when I get some money, I need to holla at him cause I need to supplement my income." Vidal said, "Hell yeah. You can flip your money." I replied, "What you mean, flip your money?" Vidal said, "When you get your check, you can make it double. Like if you get $300 on your check, you can by an ounce of cocaine, rock it up and make $6-700 dollars." That's the first time I ever heard "flip your money." I said, "That sounds good. Just tell Chris." Vidal said, "Really, it's Melvin who got the dope. That's where Chris score from too." I said, "Alright. Melvin, then." Vidal said, "I just bought some powder from Melvin. I'ma show you how to rock it up." Me, Tullie, and Vidal went inside. Vidal said, "Tullie. You got a mayonnaise jar?" Tullie said, "Yeah." Vidal said, "I need some baking soda too." He got a round pan out, filled it with water, turned the burner on, took the top off the mayonnaise jar, peeled off all labels, poured in about 5-6 grams of pure powder cocaine and about a gram of baking soda in the jar. We watched this form into crack cocaine. I was paying attention, but not entirely. There was a basketball game on the television I could see. I knew this was gonna be a part of my life, but I didn't think about this as a career move. Tullie was looking at how Vidal was doing it so intently, you would have thought he was gonna learn this as if this were the last thing he would ever do. Vidal said, "See how it rocks up? It's beautiful." From that moment on, Tullie always used a mayonnaise jar. He never deviated. That's how he learned. That's how it's going to be. If it ain't broke, don't fix it. Tullie said, "Hell, yeah. No more struggling for dollars." I said, "Hell naw." The funny thing is, over the next year I would sell more crack cocaine than Tullie because he was a basketball star at Edison, and he had to devote his time to that and homework.

So there you have it, my introduction to crack. I couldn't say no. It was the easiest money to make, even though Vidal explained that you have to hustle if you wanna be good at it, but it beats sweating in somebody's kitchen for 5 or 6 dollars an hour. Me and Tullie knew there were people on crack in Kenwood, but we thought they were just funny. We didn't realize the extent of how much money we could make off them until we got deep into it. Vidal knew before we did how lucrative this journey could be, and if done right, it would be very profitable for a long time.

Everybody is a dope dealer now. Henry had just started to sell it. No wonder he would ghost us sometimes, and come back with a couple of hundred dollars. This muthafucka didn't have no job. He just didn't want to tell us. Lester ended up getting involved with it. Carlton even started selling it. The only ones who didn't were the young ones like Phat Cheez and Tony. We hadn't corrupted them yet. It's crazy how this life will just grab you and take you. You just have to roll with it or get out of the way. I'm not the kind of guy who wants to get out of the way. I want to be there in the middle of the action, but there is a good chance this would catch up to all of us one day.

CHAPTER TEN

CAMELOT

THAT NIGHT, WE all went to a low income subdivision called Camelot on the Northeast side. It is off Walzem and Montgomery Road. It was me, Tullie, Henry, and Dembo. Vidal was already there with Melvin and his brother, Chris. They knew most everybody in Camelot, so everybody went their separate ways when we got there. Dembo and Henry went to somebody's house that I didn't know. Tullie went to this girl's house to fuck. I did the same thing. There were supposed to be a couple of parties in Camelot tonight, so we were gonna make our presence known at both of them. After I finished fuckin, I went to where Vidal was with Chris and Melvin. Tullie was already there. Vidal had been telling me and Tullie that we are a part of Big Tyme Playas. It is a gang, but Vidal never said it was a gang. He was before his time. He is trying to distance Big Tyme Playas from some street thug shit. I don't think he was comfortable with the word gang. The word was too simplistic.

To him, we were a group of homeboys that had each other's back, no matter what. There was no silly gang initiation where you had to severely hurt somebody you didn't know. That wouldn't be intelligent for all those gang members who are already into it with other crews. Why bring extra heat on yourself? I respected that way of thinking. Big Tyme Playas was affiliated with the housing project called Wheatley Courts and they were Bloods. Vidal wanted Kenwood to be a part of that, which included me and Tullie. He liked Henry, but I think he thought Henry was too close to the East Terrace gang (Crips). He thought Dembo acted a fool too much, and did not trust him at all. I would soon find out why. I met Charlie Pryor for the first time. I said, "What's up? My name Marcus." He replied, "Charlie." Then he looked at Melvin and Chris and said, "Say, we gotta gets these guns up outta here before Auntie find them (I couldn't make out whose Auntie he was referring to)."

So we all followed him to the garage. Charlie reached behind this counter and pulled out two machine guns like he was going to war. I said, "Those are pretty." Charlie said, "Hell yeah, they're fully automatic Mac-11's with 30 round clips ready to fuck some shit up. Open up your car, Chris." Chris opened up the trunk and Charlie placed them under the mat. I was saying in my mind, "Damn, I need to get some of those." They made me feel ashamed of my 380 in the car. Vidal said, "Look at Marcus. You made his day showing him those." Charlie, looking at me said, "Go ahead and get you one of them then. But you can't have one of these. Them is my babies." I wanted to ask where do I get one, but I thought that would make me look weak. I was trying to be hard like I knew where to get one. Tullie said, "Come on Marcus, let's go find Dembo and Henry." Me and Tullie were leaving and Vidal said, "I will catch up with y'all later." As we were getting in the car, I could tell Tullie was just as enamored as I was with those Mac-11's, but I didn't start talking about it. Even though I knew we were doing crazy shit, I didn't want Tullie to think about guns. He still had a dream of playing in the NBA, and I wanted to help him attain that dream.

We got back to where Henry and Dembo were, and they were heading to that party. We walked to the party a couple of blocks away and there were about 100 people already there. I went in the house and walked to the back yard and saw that girl I just had sex with about three hours ago talking to some guy, and I thought I don't give a damn. I hope he fucks her tonight. I don't want her. About thirty minutes later, Henry and Tullie left. They said something about scoring some dope and Tarsha needing Henry for something. I didn't pay attention to what they were saying because the music was real loud and I was talking to this girl. I told them I would see them back in the hood later. So it was just me and Dembo there. About five minutes later, Dembo bumped into me and said, "Come On!" He had an angry look on his face. I followed him outside, into the street, and I said, "What happened?" Dembo replied, "This nigga wanna fuck wit me. I'ma shoot these niggaz." I said "Who?" Dembo replied, "You don't know 'em." Dembo said, "These niggaz don't know who they fuckin with." All this was being said while we were walking. I said, "Where are we going?" He said, "I left this gun at m' friend house." When we got there, two blocks away, Dembo came out with a 32 caliber gun. It looked like a gun in an old Western. He was loading the gun very angrily and walking back to the party. I said, "Dembo, that gun works, dawg?" He said, "Hell yeah! I fired it last week. Come on let's go!"

He picked up the pace to a jog. So here I am following a fool who is about to commit a murder, but what is that ole saying,

"Who is the more foolish, the fool or the fool who follows the fool?" Well I guess that puts me at more stupid than he is. I really don't know what I was thinking. What you have to understand is that, with the color of my skin, I have to be more dangerous. I have to show that I'm not afraid of shit. I had to be much harder than the average black guy. If I wanna be a hard core gang member and sell dope, I have to pay dues and put in work. I thought, "This is one of those times." Then I thought, I should have walked further to my car and got my gun, but it was too late.

I was almost at the party with Dembo. Dembo got to the front lawn and raised the 32 caliber hand gun at one of the guys and said, "What was that shit y'all was talking about earlier, nigga!" Everybody stopped whatever they were doing and looked at me and Dembo. The music stopped playing. You could hear a pin drop. There was dead silence. Then suddenly, Dembo fired the gun at one of those guys. I heard a loud pop, but it didn't sound loud enough for gunfire.

Then I look at the gun, and it fell apart in Dembo's hand and burned him for a second. Everyone was still in stunned silence. Dembo bent down to retrieve some of the gun parts that fell off during the misfire. The guy that Dembo was aiming at said, "Say you just tried to kill me nigga? Fuck that nigga! We fin ta kill y'all niggaz." Two of them ran inside the house. One of them went to his car. I knew they weren't giving us invitations to the next party.

They were going to get their guns, and I bet THEIR guns work. Dembo and I seeing that, ran as fast as we could for shelter. I have never run as fast as that in my life, but I had also never run FOR my life like that either. While we were running, I yelled out at Dembo, "I knew that gun was sorry when I saw it. Fuck!" Dembo replied, "It worked the other day!" Dembo ran to his friend's house. I didn't hear them behind us, so I kept going to my car as fast as I could.

Then I saw a familiar face. It was Vidal. He said, "Why you running?" I responded, "Fuckin Dembo. He's crazy as fuck!" Vidal said, "Well fuck, come inside. A couple of us is getting head from Chancy. I went inside. I said, "Who is Chancy?" Vidal said, "This big ass, thick, light-skinned black girl. Shit nigga, just wait your turn." I said, "Alright." I was too embarrassed to tell Vidal what just happened. He was always very critical, plus I knew I was safe with him, Charlie and Chris. A couple of the Big Tyme Playas, including Vidal, knew what happened to me at the club. They were there, but I didn't even know them at the time, and they didn't know me. Why would they help me? They were already into it with East Terrace Gang (Crips) vs. Wheatley courts B.T.P's(Bloods). They don't need to make it worse.

I told Vidal, "Dawg, I'm not doing the Dembo thing anymore. Fuck that fool." Vidal said, "I don't know why you did the Dembo thing in the first place." It took too long waiting on Charlie and Chris to get out of the room and I told Vidal, "I'ma go. They taking too long." Vidal said, "Shit I'ma go wit you. I know some hoes we can pick up."

I was very happy about that. Vidal was always good for that. He knew everybody. I could either go home to Ericka or go to this new girl I was fuckin named Fatty (Olympia Wilson). I decided on neither. I went with Vidal. We picked up these girls he knew and ended up singing some Ready for the World to them as foreplay. Vidal and I have really good voices, and their panties were practically coming off by the time we got to the room. I loved the situation I was in. I'm hangin with Big Tyme Playas. I'm Kenwood. I'm getting more pussy than I know what to do with. I'm strapped at all times. I'm selling a little dope and have some power. My baby mama at home and she about to have my son. There is nothing in my life that I would change.

CHAPTER ELEVEN

MARQUIS

A FEW MONTHS passed by and Ericka and I were getting along pretty well. We had gotten married on May 8th, 1991. My mother, who is really my grandmother, was there at the courthouse as a witness to the marriage. She was very happy we were getting married. She is a staunch Catholic and she has an old school way of thinking. If you get a girl pregnant and you love her, then you better treat her and your unborn child right and marry her, and I agree with that. Mary Wilson, Ericka's mother had to sign for her to get married because Ericka was only 16 years old at the time. We had a reception at my brother, Edward Valdespino's house with his wife of 6 years, Monica Fischnar.

My boy, Robert Grant, and his girlfriend Tasha were there. Ericka's best friend, Shannon Thompson, also came with us. None of my homeboys showed up, because I didn't tell them. For some strange reason, I was still ashamed of Ericka over the Henry situation. Even though I didn't know her at that time, I didn't give her the respect she deserved. A couple of months later, my boy Robert Grant got arrested for armed robbery. It made every news channel. Ericka and I looked at each other and were astonished. We didn't know Robert had that in him. I continued working at Pizza Hut and sometimes flipping my money by selling dope. The manager at Pizza Hut was Sam Trevino. At this time, his brother, Gabe Trevino, was an SAPD Officer, who later became a high ranking official and spokesperson at SAPD.

One of the shift leaders at Pizza Hut was Gerald. He got shot in Second Baptist on the Eastside. The bullet took off a piece of his upper nose. He had two black eyes. It looked nasty. A few weeks later, he was back at Pizza Hut and selling dope out of there. When I found out about his little operation, I said, "Damn Gerald, you ain't playing around." I told him I had my homies back in the hood, and I dabble in selling dope from time to time. We are pretty much doing the same thing, but some of his customers are our pizza delivery drivers, one in particular named Don. I told Gerald, "Don making good tips tonight. You probably gonna end up getting all his money for the night." Gerald being real cool like he always is, said, "That's the way the game works, son. I didn't invent it. I just try to perfect it." I told him, "Yeah, that's good. I got my own customers. I'm not gonna step on your shit." He replied, "I didn't think you were."

A crazy thing happened one night. I was out delivering pizza. I got back to the store and employees don't come in the front. We come in the back. As I walked in the back door, I saw a bunch of commotion. As I made my way through a few frightened waitresses, one of them said, "Did you see them when you drove up!" I said, "Who?" She said "The fuckin' robbers!" I was like, "What?" Then she said, "They shot Lori!"

Just then, I looked down by the stove and there was one of my managers, Lori Bibb, laying on the floor with two other waitresses holding her hand. She had a shotgun wound in her leg. Her leg looked really bad. You could practically see her bone. The skin on her leg was opened up. It looked like a shark attack. There was blood everywhere. I said, "Ga-Dam, they must have been real close to her when they shot." An employee motioned to me to come here and said, "Yeah he was real close. It was a black guy and a Mexican guy, and we think it was a girl driver. The fucked up thing about it was that she kind of provoked them when they walked in. She saw they had guns and meant business. She told them, 'Not today guys,' and we were all thinking, What? Lori shoulda just let them get the money and go." I was thinking, "Damn. If I had gotten there three minutes earlier, I would have shot those bastards."

I always have a gun in my car. I never leave home without it, never! We had a couple of Vietnam Vets as delivery drivers and they had seen people get shot with blood and guts everywhere through combat. So they acted as if it was routine and made sure Lori was coherent and okay, until EMS arrived. Then, they started cleaning up the blood as if they had done it before. I'm pretty sure Sam Trevino notified Mr. Jack Richmond, who is the owner of this particular Pizza Hut restaurant. Mr. Richmond sent two of his district managers to oversee the situation. After a while, Lori left to the hospital. The news media left. Customers gave statements to the police. Then, they left. Waitresses who had still been there, and in shock, left. This happened around 9pm-10pm. Nobody wanted to continue working. The phones were still ringing off the hook for people ordering pizza. Gerald and I were the only ones crazy enough to continue working. The two district managers looked at us and said, "Can you guys close out the store?" We both said, "Yes." I still had fifteen pizzas to deliver in two hours. I had made more money that night delivering pizzas than I ever had before.

The next day, Ericka and I went to the Spurs game. We were always at Spurs games on my nights off. We had plenty of money. I was selling dope on the side and working. It was all good. We would just walk up to the box office and get two 75 or 100 dollar tickets, and just go in. I had lost contact with Sean Elliott. We hadn't talked in a while. So I wasn't going to ask him for a ticket, when I had the money. After the Spurs game, Ericka and I were back at my house, sitting in my car, and we were arguing about a girl paging me when my brother, Martin Valdespino, drove by.

I was surprised to see him, since he lived in California. It must have taken him a couple of days to get here. I was yelling at Ericka and told her. "You were saved by the bell, by my brother Martin." She replied, "Whateva." I said, "Get out of the car, so you can meet him." I introduced my brother to Ericka and we talked for a while, and then I pulled him to the side and showed him my bank statement. It read 3,200 dollars. My brother was surprised and said, "That's all yours. What do you do?" I told him, "I work at Pizza Hut and I save." He bought it, and said "Wow, that's great." I didn't tell him that I sell dope and I'm a gang member of Kenwood and Big Tyme Playas. I didn't think that was fit conversation for someone I hadn't seen in years. Besides, if he stays here long enough he'll probably figure that out on his own.

At this time, Tullie was playing great basketball. He was 6'6, 235 pounds and had great post moves. He was not a great leader, but he could hit jumpers like a guard from all over the court. He had gotten lots of scholarship offers. One of them was from Tony Barone, the coach at Texas A&M. Tullie was excited about that. I told him, "You gotta work on your grades if you wanna go there.

You probably gonna go to the junior college for two years, and then you can meet up with Coach Barone at Texas A&M." He knew that I always knew what I was talking about, so he trusted my judgment.

A short time later, my son was born on December 23rd, 1991. Ericka named him Marquis Duane Valdespino. He was born at 3:30am in the morning. Ericka was at her house on Calmar Street on the Eastside. Her sister, Monica Thomas, took her with their mother, Mary Wilson, to the hospital. Crazy thing was it was real foggy that night, and I was praying they got there in one piece. Earlier in the day, on December 22nd, my favorite team the Dallas Cowboys beat the Atlanta Falcons and I went to sleep thinking about Alexander Wright's great kickoff return. I got a call from someone and I can't remember who it was from Ericka's house, saying, "It's time. We're on the way to the hospital." I jumped up and told my brother Martin, "Ericka's on the way to the hospital." He was asleep and said "Yeah. Ok."

I was racing to the hospital and the fog was bad, and I was thinking I won't make it to see my son being born. I made it on time, held Ericka's hand and watched my son come out of her womb. Ericka's mom, Mary Wilson, Monica, her sister who was also her baby coach and Aunt Joyce were there in the delivery room with us. It was the greatest thing I had ever witnessed in my life. It was also the greatest day of my life. The past two years, I had wanted a son. I wanted to raise a child better than I was raised. I want to see the better side of me, through my son. It was a great feeling that whole day. My brother Martin was there with my mother Gloria Valdespino. She said twice, "Look at that little man." The crazy thing, though, is that this didn't change me as far as running the streets, hanging with the homeboys, being a gang member and selling dope.

When I go hard at something that I want, I don't stop. I wanted to be the best dope dealer, the best gang member, be with my boys and try to have sex with as many girls as I could. It was a race to knock off as many hoes as my friends, and I wanted to win. Needless to say, because of this, Ericka and I had a falling out. She kept Marquis away from me for about 5 months. Tullie and I, Henry, Lester and Vidal ended up having these four black girls stay with us for a few weeks. They were runaways: Trina, Tanya, Nikki Loving and Sharon Holloway, known as Tweety. Lester was with Trina, the light-skinned one. Henry was with Tanya. She was brown-skinned and, as usual, I had sex with the two dark-skinned ones, Sharon and Nikki. I took more of an interest in Nikki. We took Sharon to David Johnson's house, aka Donkey Dick Dave, so she could stay there for a while.

One night, we were all at Henry's house. It was me, Henry, and Lester. Then, Dembo and Kendrick came over. Kendrick did his fucking-the-door routine; he was the entertainment. He made us all laugh. The runaway girls were scared, because outside across the street at Tullie's was Henry's girlfriend, Tarsha. Ericka was there as well. Ronald Green, Tullie's gay brother, knew that the runaway girls were at Henry's house and he was getting Tarsha and Ericka amped up about being inside Henry's house with other females. The girls didn't want to come outside because they were petrified Tarsha and Ericka would beat them up. Henry and I let them know, "Tarsha will beat your ass if you go out there. She don't play." It was a funny situation, with Ronald yelling at the runaways from outside, "Come up outta there. There's people here that want to talk to you!"

It was like a two hour standoff. Tarsha, Ronald and Ericka ended up leaving and I went home later. The runaways ended up leaving about a week later. It was a mutual parting. Henry and

I ended up having a falling out. Henry stole some of my NBA basketball cards. The first couple of days I was upset about it and wanted to whoop his ass which I could have, but after a while I felt sorry for him. I'm not trying to get on my high horse or anything but there's nothing Henry could do better than me. Was he jealous? I get more hoes than him. I play basketball better than him. I fight better than him. I'm much harder than he'll ever be, and I hadn't even come close to my peak yet.

I started to accumulate an arsenal of weapons. I had way more guns than he will ever have. It was almost as though I was originally his clone, but now I did everything better than he did. The only thing he had on me, was that he had more clout than me on the Eastside. He was a little more known, but I was going to make that change real soon. After he stole from me, I found out who he really was. When a friend steals from you or owes you money, that can be a good thing sometimes. After they do that, they tend not to want to come around you anymore, and this is an easy way to get rid of someone you don't want to be around anymore. I hold no animosity towards Henry. As a matter of fact, I love the guy. Without him, I wouldn't have Ericka, and my kids wouldn't be here.

In January of 1993, I went to Pasadena, California to the Rose Bowl to watch my favorite NFL Team, the Dallas Cowboys, whip the Buffalo Bills 52-17. My real father, Joe Mark Valdespino made me a promise that if the Cowboys made it back to the Super Bowl, that we would go. To his credit, he didn't go back on his promise. We stayed with my aunt, Anne Valdespino and her husband Paul Hodgins. When I got back to San Antonio, it was business as usual, selling crack and being a gang member. I met two new homies from the Eastside, Pierre, a light-skinned homie with green eyes that fucked anything that moved and Adrian

Hilliard, aka, Mugsy. As the Geto Boys from Houston would say about Adrian, "He had the mind of a lunatic." He is still, to this day, the craziest person I've ever met. He and I might be a match made in hell. Still, I wanted to prove I was a badass, and he was already proving he was.

CHAPTER TWELVE

ME AND CHRIS

I JUST GOT back from fucking this small, black girl named Terri. It was weird, because she had her newborn son in the room. His name was Demetrius. I told her, "Let's move to the living room." I did not want him hearing us. After I finished, I went to the Eastside with Tullie on Blue Bonnet St. to score some cocaine from Melvin. Vidal, Adrian, Vidal's brother, Chris Kelly, or as Tullie would sometimes called him, Christmas Kelly, and some girl named Latrice were there at the time. Chris Kelly, by this point, had been making a name for himself as a gangster. He had been shot on the MLK Bridge and survived. I probably fucked ten girls in 1993 just because I knew who Chris was, and because he was my homeboy. Melvin Turner was big time in me and Tullie's eyes. Melvin was like his uncle, Hyron, this old school cat who was a legend. The story goes: Hyron got word somehow the Feds were gonna raid him and he fled with three of those big hefty cinch sack grocery bags of cash filled up.

That was the great thing about Melvin, like his Uncle Hyron, he never flaunted his money. He drove around in a blue, beat-up old Hyundai, and always drove the speed limit. That way, he could make trips to Houston to get the dope and wouldn't get pulled over. He was a light-skinned black man with long curly hair, like a perm. Maybe the cops thought he was white and he didn't get the "driving while black" treatment.

Nobody ever asked Melvin where he got his cocaine from. We didn't care. That was his business. He reminded me of the great mafia bosses like Tony Accardo and Carlo Gambino. You wouldn't have known Don Carlo or Tony Accardo (The Big Tuna) were millionaire mob bosses. They both dressed like they were taking their wives to Friday night bingo. Melvin dressed the same unassuming way. He didn't conduct his business in a flashy way. He just got the job done, without bringing attention to himself. The only time I saw Melvin look the part of a dope dealer was when he went out to the club. Other than that, he looked like a guy going to get some milk for his mother at the store. We would score an ounce or two from Melvin at three hundred dollars an ounce and we would make about seven hundred to seven hundred-fifty dollars off each ounce.

Chris Kelly had asked Vidal and me to accompany him to his ex-girlfriend's house, where he had been staying. Her name was Shantell Robinson. When we got there she started screaming, "Get all your shit you brought up in here! You a sorry ass nigga fuckin' wit all those hoes! Hurry up shit!" She was throwing his stuff out of the apartment and Vidal and I were just watching the action. She told us, "What the fuck y'all lookin at! Help him out! Y'all muthafuckas wanna be nosy!" Then, Chris looked at us and said "Come on. Help a nigga out." So we started grabbing some of his shit and taking it downstairs. I grabbed one of his jackets and it happened to be a Dallas Cowboys bomber, and it looked great. Chris saw that I was admiring it and said, "You want it? I'll trade you for the one you got on." I thought about it for a second and said, "Alright". My jacket was a pullover. His was a bomber jacket with a zipper. I liked it better.

So I took mine off, gave it to him and put his on. Shantell was watching us with this dismayed look and said, "Y'all can do all that trading shit outside! Get the fuck out of my house!" Vidal looked at her with his usual puzzled expression. "Ga-dam Shantell.Calm down. We almost outta here." We dropped Chris off, with all his shit, back at his house in Kirby. I still have that jacket to this day.

Later on that night, I was on Bluebonnet Street with Chris, Melvin, Adrian and Charlie and this new guy I met named Raynard. Vidal left in a geeker car. A geeker car is a ride you get from a crack smoker who will rent you his car for at least a twenty dollar hit of crack. Sometimes you can run into a problem if you don't bring the car back in a few hours. The geeker gets paranoid and can report the car stolen.

Usually after that, you catch that person and beat the shit out of him or her. It usually doesn't happen, because the geekers know better. Chris left for about an hour, and when he walked up I asked him, "Where you creep off to?" Chris said, very fast with broken English, "I just dropped a dub off at my homeboy's, T-jones. You seen Vidal? That nigga be ha-ciding right? He be ha-ciding". I replied, "Yeah he do be trying to show out sometimes." Then Chris changed the subject suddenly. He started babbling quickly and incoherently, saying something like, "Ga-dam, that bitch want money from me. They want me to go down there nigga and talk to them. Talkin about child-support nigga. I don't want to go down there and talk to them hoes, nigga." That's when I looked at him and said to him for the first time, "Damn, Chris you need mutha-fuckin captions when you talk, dawg." Then, Melvin jumped in laughing "Chris, just go down there tomorrow and talk to them. Once they hear you talk, they going to feel sorry for you and let you make it." Chris embarrassed, responded "Shut up nigga!", but everyone was laughing, including Chris.

A couple of weeks later my parents went out of town, and I had, Chris, Vidal, Pierre, Tullie and Adrian over. I had brought this girl Kesha to the crib, and she had brought her friend Teresa. I took Kesha into the front room, my parent's room. Kesha was a thick black girl, with matching titties, and a matching ass. I started fucking her and I turned around and I could see Tullie and Vidal watching me and hearing her moan. I just knew Chris, Pierre andAdrian were fucking Teresa in my room. Kesha brought her for a reason. She knew her friend was gonna get down and fuck. After I finished fucking, Kesha went into the shower to clean herself up, like all females should do. I went in my room and that's where they had Teresa at. I had a couch in there and Adrian, Chris, Pierre,Tullie and Vidal had her surrounded.

I felt bad for her. She looked like a piece of meat about to get devoured by lions. I get to my door, and Chris sees that I entered the room. Chris said, "Marcus, turn the light off." I went ahead and I turned the light off. All of the sudden you heard a smack like skin to skin contact. As soon as I heard that, I cut the light back on and everybody looked at the girl and she had a cut on her nose and was bleeding. I immediately thought back to the story Charlie had told me when Chris tried to get a girl's phone number at the bus stop. When she refused the "great Chris Kelly", he was so embarrassed that he turned the car back around and got out the car walked up to her and slapped the hell out of her.

Here, it seemed to be happening again. Chris said, "Ga-Dam Adrian!Why you hit that girl like that! We just sitting here and we tryin to talk to her and you got to hit her like that!" Adrian replied, "You got me fucked up Chris. I didn't hit that bitch! You hit that bitch!" Then Chris, laughing said, "I did right?" I tried to intervene. "Vidal, she bleeding. Give her that towel right there." Vidal handed her one of my towels. Tears were coming down her eyes. She wiped the blood and tears away. I could see she was scared and Adrian said, "You look good now mama." Then he proceeded to push her back on the bed and start to take her clothes off. I was thinking, "Damn these fools are crazy." At that moment, the bathroom door came open and Kesha was coming straight to my room. I had to short stop her ass so she wouldn't be able to see what was happening with her friend in my room.

I got her right before she got to the door. She asked me: "What my friend doin? What's goin on in there?" I said, "Hold on baby. Shit. She getting her fuck on." Kesha responded, "They ain't started fuckin yet?" I said, "I guess they just been talkin for a minute." She looked at me suspiciously. "How many niggaz in there?" I knew there was five of them but I told her "Two or something, maybe three." She wasn't happy. "That's fucked up. I brought my friend over to fuck one of your homeboys, and there's three niggaz in there?!" I tried to calm her down. "Babygirl, you seen this girl in action. You know her. You knew she came over to fuck. How many guys has she fucked before at one time, that you knew about?" She said, "Two at the most" I responded, "Well, it's three in there, so she's about to step up her game a bit.

There's a first time for everything, mama." Kesha replied "That's fucked up." At the exact same time when Kesha said that, you can hear Teresa in there hollering a little bit. Kesha wasn't satisfied with what I had told her. "Let me make sure she alright." I said, "Babygirl she's getting her fuck on. You seen people fuck before. She's good, mama. Didn't you say you was hungry earlier?"

She responded, "Yeah a bitch is hungry." I replied, "Well let's get the bitch something to eat." She said, smiling, "Oh fuck you boy." As she stuck her finger out laughing, she continued, "You better watch yourself." "Let's go,"I told her, as I started pushing her towards the door.

After we got back from eating, Kesha's sister came to pick her up and I asked her, "What about your friend?" Kesha said, "She'll get a ride home. She got plenty of kinfolk." I wasn't about to let that happen. "I'm taking her home my damn self. I don't want her kinfolk to know where I live." She replied, "Good, you smart," as she got into her sister's Cadillac, and drove away.

Adrian, Pierre and Chris left back to the Eastside and Tullie and me, Vidal and Teresa stayed the night. That night, I went to the bathroom, and when I opened the door, Tullie was in there fuckin her on the bathroom floor and I said, "Damn, Tullie, you couldn't wait til you got to the bed?" Later on in the night, Tullie and I went outside and we could hear Vidal and Teresa talking inside. Teresa was saying, "No Vidal! No Vidal!" as they were fuckin'. The next day, Tullie and Vidal went back to Kenwood and I took the girl home. I ended up smoothing things over with Teresa about my homeboy's actions, and she gave me her number and said I was real nice and everything.

A couple of days later me, Vidal, Chris, Melvin, Charlie, Raynard, Tullie, Adrian, Pierre, and Chris' little brother Kevin, were all hanging out on Bluebonnet St. Chris Kelly, had fucked X's girl from Crockett St. and they had a little crew called the Crockett St. Boys. X was one of the main leaders. X, as you can imagine, was pissed off at Chris. We heard that the Crockett Street boys wanted a little revenge on BigTyme Playas because of that situation, and probably some other shit I didn't know about. We were outside for a while, and Chris had disappeared and amazingly nobody noticed as other members of B.T.P. Gang were showing up there that I didn't recognize. A

ll the sudden, about15 minutes later, this guy jumps out of the bushes, by one of the houses, yelling "Tha-tha-tha-tha-tha-tha!" pretending to shoot at us with an AK 47 in his hand, and a blue bandana on and making loud noises like bullets were coming out. Everybody jumped back for a second. We was scared for a couple of seconds, like it was a real deal. Then the man pulled down the blue bandana, and to everybody's amazement, it was Chris Kelly. He was wearing the enemy's colors at the time, but we didn't know it was Chris at first, until he pulled down the blue bandana. Chris, in anger, told us, "All y'all just slipping, nigga! I'd a killed all y'all niggaz. All y'all just chillin and shit. What if X and them came down? Fuck they'd a killed all y'all niggaz. What the fuck is y'all doing! Niggaz come at us. We gotta be ready, Nigga!" and he emphasized again, "All y'all niggaz woulda been shot."

I had been behind a car the whole time and had pulled out one of my guns, a 38special. I responded to Chris. "Chris, I woulda killed your ass," as I was pointing my gun in his direction. He looked at me with an astonished look, like,"Ah, shit yeah! Marcus had a gun." He said very loudly and proudly "See, look at Marcus. He ain't been here that long and the nigga is already down! I woulda shot a bunch of y'all right here and that nigga woulda shot me. What if they come down here right now, nigga? All y'all be dead! Shit, Marcus be strapped. That nigga is down. All of y'all woulda been dead." I replied, "Chris you right, but you'da been dead, 100%, right there on the spot. You wouldn't a moved no further. Yeah, you'd a killed half of us, but I d' a shot the shit out of your ass. I don't miss." Chris said, "See, that's what I'm talkin bout!"

Melvin got embarrassed and pissed off. Melvin told Chris, "You got me fucked up." Then Melvin reached in his car and pulled out his two 9mm guns with 16 shots in each of them. Melvin said, "I don't need no niggaz to stand with me. I got 16 shots in each gun. I got 32 gang members with me, nigga." As he was looking around at everybody, he repeated. "I got 32 gang members, nigga. I don't need all these niggas with me! When my bullets run out, then I'll just die. But I'm gonna kill a whole lot of muthafuckas, before they kill me." Everybody was silent. Then Vidal broke the silence and said, "Hell yeah!" That's right, but that's why I ride with Marcus. He always be strapped and he the only one in the hood with license and insurance. Let's go to the club." Vidal was always one to try to break up moments of tension with his humor, and this was no exception.

Thinking back on that, I remember at that time, how that made me respect Melvin even more than I had previously. He didn't need to ride with his crew all the time. He always rode with his two 9 mms, and if he got into a situation, he would handle it himself. He had both his guns and his bullets that he called his 32 gang members.

We got into our cars and we were going to the club, the Main Event on Ashby. We went around by the Wheatley Courts, and Melvin drove by around all of our cars and said,"The Main Event, The Main Event." We were at the Main Event for about thirty minutes, and Charlie walked up to me, Tullie and Vidal and said, "This nigga, Melvin, gave his phone numba on a hundred dollar bill to this fine ass bitch." Tullie said, "That's a little steep for me. I'll try it with a 20." We were all laughing. Then, I saw Willie Heights. He went to Fox Tech High school, and my grandmother who adopted me had taught Willie Heights at Bowden Elementary. So, I have known Willie for a long time. I said hi to Willie but I wish I would have said more to him because a few months later he ended up getting shot and killed on the Eastside. Rest in peace, Willie.

I ended up fuckin' Monica Heights, his cousin. Monica Heights was black and beautiful. A few months after that, I went back to her apartment. After I fucked her, she went to sleep and I was sitting on her couch, and she had a bunch of letters from the jail house from some fool named Chris Crisp. I was being nosy, so I just picked up one of the letters and it read, "I can't wait to put my face in between those legs again." I thought to myself, my dick was just there. I see why he's writing her. She got some good pussy. After I read a couple of the fuck pages from the jail house, it made me wanna fuck her again. So I went back in there and woke her up. I was hard again, and she wasn't even trippin. I ended up hittin' it over the next year. That was some good pussy.

The next day, I went to the Wheatley Courts and Chris Kelly wanted me to give him a ride. The ironic thing was, he was fucking Jackee Coleman, the one who was with me at the club incident a few years ago when I was a nobody. Not anymore. Chris stayed with Jackee in the courts. She went from Joe Rick to Chris Kelly and who knows who else in between. Jackee was with Chris. I could care less. Everybody fucks everybody. It's a fuck fest in the ghetto. Unless you make that girl your wife and you invite your family and her family and walk down that aisle with her, it don't matter. Nobody I knew did that anyway. It's a free-for-all with sex. 70% of black women aren't married. That's part of the reason why the black community is in despair. Hardly any black women I knew were married. I've been hearing all the time on CNN, MSNBC, everywhere, that 72% of black children are born out of wedlock. I don't know what it was at that time, but it sure doesn't seem like it's changed much to me. That 72% and 70%, those statistics kind of go hand in hand. They feed off each other. Martin Luther King is probably rolling over in his grave. Those numbers have tripled and, I repeat, tripled since Dr. King's death, and it's supposed to be better for black people? Ain't that a bitch!

Chris asked me to take him somewhere. He had an old Impala with some rims on it. It was a nice car, but when he could avoid using it for a simple errand, he'd do that because his car attracts attention from the police. I was over there with Vidal as usual. He was with Nena Clayton, his baby mama. So Chris asked me to give him a ride to get something real quick. Chris had been shot a few weeks ago. I'm not even sure who shot him.

He gets in the car. He has red house shoes, red Dickies shorts and a white wife beater and he just got his hair did. It was like in some lil dookies or something with rubber bands. So his hair was perfect and he had the golds in his mouth. He said, "We just gotta pull up here and pick up something right quick." I said, "Chris you ain't gonna believe this, the fuckin police is behind us." Chris responded, "What! Lose them hoes, nigga! Step on the gas and turn the corner. Let me jump out this bitch! Go nigga! Go nigga! Pull over, pull over, right here!" I did what he said and tried to elude the police. I was in it for life. I was in that frame of mind. I didn't give a fuck about no police. I 'm trying to speed up a little bit.I was about to pull over and I was gonna stay in the car.

I didn't have any warrants. I had my license and insurance like Vidal said. Chris suddenly changed his mind and said, "You know what nigga? I ain't got nothing but a couple of ticket warrants. I'll sit my little two or three days in jail. Nigga look at me. I just been shot, my hair just got did.I got on my red Dickie shorts on. I got my red house shoes on,nigga. You know what I'm saying? I just got out of the shower. I got my wife beata on Nigga! This is how you go to jail nigga. Just like this. I'm a star, nigga. I'm gonna walk up in there just like this!" I replied, "Shit, alright." I was just gonna pull over for the police.

So the police cut on the sirens. At that time, they had been following us for about 3 blocks and I guess Chris just gonna go to jail. Fuck it. Then, all of the sudden, he changed his mind for the third time as reached for his right pocket and said, "Naw! naw! Man, that bitch got my keys! Hell naw nigga. Go go go!" He was worried that Jackee would ride around in his car for the three days while he would be in jail. Maybe she might go see another nigga or wreck his car and shit. Chris continued: "That bitch gonna be drivin' my car nigga, for 3 days! Pull over nigga!" I quickly pulled over. He got out of the car and ran, and the police didn't go after him. They went after the driver of the car which was me, and they pulled me over and the police officer ran to my car and said, "Put your hands where I can see them and step out of the vehicle!" Then the cop asked me a fucked up question. He said, "What is he running for!" I said, "I guess he didn't wanna see your ass."

The cop replied, "Shut the fuck up and quit being smart. Who was that?" I said, "He's a friend of a friend. He asked me to take him to the store. I don't know his name." The cop replied, "You mean you are that fucking stupid? You put somebody in your car and you don't know his name!" I replied, "What did you want me to do, grab him before he jumped out? That's your job." The cop responded, "Shut up, smart ass." The police hemmed me up for about 30 minutes, running my name and searching my car. I left my gun with Vidal. After that, I just went back to Kenwood. Later on that night I picked Vidal back up from the Wheatley Courts and was back at another party.

It was about midnight and everybody was at a party at Hays Street. Me Tullie,Adrian, Chris, Melvin, Vidal, Charlie, Pierre, Raynard, Chris's younger brother Kevin and Ralph and a bunch a girls. Chris was the shit at the party. He had just been shot a few weeks ago driving in a car on Martin Luther King bridge while being shot at by another car. While Chris was holding court, there were a lot of girls around him and I was sitting next to him. He had small very visible holes in him from the gunshots he had taken in the car drive by, and he was telling the girls to put their fingers in his bullet hole wounds and some of them were freaked out by it and some of them were attracted to it, like I'm touching a real gangsta that just got shot.

As I'm sitting next to him, I told him, "Chris it seems like everyone wants to shoot you. Sitting next to you, I'm putting myself in the line of fire. I'm in danger. I'm a target now, we all like targets." He replied, "That's how gangstas really do. You know what I'm saying? Sometimes you gotta put yourself out there and let everybody know that you don't bar none. That you ain't no hoe! You ain't no joke. You know what I'm sayin?" I said, "I do. I just want to avoid the getting shot part, but I gotch you." Just as I was saying that, a Cadillac passed by and a whole buncha niggaz was in the Cadillac and half of us was watching the Cadillac and the other half was still drinking and having a good time. As soon as the Cadillac got to the end of the block, it turned around and that's when I said, "Chris, that Cadillac turning around."

Chris had a 9mm gun and he cocked it back, and I pulled out my 38, and Chris let it be known that we might be in trouble.

"Everybody head to the back of the house!" Everybody started heading to the back of the house and some of us just got behind cars parked out back, and me and Chris had our guns pointed at the Cadillac but they couldn't see us. The Cadillac passed by with no incident and everybody was relieved. That pretty much describes some of the essence of the hood, that we could still party on the front lawn of a place knowing that we have beefs with other sets and not give a fuck. It gives you an adrenaline rush when a car passes by and then they make the block and turn around and anything can happen at any second, and all of our lives are on the line. We're willing to take that chance and have a good time. It's a crazy existence.

That night I met this girl named Kim Cypher who supposedly had a baby by my old homeboy David Johnson from the East Terrace. We were vibin' pretty good. What I didn't realize at the time was that Ralph was trying to get at her. Kim was like 18 years old. Ralph was always a nigga that liked young hoes for some reason, so Kim was old for him. At the end of the night I told Vida, l "Let's go" and Kim came with me and Vidal said, "I don't know. Ralph's gonna be mad at you." I said, "I don't give a fuck. I got a gun too. Its survival of the fittest .You let the bitch decide." I dropped Vidal off at one of his hoe's houses, and I took Kim back to her apartment off Broadway and fucked all night.

I always liked hanging with Chris Kelly. It was always an adventure. You never knew what was gonna happen. I never had any problem with Chris. He knew I wasn't to be played with, and I definitely knew he wasn't to be played with. It was a common understanding. Years later, Chris spent a few years in the penitentiary. I give Chris some props. He is in his mid- thirties and still one of the only niggaz from the early 90s still surviving and thriving in the streets.

CHAPTER THIRTEEN

KENWOOD

TULLIE ENDED UP going to Clarendon Junior College. He got a full scholarship, but before he left he worked out with Coach Nevil Shed. Coach Shed was a center for Texas Western University in 1966, which later became known as U.T.E.P. They were the first all-African-American starting five to win the N.C.A.A championship. They beat Adolph Rupp's Kentucky team, led by future Los Angeles Lakers coach, Pat Riley. They had to endure racism and lots of hardships along the way just to get to that point. His was a tremendous story. Coach Shed was selected in the 4th round by the Boston Celtics, and he backed up the great Bill Russell. He won an NCAA championship and an NBA Championship, and is a better human being than his basketball accomplishments alone merit. In 2006, Hollywood made a movie about the college championship season for Texas Western University, starring Josh Lucas and called Glory Road. Tullie and I went to see Coach Shed at the University of Texas at San Antonio to ask him if he could work with Tullie on how to improve his game. Coach Shed agreed and we worked with Coach Shed two weeks before Tullie went to college. I learned a lot about post moves and what big men are supposed to do in certain situations from Coach Shed. It was a great learning experience for Tullie. He had skill already. Coach Shed perfected Tullie's game in the post. With Coach Shed's tutelage, Tullie was more than ready for college basketball.

Meanwhile, back in Kenwood, the hood was growing every day. I had gotten there in 1989, but it seemed like everyone just started coming out and wanting to hang together every day. Henry had moved to the Glen. There was Jamal Montgomery, aka Chubby, Kevin Wallace, Carlton Wilson, Erik Twyman (Stix) Maurice, aka Scarface, Dongi Lomax, Devlin Jefferson, aka baby Tyson, Shawn Thorton, who lives with his girlfriend Denise Lomax and her daughter Destiny Lomax, Jumbo, The Crawford boys— Peanut and Omari, and two Mexican boys who used to come around often, Eric Piceno and Zeke Luna. Tullie used to say if a nigga ever get into it with Devlin, you better come correct and wit everything you got to even stand a chance fighting his ass.

Tullie was gone for a few months, but I knew he was homesick. He liked being around us too much. We were his family. When he was gone, part of my life was about keeping up with Vidal by trying to fuck as many hoes as he did. One day, I went to fuck this fine, thick ass black girl named Sabrina, on Lucas St. I took my SKS machine gun with me everywhere I went. An SKS, upon striking you, will take your arm off and tear you a new asshole. People probably think I am crazy. I took my SKS from the front seat of my ride in broad daylight, put it over my shoulder as if were in a war zone and walked up to Sabrina's apartment and knocked on the door. I wanted to fuck so bad, that I forgot to lock her front door and I left my SKS on the couch. While I'm in her room, the front door opens, and then slams real hard. I stopped fucking and said, "Who is that?" She said it was her little brother. I said, "Oh O.K.," and continued. I was relieved it wasn't another nigga or her mom. Then I thought, what if that boy grabs my gun and shoots himself? I will be on the news for some kind of negligent homicide. I jumped up and said, "Oh, shit! I left the gun in the living room." She said, "We'll get it baby. I want to finish." I opened the door, my dick hard as a rock.

The little boy saw me as we stared at each other for a second and I got my gun off the couch. I was thinking, what could be going through this little boy's mind? This here white man with his dick hanging out was coming out of my sister's room getting a big-ass machine gun and going back into her room. That must have split his wig. I went back in the room and finished. When I was leaving, the little boy wasn't there anymore. He was probably at his friend's house telling him what just happened. I got back to Kenwood and told Vidal what had happened. He said, "Ga-Dam, Marcus. Don't be stingy with the hoes. Do she have a friend or a cousin or something?" I replied, "She probably do. I'll find out." Vidal asked me, "Why did God make pussy so good?" I said "That's a good question. That is the first thing I am going to ask him or her when I get up there."

That's how we talked to each other and how we did things. Me, Tullie and Vidal shared pretty much everything with each other. Vidal went back to Wheatley Courts with Chris, Melvin, Charlie, Omar and Sleazy. Years later, when I would head back to the Courts, Omar and I would talk sports for hours. I stayed in Kenwood till about 4a.m. I was fucking with Meshion Mathis a little bit. She stayed next door to Tullie, with her children Tiffany, La'toya, Marcus and Larry. Her kinfolk were big time gangsters on the Eastside, Andre and Ray Mathis. She climbed through

Tullie's window to give me some pussy a couple times. She would tell me while she was fucking me that she loved sucking on white skin. I guess to her it was an aphrodisiac because she was real dark and I was real white. She liked looking at our skin together. I grew fond of her sons Marcus Mathis and little Larry Williams.

I used to take them to the store and little Larry Williams used to always say, "I'm gonna be a bad-ass nigga!" He was 3 years old and everybody thought it was cute that he said that. They would make him repeat it. His momma, Meshion, would say, "Tell Marcus. What you gonna be?" Larry would say it again. "When I grow up I'm gonna be a bad-ass nigga!" Everybody would start laughing, including me. At the time, I didn't know any better. A few years later her son, Marcus Mathis ended up going to the penitentiary, for what I don't know. I used to fuck Wylette Brown a bunch of times too. Her brother Willie Brown, his friends Willie Collins and Michael Adams were on crack and were good loyal customers. Wylette had some good pussy, but I felt sorry for her one day when she and Tarsha Kyle got into it and Tarsha beat her up real bad. Willie stabbed Ronald once and Wylette said something to Ronald like my brother gonna stab you again. "What did she say that for?" Ronald said. "You black bitch! You and he ain't gonna stab a mutha fucking thing!" And Ronald commits to whopping her ass.

The next day I fucked some girl named Samantha Hastings at the Suzanne Motel on Commerce St. and after that I went home to be with my wife and child. I still tried to maintain a family life despite all the madness. It was sometimes boring when Tullie was in college. One time, Chubby and Kevin called me because they were into it with some niggaz and I told them I wasn't coming because I'm doing family time right now. I figured they're big boys. They can handle it. They got mad, and

I understand why, but unless your name is Tullie, Vidal, Phat Cheez or Tony, I wasn't in a hurry to get there. What I love about all my homeboys is that there is no bitch in them. Try and pull a hoe card out of them, and see what happens to you. To cure some of my boredom, I went to hang with Adrian Hilliard and that almost became my downfall.

CHAPTER FOURTEEN

CRAZY ASS ADRIAN

I FIRST MET Adrian Hilliard through Vidal. Vidal told me some wild stories about Adrian being crazy. Vidal said that one time Adrian was taking too long to get ready and they started to drive off because they got tired of waiting for him. They were going to the mall and they wanted to hurry. Adrian started shooting at them, because he got mad that they were gonna leave him. So, they had to turn back around and get him. Another time, there was a cop on the highway and Vidal and some of the homies were in somebody's yard and you could see the highway from the yard and they were daring Adrian to shoot at the cop. One of them said, "I bet you won't shoot at the police, Adrian!" You can't dare a throwed-off person like Adrian, so he started shooting at the police, much to everybody's amazement. So, needless to say, Adrian's not to be played with and is CRAZY.

The first time I met Adrian, me and Vidal picked him up on Rio Grande St. He was walking with his girlfriend and he had a backpack with him, and we got off the road for a little while and I started talking with him. I showed him that I was always strapped, and I let him see my 38 handgun. Then, he looked at me and said, "Yeah that all good, but where's your backup gun?" I was thinking to myself, "Is this man for real? My backup gun?" I told him right away, "I carry a deuce 5 in my glove compartment in my ride(a deuce 5 is a handgun)." He replied, "That's tight. Every nigga gotta have a backup gun." I was impressed because that was the first person since my father that had told me that every man worth a piss should have a backup gun. In his backpack, Adrian had two 45s. That's the Dirty Harry gun. So, that was my introduction to Adrian. Here he was walking with his girlfriend with two guns in his backpack. Vidal, with his usually funny self, upon hearing our conversation said, "Oh lord, y'all might be a match made in heaven."

A few days later, Adrian had got this girl to come see him and they were at my house. Me and Tullie were just chillin' and waiting on him to finish fucking. We all have this thing where everybody likes to watch everybody fuck. This may seem sick to some people, but we were young men in a gang world, with a gang mentality, living a crazy lifestyle. So Adrian is in my room handling his business and Tullie wants to watch Adrian fuck. Tullie is crazy because he just finished watching Adrian fuck Tarsha Kyle the other day and making her yell Mugsy. We all fucked Tarsha before, so I guess it wasn't a big deal to Tullie. He wanted to watch Adrian fuck a new hoe. Tullie slowly opened the door and I followed closely behind. Adrian could hear us and told us very loudly, "Say, I need my privacy. I'm trying to fuck my girl!" We said alright, we'll leave. So, we left the room.

Tullie would not listen and was determined to watch. So Tullie went back in the room with me a good distance behind, and Adrian said, "I told y'all niggaz. Get the fuck outta here! I need my privacy!" So, we left again. I was a feeling a little uneasy about the situation. I remember Adrian talking about pulling the juice on us like the movie where a guy turned on his homies. So in my eyes, we're giving him food for thought. It seemed this was all a big game for Tullie. He was laughing and he went back in. Adrian saw him again and was even more upset. "I'm tryin to get my fuck on! Get the fuck outta here! I'm not gonna tell y'all again!" So, we left the room again.

We knew Adrian was crazy and likes to shoot at people, even his hom boys, and it just dawned on me that there is a duece-fivein there by the window with Adrian and he knew it. I told Tullie. "Adrian's pissed off.We need to get that gun away from him." So we proceeded to go back in the room and you could hear the girl yelling out in ecstasy,"Mugsy, Mugsy!", and then he saw Tullie and he told Tullie very angrily "I told y'all niggaz not to becoming up in here!" Tullie tried to grab the deuce 5 off the windowsill, but before he could reach it, Adrian beat him to it and started shooting. Tullie ducked and ran outta there as fast as he could.

I was already outside waiting on Tullie, hoping he wasn't shot but I kind of knew Adrian was just scaring us. Adrian shot two holes in the corner of the ceiling. I could hear Adrian yell, "I told y'all niggaz.I'm not playin round with y'all!" Tullie and I were outside laughing and I remember saying, "Why are we laughing?""I don't know," Tullie said. "Shit, that nigga is crazy!" I said, "I told you." About thirty minutes later, Adrian came out of the room and everything was all good. I was thinking, "Damn, how many more days do I got to spend with crazy ass Adrian."

We went to Kenwood later on and Tony and Phat Cheez were there. Phat Cheez and Tony were Tullie's nephews. I met them when they were 9 and 10 years old and neither one were punks. They were tough kids. Me and Tullie and Phat Cheez decided to go to the store, and as we were leaving I saw Adrian and Tony playing a hitting game. The object of the game was to hit one another on the arm and see who gives up first. We left for about ten minutes and when we came back we saw Tony in the living room, crying and holding his arm. I looked at his arm and it was black and blue. Tony doesn't cry for shit, so for him to be crying it meant that it was a significant hit by Adrian. Tullie and Phat Cheez became irate. Tullie said, "Where is Adrian!" Tony responded, "In your room." Tullie went straight for his room. Tullie told Adrian very loudly, "You hit Tony?" Adrian said, "Yeah." Tullie responded, "You know that's my nephew right? I ain't really trippin hard because Tony wanta put himself in a grown man's position. He wanna play with the big boys, then once in a while he gonna get dealt with like a grown man. You know what I'm sayin? But let me tell you something, dawg. Don't ever put your hands on that boy again! If my nephew fuck up! Then you come and tell me! If you ever hit him again, thenit's gonna be me and you, nigga!" Adrian responded with, "All right nigga. I respect that. That's your nephew." I was very happy Adrian respected that Tullie was defending his kinfolk. I jumped in and completely changed the subject the best way I knew how. I said, "What's up wit them hoes tonight? We need to start getting ready for the club."

Later on that night, we all went to the club. This Mexican girl was dancing nasty all night with Adrian and Tullie. So she comes back with us from the club. We are in two different cars and she starts putting her ass in the window sill of the first car that has Adrian and Tullie in it, while I'm driving the second car with Omari, Peanut, Phat Cheez and Tony. I remember thinking, "We all are gonna fuck this hoe." The crazy thing is that I looked in the back seat and saw this little girl who couldn't have been more than 10 years old in my car. I was so busy getting phone numbers at the club and talking to Tullie, I didn't notice the little girl get in the backseat. I looked at her through the rearview mirror and said, "Who are you?" Omari answered for her and replied, "She her little sister Marcus from the one Tullie with." I replied, "Shit how in the fuck her little sister get in the car with us?" Nobody replied. So I got this little girl in the car with us. She was a trooper though. She wasn't scared. I looked back at her again and asked her, "You alright?" She said, "Yes."

Not being worried at all, we arrived at Tullie's house on 150 Horace St. The older sister who was riding with Tullie and Adrian started booty shaking on the stairs while walking to Tullie's front door. Everybody gets in the house and her little sister sits on the couch. Adrian and Tullie take the older girl to the back to Tullie's room. As Tullie passes by me he said, "We finta tear this pussy up." I could tell Adrian was happy too. I was in the living room with Peanut,Omari, Phat Cheez,Tony and the little girl. About two minutes later, you heard the most fucked up word that no nigga that's about to fuck wants to hear. She yelled, "NO!" Then I heard her say, "Can you just take us home? Me and my little sister are tired."

As you can imagine, Adrian wasn't having that. He yelled, "Fuck you bitch! You ain't finto play with a nigga! Doing all that stripping and shit! You fins to fuck, bitch! You gonna give me some pussy!" Amazingly, it seemed like Tullie kind of agreed with Adrian because he didn't say a word. I walked back there to see what washappening and I saw Adrian throw her on the bed. She started fighting back. She yelled, "No stop! Please." He pulled her panties off. She was kicking and Adrian started slapping her. Adrian yelled, "I'm gonna teach your mutherfuckin ass a lesson!"

There was a mac11 in the room(a Mac 11 is a fully automatic machine gun with 9 mm bullets, and a 30 round clip).

Adrian grabbed the gun and started putting the tip of the gun in her pussy, stroking it and telling her, "You like that bitch!" I said, "Adrian, what if that gun go off? You know there is always one in the chamber!" Adrian said, "I don't give a fuck! That's what that bitch might need and learn not to play with real ass niggaz!" Tullie was getting uneasy. "Adrian! Put the gun down. Let's just fuck her!" So Adrian puts the gun down and he starts fucking her.

At this point, everybody is at the door watching. Tony, Phat cheez, Omari,and Peanut. Then, I thought for a second. They left the little girl in the living room. I looked at all of them and said very loudly, "Where is the little girl at?!" Everybody looked around for a second and looked at each other like they didn't know. So I ran back down the hallway and there she was in the kitchen, with the land line phone to her ear. I instantly grabbed the phone from her and put the phone to my ear to see if I could hear someone talking on the other end. I didn't want to say anything on the phone because then I would incriminate myself, just in case she dialed 911.

Then my voice would be on every news channel in San Antonio with a 911 rape call, forever. So, I hung the phone up and looked at the little girl and said with a stern voice, "Who were you talking to?" She stared at me with a terrified look and said, "Nobody." I replied, "You had to be talking to someone. Why did you pick up the phone?" Looking petrified, she didn't say anything.Then Omari jumped at her and said, "Naw little bitch! Who were you on the phone with?!" I said, "Omari get back and calm down!" I looked at her again and said, "Who were you on the phone with? Your mom?"She started crying and again said,

"Nobody". That's when I had enough of this situation and said, "They gotta go."

I told the little girl, "Go sit on the couch." I started walking down the hallway and saw Tullie and he said, "What happened?" I told him very deliberately, "They have to go right now. It's over. Your momma has worked too hard for this house to throw it away on some bullshit like this. They got to go, and I'm not taking them home. Tell Adrian he has to take them home."

Tullie went in the room and told Adrian."Say dawg, they have to go and Marcus said he ain't going to take them home." Adrian stopped fucking and responded, "Fuck it, I'll take them home. It ain't like I ain't never took a stupid bitch home before." Adrian put them in the geeker car that he rented out for a 20dollar piece of rock. I could imagine the terror going on in the little sister's head, listening to her big sister getting raped.That's the main reason I cut that situation short.

We left Tullie's house for 24 hours because we didn't know if the girls would find their way back to the house with the police. When I saw Adrian a few days later, he told me he did not take them all the way to their house. He said he dropped them off a few blocks away from it. I told him good move, but you don't have to be in the business of taking pussy. I told him we get so many hoes already. He told me "Yeah I know. Sometimes I get full of that alcohol and I lose it, plus the bitch was playing with us." That wasn't the first time I saw Adrian slap a female. A couple of days before that, he slapped my wife's cousin, Ebony Steele around in the parking lot of the YMCA. Just another day in the life of Adrian Hilliard. What the fuck could possibly be next?

A couple of days later, I picked up Adrian from his house on Blaine St. I was always very wary of how crazy Adrian was. I didn't fear him. The only things I fear are God and sharks. Fear of sharks needs no explanation. Some people would ask me why God? I'd tell them it's because it's the unknown. If he or she is out there, they will put a stop to what I'm doing and punish me for all the things I've done. With Adrian, I was not afraid. I just knew I had to exercise the appropriate caution.

Like I said before, he used to tell me, Tullie and Vidal that he was gonna pull the juice on our ass one day, like the movie, meaning he would turn on his own homeboys and kill us. Out of all of us, he would make sure he was the last one standing. Tullie told him, "Adrian, you got me fucked up." Vidal said, "I told you he was crazy." Adrian said, "Alright nigga. You gonna see." I didn't know if it was bullshit. He'd turn on his friends? We would die for him and he'd die for us, so I don't even know why he'd focus his lips to say some shit like that. The crazy thing is, I kind of gravitated toward that. Because of the color of my skin, I had to put in more work than the average street thug. I'm gonna have to show him. He ain't gonna have to pull no juice on me. Fuck that. I already showed Adrian how I get down, so he knew he'd be in for a little war if he fucked with me.

One night, we had a party at Tullie's house and Adrian was already full of beer and drunk. Tony wanted some beer. I didn't think it was a good idea because Tony was just 14 years old. I always felt responsible for Tony and Phat Cheez. They are Tullie's nephews, but I always felt they were my nephews as well. I had a cup of beer in my hand and I don't know why because I don't drink and never have and neither does Tullie. Tony was looking at me funny because he knew I didn't drink. He walked up to me and said, "Marcus let me have some. You is not finta drink that." Adrian, already drunk, jumped in the conversation and said, "Why don't you go on and give the little nigga the drink."

I looked at Adrian, then looked at Tony as he was waiting for my approval with anticipation and I said, "Here, only drink this one cup, Tony", as I handed him the cup of beer. He grabbed the cup, very excited, and ran back to his friends. Adrian looked at me and said, "I heard that shit before." I said, "What?" He said, "Menace II (Two) Society. I just said go on and give the little nigga the drink. That's from Menace II(Two) Society." Adrian started laughing. I thought about it for a second and said, "Oh yeah you right. That was from that movie. Adrian, you silly dawg and drunk. Let's go get some hoes and go to my parent's house. My parents out of town." I forgot who Adrian fucked, but I fucked this tall, black girl from the Wheatley Courts, Etanya Erving, and the next day these two sisters, Joanne and Nikki Pierson.

CHAPTER FIFTEEN

CRAZY ASS ADRIAN II

A FEW WEEKS later, I picked up Adrian from his house. I thought we were on our way to Kenwood to be with Tullie and them, but Adrian told me he needed to make a pit stop at somebody's house. I can't remember if it was on Burnet or Hays or one of those streets. As I headed down the street, he asked me, "Are you strapped" and I said, "You know it." He said, "What you carryin?" I told him, "My 38." He asked me, "You got some extra bullets somewhere." I said, "Naw, I just got my six that's in my gun right here." "You still got that deuce 5 in the glove compartment, right?" I replied, "Yeah." With a very puzzled look on my face, I said, "Damn fool, what are we getting ready to get into? If I need more than 6 bullets in my gun, what are we gonna do, go to a war or something?" Adrian said, "Naw nigga we just gotta check this fool, but I don't know how many niggaz are in there. I wish that nigga Tullie was with you. Just put the deuce 5 in your pocket somewhere." I knew I would probably regret this. "Damn Adrian, what the fuck are we doin'?" He said calmly, "Don't worry 'bout it. Follow me."

So we walked up to the front of the steps to the screen door of this house, and the door was wide open. Next thing you know, this skinny black guy appeared at the door. When he saw Adrian, he had one of the most scared looks I've ever seen, and Adrian hits him in the head with the gun and yells, "Nigga did you think you was just gonna talk about me, nigga! You think you can just play with me! I'm not to be played with nigga!" The guy said, very anxiously, "Naw, naw, naw! You got it all fucked up. You got it twisted, Adrian." Adrian cut him off and replied, "Call me Mugsy, you hoe ass nigga!" The man replied with terror in his voice, "Alright, alright, Mugsy. Mugsy!"

Adrian then sits his ass down on the couch and pops him with the gun again a couple a times and I told him, "Damn Adrian what this fool do?" Adrian said, "This nigga been saying I can't handle mines. He been bumping his gums sayin that I ain't all that. That I aint real a real ass nigga!" Then I looked at the dude and said, "What the fuck was you thinking about? Why would you say some crazy ass shit like that?" He looked at me and said, "I didn't say no shit like that. Adrian…I mean Mugsy, got it twisted." He could barely speak at this point. He was bleeding so badly from his mouth. Adrian yelled at him, "That's not what they told me and why would you even say some shit like that when you know I know where you live? You little dumb ass nigga!" Adrian looks at me and says, "Marcus get in on this shit. Pop his ass."

I shook my head. "I'm not breaking my gun over this little fool's head." Adrian looked at me with a disappointed stare, and I said, "I'm gonna use your shit." I grabbed Adrian's gun and yelled, "Who else in this muthafuckin house? Anybody else in this muthafuckin house?"He replied, "Ain't nobody here." That upset me, because I always wanted to make sure we didn't get into anything we couldn't get out of, and I didn't trust him. He probably would have said anything at this moment. "Don't lie to me little bitch!" I put the gun in his mouth. Adrian got excited when I did that, and said, "Look at my nigga right here. Make him give head to the gun!" I wanted Adrian's approval, so I proceeded to slide the gun in and out of his mouth said, "Yeah he does give that gun good head." At this point, the guy looked like he wanted to pass out, and then Adrian looked at him and said, "One of these days you might wind up in the penitentiary and you gotta give good head to them big niggaz up in there or you get killed."

I said, "I guess he getting his practice on. Hold up. I think he's tryin to say something." Blood was coming out of his mouth profusely, and then he said something I could barely make out, but I think he said, "My auntie in the back room." I thought oh shit someone is here. Adrian, with a puzzled look, motioned to me to check the back and make sure nobody was back there. As I went back there, I heard a television with a soap opera going on and sure enough this big fat black lady was snoring away, with a fan on full blast.

My first notion was, let's hurry up and get the fuck out of here, and my second notion was how the fuck could you sleep with some shit like this going on in your living room. I went back down the hallway and told Adrian, "Yeah there somebody in there, his aunt or something." Adrian said, "What!" and popped him on the head one more time as hard as he could and said, "How the fuck you gonna lie to me like that? You lucky I don't kill your mutherfuckin ass!" With that last hit, it seemed like he got knocked out, but he was still conscious. As we were about to leave, Adrian told him, "I know you ain't gonna tell nobody like the police, right nigga? Don't do that. Do it gangster style nigga and come back at me. Come back at me nigga! Come back at me nigga!"

Adrian was staring him down with a menacing glare. The man looked like he was ready to die. I looked at Adrian and said, "I wouldn't hold your breath on that happening. Let's go." As we walked out of the house, I was praying nobody saw me walk out of this house and walk toward the car. We got in the car, and there was blood all over Adrian's gun. I said, "Hell naw. You ain't gonna put that bloody ass gun in my car anywhere." I reached back and got a trash bag and I said, "Put your gun in here. You gotta contain that blood, cause if he a hoe ass nigga and calls the police, that blood will get us fucked off." Adrian responded, "Marcus, that's why I like to hang with you dawg, cuz you smart." I didn't say anything after Adrian said that. I was excited and scared at the same time, but I felt like I was a part of something that was bigger than me.

About an hour later, me and Adrian left to my house. Vidal was back at the Eastside, more than likely to gamble or fuck a hoe and Tullie stayed to fuck this light-skinned black girl I already fucked. I told him just work your jelly and she will give up the pussy. After we got to my house, we left again to get something to eat at Wendy's on Broadway, and this truck pulls out and almost hit us as we were coming out of the parking lot. The truck moved into our lane. He had to have seen us, but he didn't give a shit. I looked in the truck and saw two white guys that lookedlike a couple of buffed Willie Nelsons. We were side by side and the driveryelled, "Hey! What the fuck asshole!" as they sped off in their white Ford truck. I don't think they knew who they were dealing with. Adrian yelled, "Fuck that old white man! Go after them!" I said, "Fuck!" As I raced after them, I'm thinking we got food in the car and shit. We had just left my mom and dad's house and it was right down the street. We didn't bring any guns with us. I remembered I had the deuce 5 in the glove compartment. It's a small gun and Adrian left his gun at my house, and we were kinda slippin' .

We were talking to some hoe and we forgot our guns. Adrian said, "Let's get them muthafuckas!" So, we're chasing after them on Broadway going towards downtown. Adrian yelled, "Where the guns at?!" I replied, "Adrian, we didn't bring any guns. You was talking to that hoe remember?!" Adrian looked at me as though he had just remembered something. "Marcus, I know you got a gun in this car!" I said, "Yeah in the glove compartment!" Adrian reached in the glove box and as he pulled out the duece five he said, "This is it? Shit, it's gonna have to do." We were still chasing them and Adrian stuck his head out the window and started shooting at them. We were so close to them I could see them ducking their heads as they were being shot at.

They had a Dixie flag bumper sticker. And then I noticed they had a shotgun on the back window. There were seven bullets in the clip, and Adrian just shot all seven of them very fast. Then he yelled to me, "Fuck you ain't got no other clip!" I said, "Naw, that's my back up gun. You know that already, and you see that big ass gun they got in the window? I'm turning around dawg. We slippin!"

As I started to turn around, I stopped in the middle of the street and they stopped as well and started taking down the shotgun off the rack at the window."Adrian, they taking the gun off the rack." Adrian yelled, "Well then turn around then nigga! Get to the muthafuckin crib and get our guns!" I started heading back to the house to get to our guns. I was running red lights the other way we just came from. I was flooring it. They started shooting at us and this time we were the ones ducking. Adrian vowed, "I'm gonna kill these white boys when we get to the house!" I was just hoping we would make it to the house. I turned on Mulberry Street and I thought we lost them because I didn't see them anymore. Adrian said, "Hurry up Nigga!" "Adrian, I'm going as fast as I can." Maybe they were still following us and were waiting for us to stop so they could shoot us at point blank range. I didn't want to die by Mulberry St., near where I grew up. I also thought, what if the car died on us and didn't want to start back up. We would be dead for sure.

It's incredible what you can think of before you might die. We went one more mile and we were home. I was still going fast in the residential neighborhood because I had to make sure we had enough time to go in and get the guns. We pulled up to my house. Adrian and I jumped out of the vehicle and ran inside as fast as we could. I got the SKS machine gun and Adrian got his 45. We were waiting outside for them to come down the street and Adrian said, "Soon as they come down the street, we gonna start dumpin' on their ass!" So we waited for about five minutes out there, and if we saw them and started shooting at them I was starting to think ahead about things like, "What are we gonna tell the police?" I thought, we're gonna tell them these guys started shooting at us and chasing us and I have the right to defend myself as well as my home, even though Adrian was the one who started shooting at them first. Adrian wasn't thinking about shit like that because he's crazy. So we waited for a few minutes and they didn't come down the street, so we started laughing about it. I finally told him, "Let's eat dawg." The Wendy's was cold but I didn't mind. I was glad that I wasn't dead and that I didn't have to shoot anybody and I didn't have to talk to the police. Another day of craziness with Adrian Hilliard. That was to be expected.

Later on that night, Adrian wanted to do something crazy and I was all in. It's crazy because after you get that sense of adventure, being in a shootout or something, and nobody got shot, we didn't die. We were shootin at people but we still had a taste for blood and excitement. Adrian said "We still got the SKS right?" I replied "Of course. What did I do pawn in the last 30 minutes?" He said "Ok smart ass nigga. Let's ride up to jolly time and see if them crip niggaz is standin outside. Let's blast some of they ass." I said "Fuck it lets go." Jolly Time is a place where crips tend to hang out. You have to remember, I represent Kenwood first and foremost I also represent Big Tyme Playas (B.T.P.) which is affiliated with Wheatley Courts (Bloods) and Adrian represents (B.T.P.). We drove by jolly time and we didn't see a whole lotta people out there ,so we kept driving and we were on E. Commerce and we passed by the Players lounge right across from Lindbergh gym and there was a bunch of them crips out there. It looked like a gathering a party or something. So when we saw that, I was kind of feeling the fuck it mode I was trying to impress Adrian and I remembered my club issue a few years ago and how ETGs wanted me and Tullie dead at that club one night. It's amazing how humans can rationalize anything to justify bad behavior but that's what I was doing at that point. We pulled down this real dark street alley and I got out the car and I let Adrian drive and I went to the trunk to grab the SKS and I sat in the back seat. When I was doing that Adrian said "Hell yeah, we gonna do this gangsta style. I know you a down ass nigga. You downa than most of those niggaz." I appreciated what he was saying to me. My mind was in another world. Right there at that point. I didn't give a fuck about nobody. I put on a red bandana over my face, and I had a cap on with my jacket. I made sure that if I drove by, and started shooting at them, they wouldn't be able to describe me. As we got closer to our destination at the player's lounge, anxiety started to set in and I began thinking this really isn't my style. I'm gonna start shooting at somebody just cause they wearing the wrong color. I was thinking if you're gonna shoot somebody. You outta have the heart to walk up to somebody and look at them and pull the trigger. But at that point we were almost there and it was too late to turn back. So as we get right up there Adrian yells out the car window "Whats up you crip ass niggaz!" Right as he said that I began to spray a hail of bullets from my SKS. I fired about 10, 11 shots and everybody just scattered and ran. They looked like roaches fleeing an atomic bomb or a grenade or some shit. I kept firing and Adrian had my 38 and was blasting and when I stopped shooting for like 2 seconds, Adrian yelled "Shoot them crab niggaz!" I heard girls screaming and I saw a group of people that stopped running like if somebody had been hit. I didn't want to shoot at them because that would have been too easy a target. I was trying to hit the ones that were still running for cover and when Adrian said that. I started shooting again, but after firing a few more times I told Adrian very loudly "Go go go!" And we drove off. Adrian was feeling a sense of euphoria and the adrenaline was running through me but I still had an empty feeling. I didn't mind shooting at people, but next time I wanna know exactly who I'm hitting. Adrian drove straight back to my house. I asked Adrian. "You think we hit a lot of people?" He said "Hell yeah, nigga. We got show them hoe ass niggaz we ain't no joke nigga!" After that, I told Adrian "I don't wanna do nothing, I don't wanna do shit for about a week. We need to lay low for a while and don't tell anybody." He agreed. Thank god. I had a hard time sleeping that night because I was thinking that the police would be knocking on my door that night but they never did. A couple days later, we got feedback about that shooting cause in San Antonio the black community is a small world. It's a small, small percentage of San Antonio and everybody knows everybody. By some miracle, nobody died, but we heard that some girl got shot in the leg. I don't know if it was Adrian's bullet or mine. I never talked to anybody about it. It really wasn't my style. No more drive byes for me. I need to follow my own advice from now on. If you have beef with somebody. Have the courage to walk up, look them in the eye and shoot em. Just don't shoot people that might be associated with the people you have a problem with. It still fucks with me a little bit to this day.

A week later me and Adrian went to bluebonnet St. at around 3:30am and nobody was there. I was sitting in this chair outside one of the houses for about 15mins when a geeker walked by and wanted to know who was holding some dope. I didn't know her but Adrian did. I wasn't about to sell to somebody I didn't know. So Adrian gave me the okay she was good people and I had about 60dollars worth of dope left and she wanted a 20. So about 5minutes after I served her I gotta page from this girl I been fuckin named Olympia Wilson aka (fatty). Don't be fooled by her nickname she looked good I still have pictures of her today. There was still pay phones on the corners and there was still an ongoing problem with Chris Kelly and X, the Crockett Street boys and New Light Village. So when I got the page I started walking to the pay phone. I called Fatty and I was trying to hook it up for Adrian with her friend Tracy. As I was on the phone we heard a couple of cars coming and as I turned around we saw a couple of Cadillac's and we both got a little worried cause we knew we had beef with different sets. The Cadillac's pulled up right where we were sitting and we're very lucky that the City of San Antonio doesn't care about the grass on the East side on public streets cause the grass was real high. Adrian and I ducked down into the grass. I was on the phone with Fatty, but, left the pay phone dangling. We both had guns. I had a 38 and he had a 45, but I knew our guns were no match for a couple of Cadillac's loaded with a bunch of machine guns. We still had no idea who they were. The Cadillac's started approaching down the street where we were, at the pay phone and I told Adrian, "Hey do you think they saw us?" He said "Say whatever you do, don't look up, just look down. All of a sudden we heard pow! pow! pow! pow! pow!, five or six shots from a high powered gun and I thought are they shooting at the house or are they shooting up in the air to try to scare us out of the house. We were face down in the grass. Then we hear the Cadillac and they start rolling towards us. Toward the pay phone. I could still hear Fatty on the phone with a muddled voice probably wondering why I left the phone. I was thinking What if they got to the pay phone and picked up the phone and asked her questions and she asked where is Marcus? Then they would now we were just there or still here. Adrian said "Marcus keep your white ass down. They can probably see you through the grass." They slowly rolled by the pay phone. I almost shitted on myself thinking were gonna take a whole lotta bullets coming at us and this is where I might die. I had my gun ready just in case they saw us but they drove away real slow. We stayed in the grass till we were sure they were gone. The moral to this story had Fatty not paged me, we wouldn't have walked to the payphone at that specific time. We would have been in a shootout and more than likely been out gunned. It's like somebody wants me to live. Thank God for fatty Wilson, she saved my life. She used to fuck with this nigga in the penitentiary named pork'in beans. What the fuck kind of name is pork'in beans?

Sometime in 1996, Adrian and I had a fall out. He wanted a Mac11 Machine Gun that I had and I said Okay but it wasn't completely mine. I told him it belonged to Kenwood, meaning I had to ask Tullie because we had a certain number of guns and I wasn't going to just give it away. A Mac11 with a 30 round clip just doesn't grow on trees. Besides he didn't just want to borrow it he wanted to keep it. He got real upset with me that I didn't just give it to him. He said over the phone "Nigga you act like you need Tullie's authorization or something!" I replied "Yeah, I do Adrian. I want to build something like an organization with my homeboys you included. I don't want to do shit without thinking. Like shoot first and ask questions later. Let me check with Tullie." Adrian said pissed off "That nigga ain't God!" and then he hung the phone up on me. I never spoke to him again after that. A crazy thing happened a day later. I was watching a basketball game at my house in the front room getting ready to go back to Kenwood and a Cadillac pulls up in front of my house. I turned off all the lights to get a better glimpse of it. I didn't recognize the Cadillac at all. I went to my room and quickly grabbed the SKS assault rifle and ran back to the living room. Then I looked out the window again and much to my amazement I saw Pierre, Adrian and two other guys I didn't recognize. I thought to myself what are these idiots doing? Do they think they can just come and take a gun away from me? They know how I get down or at least Adrian does. But Adrian you gotta love him but he's a real whack job like character in the movie Goodfellas, Tommy DeSimmone. I went to the living room and the window was open. I heard Adrian tell Pierre "Bring that nigga out here. We don't have all fuckin night." I thought I'm not about to walk outside and negotiate with Adrian Hilliard. I opened my front door and stuck the barrel of the SKS out first, then the rest of my body. I glanced at Pierre he was scared as hell. He turned around and ran yelling" He got the SK!" As soon as they saw Pierre running, they all ran like hell, got back in the Cadillac and took off. I don't know what could have been going through Adrian's mind. Like I said I never talked to him again. In December 2003 Adrian Hilliard, was shot at Santa's Place night club in the leg. In a dispute I have no knowledge about. He spent one night in the hospital. He lost a lot of blood, the bullet probably hit an artery. He went home the next day, when the he probably should have stayed at the hospital for a few days. I was told He was at home in his recliner chair when his baby momma Tiffany found him dead. He probably had internal bleeding or a blood clot. What a horrific site that must have been for his baby-momma to see. The crazy thing is everything I ever went through with Adrian. If he had called me that night at Santa's Place ,and said Hey Marcus, these niggaz is trippin I need you to come get me and stare these niggaz down and see what they gonna do. He wouldn't have had to tell me to bring a gun, he knows that's how I walk. I know I would have come up there and made sure he was alright. I would have never turned my back on Adrian if he was in trouble. I still would have got down with him against whoever they were. Regular people don't understand this. If there are points in your life where another human being would die for you and you would die for him. You don't ever take that lightly. I think It is like how soldiers feel about each other in combat. Once a brother always a brother. Adrian used to always bring up the rapper D.J Quick who got either stabbed or shot right here in San Antonio. He was so proud the niggaz in San Antonio showed D.J. Quick that we get down to. The way Adrian talked about it you would have thought he was a kid at Christmas about to open presents. Those were six years of my life where that was the case with me and Adrian. For as long as I've known Adrian he always felt real bad for this old lady at the bus stop who got shot in the crossfire. It was at the bus stop at Windsor park mall. I don't know the entire situation, but apparently she got caught up in a gang shootout, where he was involved in the shooting, or was there at that time. I didn't ask him about it. It was none of my business. I never asked any of my homeboys if they did any dirt, because if they tell me and I get questioned by the police then I would know what happened. And I don't want to know what happened. A regretful situation for Adrian. He would mention that lady to me quite a bit, so I know that fucked with him a lot. He was always very remorseful. I'm sure he took that to his grave. I love you homeboy (rip) Adrian Hilliard.

CHAPTER SIXTEEN

CAN'T FUCK WITH THE "WOOD"

WHEN TULLIE GOT back from college, we were dealt a devastating blow. Tullie's mother passed away one night in her sleep. It was a very emotional time with Tullie and all his siblings. Tullie was somewhat at a crossroads. His mother meant everything to him. She was the reason he was at college. His mother pushed him to be the best. Tullie and I debated only one time about whether he should go back to college. I told him that's what his mother would want. He already knew that. I told him I thought he had a shot at playing professional basketball if not in the NBA, then playing overseas somewhere making quality money. Tullie's game at this point, after two seasons at junior college was dynamic. He had both a left-hand and right-hand jump hook (Thanks, Coach Nevil Shed.). He was a power forward, but he could shoot the ball like a two-guard. At 6'6", he was an undersized power forward, but he was always in the right rebounding position to foul out guys who were 6'9" and 6'10.

The only thing he was lacking was that he only had a 25 inch vertical. That's not NBA standards, but his skill set was such that he could play professionally somewhere. The crazy thing about this is that Tullie understood everything I told him, but the allure of being with your friends who you consider family is overwhelming. People will look at this, and say: What a stupid decision to not go back to college, right? What they don't understand is that when you grow up in a ghetto, you make longtime friends. That sometimes transcends your own blood family. When you have homeboys that love you and would die for you at any moment, that can trump a coach yelling at you at some far-off college. The ghetto environment clouds your judgment on big picture thinking. When you're poor, and there is death and despair around you, you live in the moment, not 5 or 10 years down the road.

Me and the homies loved Tullie, and he loved us. We would lay down our lives for him, and he would lay down his life for us. Try and go find that camaraderie somewhere else. You can't. I had the same feelings as Tullie. I loved being around the homies as well. There are not too many days that went by where I didn't want to be in Kenwood, selling crack, fucking hoes, and playing basketball. It was almost like breathing. Those things had to be done. For my own selfish reasons, the one thing I regret about Tullie's decision is that I didn't encourage him enough to go back to college. Part of me wanted him here with me and the homies. I had a strong influence on Tullie because he respected my mind. If I had been adamant with him about going back, he might have. That fucks with me to this day.

A couple of years later, Tullie and his siblings sold his mother's house on 150 Horace St. They split the money eight ways. Tullie gave me five hundred dollars of that money. That's some powerful shit. Think about that for a second. He gave me a percentage of his mother's house money. That confirmed what I already knew. I had a friend for life. Tullie and I used to always see a few of the little homies of Kenwood walking around. One night, me and Tullie were driving on San Pedro by Taco Cabana and "Jack in the Crack".

It was about 1 in the morning, and we saw Scarface, Dongi, and the Crawford boys, Peanut and Omari walking by, and I said, "What the fuck are they walking around on San Pedro this late at night for?" Tullie said, "I don't know. They probably scaring people. They blacka than a mutha fucka. They looked like four Grim Reapers." I looked at them and I thought. Holy shit. His assessment is right on. Two of them had hoodies and they were dark-skinned. They were scaring the citizens of San Antonio right now. I said, "Yeah, but they too young and little to be Grim Reapers." Tullie said, "Yeah, they the young version, like the Grim Mites." I started laughing. Tullie yelled out from the car, "Grim Mites!" They looked hard at us first, then they realized it was me and Tullie. I told Tullie that we gotta get them on our team somehow, implement them in our program. Tullie said, "We'll talk to them tomorrow, but I can't do it now. I'm on a mission. Time to go fuck now." I said, "Alright."

The next day, we talked to them about it and Omari and Peanut were intrigued with me and Tullie. Scarface and Dongi were receptive as well, but I knew we had two soldiers in Peanut and Omari, down for whatever. A couple of nights later, me, Tullie, Chubby, and Omari and Peanut were walking back from Dongi's. Peanut and Omari kept talking about some Mexican boy disrespecting them and fucking with them at school. Peanut said, very intently, "I can't wait to see this fuckin' fool tomorrow. I'ma fuck his ass up, right in the hallway or outside or whenever

I see his ass!" Omari said, "You know his little brother gonna jump in. That's what them Mexicans do. They ain't fin to fight one on one."

Chubby said, "Don't get them all twisted like that. Sometimes them Mexicans down for theirs, and fight you without anyone jumping in." Tullie said, "I'm tired of y'all talkin' about it. Y'all been about this for the last 10 minutes. When you see them tomorrow, bust that ass! Don't TALK about it! BE about it!" After hearing that, Chubby gave his famous giggle. I asked Peanut, "Where do they live?" Omari jumped in. "They live right around the corner." Tullie responded vehemently, "What?! They live in Kenwood? Why the fuck y'all didn't say that earlier? Fuck waitin' for tomorrow. Go whip they ass now!" I said, "Tullie, it almost 9 o'clock. Those kids got school tomorrow. Their parents are probably home." Tullie replied, "I don't give a fuck! What's a little fight before Mommy tucks you in?" Everybody laughed. I said, "Fuck it. Let's go." When we went to the house, you could see in through a window that they were all eating as a family, the dad, the mom, the two brothers, and what looked like a little girl in a high chair. I was thrown off. Shit. We were about to disturb their family. Tullie told Peanut. "Hurry up, go knock."

Peanut knocked on the door. The mom answered looking a little strangely at Peanut. "Yes, may I help you?" Peanut responded "Can I talk to Richard? It's something about school tomorrow." The mom, looking a bit puzzled replied, "It's a little late but I will get him." Just then, her son came to the door. He looked very surprised to see Peanut. Without any hesitation, Peanut grabbed Richard while moving his mom out of the way and started punching him on the patio. The mother started screaming for-help from her husband. Richard's little brother showed up first and began going at Peanut.

Omari intercepted him on the way there and began fighting with him. The dad, with an astonished look at first, came out. When he realized what was happening, his look changed and he became very irate. He started charging at Peanut, who was engaged in contact fighting with his son. Chubby, who is 6’1 and 240 pounds, grabbed the dad on the way to protect his sons and started throwing combination punches at him. I was witnessing all this, standing right outside the gate. I had my 38 revolver on me. If I had gotten in the fray, my gun could have accidentally gone off. I was put into the position that if any of these people retrieved a gun from their house and tried to shoot one of my homeboys, I would have to shoot them before they could get a shot off. I would have gladly done it. You’re not going to attempt to shoot one of my boys. They could have had some crazy uncle come out of the house with a gun. I would have shot him.

Tullie went in the gate and got a lick in on the dad a few times. Tullie knew I had a gun and that I had to stand and watch to make sure everything went alright. The mother didn’t call 911. She just stood there and watched her husband and two sons get whooped. I was a little surprised she did that. We just took an entire family out of their house, and beat the shit out of them on their own front lawn. I give them some props. They fought courageously, and were still taking punches when they were down. Meanwhile, Peanut and Omari were very proud to have handled their business. Peanut said, “That’s what y’all mutha fuckin ass get! Y’all got fucked up!” Omari said, “Say something tomorrow now, bitches!” Chubby said, “This is Kenwood, bitch!” while looking at their mother who was crying, with a horrified look on her face. “You betta recognize!” Tullie said, like a proud papa, “That’s how you do it. You yank them hoes out of their house and teach them hoes a lesson!”

Chubby kept on yelling, "Kenwood!" As we were leaving, I aimed my gun and fired two shots in the direction of their house, at the bottom of their steps. That was a warning to them on two fronts. If you call the police, we will come back for you and this time it won't be an ass whooping. Number two, you don't get gangster and call any of your relatives because they will get shot. The looks on their faces after I fired the gunshots was unbelievable. Their faces were terrified and suggested they weren't going to do either of those things. I felt power and evil rushing through me at the same time. I was very proud of walking with my crew. The next couple of days passed by and they had a For Sale sign outside their house. I don't think those boys ever went back to Edison H.S.

A few days later, Nikki Green, who is Tullie's niece, started living at Tullie's with her husband Arthur, after Tullie's mama passed away. Arthur invited two of his kinfolk from Arkansas to visit. Me and Tullie didn't care at the time who Arthur invited. We thought they wouldn't be crazy enough to get in our way or anything. They would get killed. So when they arrived, they got out of the car and greeted Arthur with much love. Then Arthur said, "This Nikki's uncle, Tullie, and his boy Marcus. This my cousins, James and Gary." Me and Tullie both said, "What's up?" They could see I had my SKS machine gun with me. One of them blurted out, "You ever seen that HBO special on gangs, called Bangin' in Little Rock?" Me and Tullie looked at each other. We both saw bits and pieces of it, and we said, "Yeah, we seen it." Then the other replied happily, "That's us, nigga!" Tullie responded to them. "Oh, ok. So you know the game, then, huh?" I said, "That's pretty tight. Y'all got your little fame and what not?" One responded, "Yeah that's all us down there. We run that shit." Arthur jumped in and said, "Let's go inside and talk for a minute," as he put his arms around his cousins.

As they were walking away, Tullie and I looked at each other, like Oh lord. I hope we don't have to put them down. I said, "Man, I hope they don't get out of line." Tullie responded, "Hopefully Arthur will tell them what time it is. So just play it cool with them. Don't start none, and it won't be none." The next day, me and Tullie and Carlton, Phat Cheez and Peanut were sitting at the table, in front of Tullie's house, talking about what else, basketball and hoes. Tullie said, "Damn, nigga.

I was locked up for my three days because I couldn't pay my parking tickets. Them Mexicans in there was crazy. I told them, the Spurs can win it all. They got the best team in basketball. Now that Jordan done left to go play baseball, for what, I have no idea. We got David Robinson, Sean Elliott. Shit, we got that white boy that be shootin' his ass off. Ronald be lovin' his ass, Vinny Del Negro. Oh, and don't forget about the point guard, Avery Johnson. He faster than a mutha fucka. He pass that ball quick. Boy. Say, that little nigga good. I said that in there to the Mexicans. That Mexican in there said, 'That's the problem, the fuckin' point guard. He can't shoot, and he ain't bigger than us.' He was pointing to his homeboys. I looked at him, and I said, 'You talkin' bout Avery Johnson?' The Mexican boy said, 'Not Avery Johnson. Average Johnson.'

I laughed my ass off. Them Mexicans in there callin' Avery Johnson, Average Johnson." We're all laughing. Tullie continued, "Then I asked one of them. Say man, when you getting out? You know what he said? He said, 'I don't know dude, whenever.' I said, What the fuck? You don't know when you getting out? Shit. Your ass betta find out. I know when I'm getting out." Carlton said, "That's crazy, man," and we're all laughing at this point. I looked around, "Where them Arkansas fools at?" Tullie replied, "They in there. They in the house with Arthur and Nikki." Carlton said, "You see them 9mms they walkin' around with? They the Glock 9s, the police issued ones. They got 17 bullets in each clip. Them fools look like they don't play around," as he took another drink from his beer. As I clutched my SKS, I said, "Yeah, I don't play around either."

While we were sitting around, my boys, were playin dominoes. I don't play any sort of table games. I quit playin video games years back. I don't shoot dice, I don't drink. I don't smoke cigarettes, smoke marijuana, or do any types of drugs. I am a very serious person. I try stay on top of my game at all times. I don't want anything going in my body that would distract me from the task at hand. I'm able to clown around with the best of them, and still maintain my respect and authority with my boys. Tullie said, "Shit. I gotta go. If they do anything stupid, you can shove them 9mms up they ass." I said, "Where you going?" Tullie replied, "I'ma go help this girl move real quick and get some ass." I replied, "There you go, Mister Super Save A Hoe. When a bitch in need, you call Tullie." I continued, "Nigga, you should be in a commercial. When your man trippin', and ain't givin' you no act right, call Tullie. When you need to move furniture and give up some ass, call Tullie. When your parents trippin' and they gonna kick you out their house, call Tullie!"

I scrolled my thumb and forefinger across the air like captions and said, "Just have yo pager and phone number go across the screen." Everyone's laughing. Tullie said, "You crazy, dawg. I'ma holla at y'all later," as he was getting into his car. Just then, we all got up from the table and started walking away, and simultaneously the front door opened. Arthur and his two cousins came out, and went to the table as if they were looking out the window and waiting for us to leave.

When I was just about to exit the front gate, one of them said, out loud, "The little niggaz left. Now it's time for the big niggaz to sit at the table." I stopped dead in my tracks and turned around, pulled my SKS(machine gun) off my shoulder and put it up in firing position and said very angrily, "What the fuck did you just say?!" They quickly looked toward me, and saw a machine gun pointing right at them, and one of them said, "Naw, we didn't mean nothing by it, nigga." I wasn't falling for that shit. If I put my gun down, then they shoot at me. I replied, "What the fuck? You din mean nuttin' by it? You said, the little niggaz left, now the big niggaz get the table. Fuck that nigga! Who the fuck you think you is?! Comin all the way from Arkansas, talkin that shit! This is our hood, nigga! Ain't no little ass niggaz here! You got us fucked up, bitch! Let me tell y'all something, y'all little niggaz. Take y'all ass out them seats, and take y'all mutha fuckin' ass back to Arkansas or whatever the fuck rock you crawled up out of, and get the fuck up out this yard!"

Carlton standing way off to the side, took another swig of beer and said, "Shit, you mighta fucked up. This boy a fool.He been waitin to use that gun again." I'm standing five feet away from them, and my gun is planted right on their every move. I could see both of their 9mms on their waistline as they stood up. Any sudden movement by them to retrieve their weapons and my SKS would chop both of them up and they would be food for worms. I yelled, "If any of y'all raise up a gun, you will get a SK bullet in your muthafuckin' chest. Now slowly walk out this yard, and go real quiet to y'all car. I'ma walk you to your car like I'm the muthafuckin' valet."

I couldn't take my eyes off them, for one false move by me and I could die. I was walking backwards and praying that I didn't trip on anything. I needed help. I yelled for Peanut and said, "Peanut, you got that deuce 5 I gave you?" Peanut responded, very eager to join in on the fun. Peanut yelled, "Yeah!"

I said to Peanut as I was walking backwards, "Make sure yours is ready. Cock it back. We walkin' these little niggaz to they cars!" Peanut replied, "It's already one in the chamber, Marcus!" I said, "Good." As I'm walking backward, I'm in the middle of the street.

I had to keep a safe distance between me and them. If I'm too close they could charge me. Then I'll be on the ground with these fools and then anything can happen. When they got to their car, I was still in the middle of the street and cars were going around me, probably scared as hell. Peanut yelled, "What do you want me to do now, Marcus?" I replied, "If any of them make a sudden move, start shootin' Peanut! Say Peanut, they called you a little nigga, Peanut. Is you a little nigga, Peanut?" Peanut responded vehemently, "Hell naw!" I yelled to the Arkansas boys, "That's some crazy-ass shit! You come all the way from Arkansas to a place you don't know shit about, and you gonna disrespect the killers that are here! You should be shot on stupidity alone!" One of them said, "I told you, we didn't mean nothing by it, nigga. We big niggaz too."

I replied, "Yeah, but you don't call nobody no little nigga you don't know. Let me tell you somethin' little nigga! The only reason you gone make it out this muthafuckin' hood today is you happen to be family with the man that fucked and married my homeboy's niece who happens to live here. Other than that, y'all would be two little dead niggaz right now! Let me tell you something about me, I don't give a fuck about anything except my hood and my homeboys and you almost found that out today bitch! Now get in yo ride and take y'all muthafuckin' ass outta here! And if I ever see y'all here again. Arthur! You listenin right dawg? If I ever see them again, I'ma blast the shit outta them. Now take y'all little niggaz' ass on!" They got in their car and drove off and everybody had a relieved look on their face.

But no one was more relieved than me. As Peanut was walking towards me, I looked at him and said, "You see, that's how you do it. Cooler heads prevail. No shots were fired. But you stood your ground and didn't take no shit." Peanut replied, "Hell yeah. I was gonna shoot one of them hoes if they pulled their guns up." I asked, "Which one would you have shot?" He answered, "The one gettin in the passenger seat because I know you woulda torn up the one in the front, that driver." I replied, "Good, Peanut. I would've torn both of em up, but I would've started with that first one. You right, the driver. See you know what you doing. I was worried at first. Now, I'm not worried about you at all," telling him as I put my arm around him. I felt like a proud papa at that moment. You see, I will protect my domain, my hood and my family at all times and at all costs. This is the life I've chosen and I don't feel bad about it. I'm in beast mode and I'm not to be played with.

CHAPTER SEVENTEEN

EDEN ROC (THE TAKE OVER)

WE WERE HAVING a good time selling dope in Kenwood, gang-banging and pretty much running around doing whatever the fuck we wanted. We had a few sources we would score cocaine from. Tullie knew all the connections. We would sometimes score from Melvin or we would get it from this Mexican boy in Kenwood, named Ramon. Tullie would sometimes score from people I didn't know, nor did I want to know. On our team, at the present time in Kenwood, was me, Tullie, sometimes Vidal(Vidal would spend half the time on the Eastside), Chubby, Kevin, Phat Cheez, Tony, Omari, Peanut, Dongi, Scarface, Shawn, Carlton, Eric Twyman (Stix) and three Hispanics, Jumbo, Erick Piceno, and once in a while, Zeke.

Everybody that I just mentioned was down for the cause. At any moment, any of these individuals would lay down their lives for each other. There was no gang initiation, where we had to fight each other or shoot someone you don't know. If you did that, you might get life in the penitentiary, and for what? That's some dumb shit. Just be down for yours at anytime, anywhere. Don't be no hoe. Be ready to shoot and kill anybody coming after us and if you lay down your life, so be it. You did it with honor and respect and you will never be forgotten. Me and Tullie weren't satisfied with our situation about selling dope in Kenwood, hustling, going to different apartments and serving to different customers. We wanted our own apartment complex to call home, besides Kenwood. We wanted to expand our brand. Tullie's brother, Ronald Green, gave us the best option for that.

He moved into a place called Eden Roc Apartments, off of Jackson-Keller. This was where we hit a gold mine. Ronald attracts all the crack smokers, or geekers, to his house. He smokes dope, and his brother sells it. That's a great attraction for any geeker to gravitate towards Ronald's apartment. By using Ronald's apartment to sell dope, Tullie and I made thousands of dollars. Ronald doesn't do this out the kindness of his heart, mind you. He gets a great perk, FREE DOPE!! Tullie also knew some Mexican girl who stayed at Eden Roc. Tullie was accepted by her family and her dad called Tullie, Shaq. It was funny how he said it, and how he responded to Tullie.

When we found out there were more geekers living at Eden Roc, it made our transition easy. We had more places to move around on the property. It would make us harder to detect, by the police and anything to make the police have to work harder and make their life miserable was okay with me. Tullie also started fucking with this light-skinned black lady at Eden Roc named Donna, a mother of four. Me, Tullie and Vidal were very similar when it came to fucking girls. It was a contest. Who could knock off (fuck) the most females? Vidal might be winning because he'd be on the Eastside more than me and Tullie. But Tullie and I couldn't be that far behind him, the way we were going.

One of my first days at Eden Roc, I was outside and I happened to look up and saw one of the most gorgeous and finest girls I ever seen in my life. She was brown-skinned, perfect ass, not too big and not too small. Big ass tits and a beautiful face. I couldn't take my eyes off her. I said to Vidal, "Look over there, dawg. Look how fine she is." To which Vidal replied, "Yeah, she look good, but she looks a little young." I said, "How do you know?" He said, "Don't look at the waist, look at the face." I said, "Yeah that's true, but she looks so good. She has got to be at least 17 or 18 years old. Damn, who gets to fuck her?" Vidal said, "You take your chances with that shit. You know that statutory rape shit. Ain't no piece of pussy worth sitting up in jail. Ralph be fuckin' with them young hoes and most of the time he get away with it, because there ain't no daddies and most of the mommas don't care. But it just takes that one momma to pursue your ass and get you locked up. Your ass will be getting fucked by some big ass nigga named Tyrone in the pen."

Later that night, I found out her name was Tandelyn Tonette Green, but everybody called her Tan and she was just fourteen years old. I was devastated. I told myself, there is no way you can talk to a fourteen year old. I'm 22 years old. I sell dope, and my boys and I fuck new hoes every week. Why would I jeopardize my freedom for a fourteen year-old.Then I found out some dirt on her.One of my little homies, Kevin Wallace fucked Tan in the laundry room two years ago. That means at twelve years old she was already fuckin. Then I found out she fuckin with some guy named Eli, and he is 25 or 26 years old.

After I found that out, I said to myself, I got to have her. You have to understand, Tan is a bopper. That's a girl who's young and will not mess with someone her age. To her, they are little boys. She has to be with a nigga with money, drive a nice car and sell dope. He has to have some power too. A bopper usually won't settle for less. I'm not preying upon some fourteen year old virgin. This is a girl that's been around the block, knows what she wants, acts more mature than her age and is comfortable in her own skin. So I decided to jump all the way in on this one. I was gonna make her mine, regardless of anything. Considering the way all my homies think, if I didn't want her, there would be a fuckin conga line waiting to fuck her. There I was again, thinking about how most humans can rationalize any type of behavior if they want to pursue it. Just as I was thinking all this through standing outside, there she was about 20 feet away from me looking good as ever. I walked over to her. I said, "Say girl what your name?" She said, "Tandelyn Tonette Green, but I just go by Tan." I said, "I know. I did some research." She said, "Research or stalker?" I replied, "Baby girl, I'm a protector and a provider. The last thing I am is a stalker." She said, "You're cute. What's your name?" I said, "Marcus." She said, "That sound's black. You black?" I said, "No I'm half white, half Hispanic. Maybe my soul is black or maybe I was black in another life. I don't know." Tan said, "You sound black." I said, "I know mama. Everybody say that, but this is just me. What you doing tomorrow?" She replied, "I don't know. I think I'm gonna go with my friend Anne to the mall. What you gonna do?" I said, "Be with you and make sure your ass get to where you need to get and be safe and sound." She said, "Oh, you one of those confident types huh? Thinking you can get a bitch just cause you talking to her. How you know I want you?"

I responded, "Look, all I know is I want you and I'm going to do everything in my power to have you, and I'm going to keep pursuing you till I get you, comprende?" Tan said, "There you go with that confidence. Well, Mr. Marcus, we'll see. I gotta go in right quick." I said, "Go write your number down. I'm gonna wait right here." She said, "Alright." She came back one minute later. I said, "Me and my boys going to Taco Cabana. You want something?" She replied, "What do you usually get from there?" I said, "I just fuck with them fajitas." She replied "That's what I want. Two chicken fajitas." I said, "I'll be back in 30." She said, "Okay." As I'm walking away, I turned around and said, "Oh shit, do I just call you or knock on the door when I get back?" She said, "Just knock. I'll be in the living room." I said, "What about your mama?"She said, "Don't worry about her. She don't be giving a fuck. She probably high right now." I said, "Okay, see you in a while baby girl." She said, "Alright."

When I came back I knocked on the door, and a few seconds later this big black man answered. He was about 6'4 and 300 pounds. I said, "Tan here?" He opened the door all the way for me. I walked in and saw Tan and said, "Here you go." As I handed her the bag of food, Tan's mama, with a surprised look on her face, told Tan, "Oh you got men brining you dinner now?" Tan jumped in, "Mama, this is Marcus. Marcus, this is my mama, Sharon." I said, "How you doing ma'am? Nice to meet you." Tan said, "This is my sister Sharae, her husband Edward and my two nephew's, Mit and Tony." I said, "Hi, nice to meet y'all, but Tan I gotta get going. I'll see you tomorrow." She said, "Alright." I quickly walked out the door and shut it. I wanted to hurry up and get outta there.

All I wanted to see was the mom's reaction, and I don't think she's going to be a problem. It looked like she smoke dope and maybe even more. The next day, I was at my boy Erick Twyman's house with Kevin, who was talking to Anne at the time. Tan and Anne walked a mile to Erick's house. Kevin fucked Anne and I fucked Tan. After a month, we started getting almost half of Eden Roc geekin. My goal was to have everybody in this complex on crack. A few days later, me and Tan got back from eating and saw Ronald outside talking to this white family. It was a mother, father, son and daughter. I told Tan, "Uh oh, we got some white residents in Eden Roc." Tan replied, "And look at Ronald. He gotta be the one that's there to greet them."

We walked up on their conversation. Ronald looking at the mom and talking, "Oh yeah girl, that's right. I'm glad you said that. Oh, and trust me we'll get together tomorrow. Y'all gonna be safe in here, ain't nuthin go on here." The mom replied, "Well that's good to know, and it was nice meeting you Ronald." Ronald said, "Vice versa y'all go on to your apartment. Check it out to make sure it's alright." The mom said, "Okay." As they were walking away, Ronald said, "Okay bye." Then Ronald turned to me and Tan and said,"Ohhh, white people stink." Tan and I started laughing. Ronald continued, "They smell like a wet dog. Oh, I think I need a shower after talking to them." I said, "Ronald I heard you with that bullshit. Nothing go on here. Everything is fine." Ronald laughing said, "Shit.

They both smoke. You gonna have them at your disposal, anytime. They gonna be like pets to you." I said, "You right." Ronald said, "You want some chicken? I just made some." I replied, "I'll be in there in a minute Ronald. I'm a go talk to Sharon," Ronald said, "Tan, that reminds me. Tell your mama to come over. I need to tell her something." She replied, "Okay Ronald."

Later that night, Peanut, Chubby, Kevin, Tullie and Omari were chillin' at Ronald's. Omari, had just recently got the nickname Murder1. I went home for a few days and the story I was told was that Omari shot a geeker when told to by Tullie. The bullet missed the intended target, the head and grazed the man on his shoulder. The man was scared and relieved at the same time, relieved because he did not get his head blown off and was scared to death because he just got shot. He quickly ran off. They haven't seen him since. Tullie was kind of surprised that Omari shot on command, but was happy he did so. So after that, Tullie gave him the nickname Murder1. They were all in Ronald's living room when I walked in from Tan's house. Tullie sarcastically said, "So how's your other family?" I said, "They alright. Crazy as usual, you know Sharon got her man staying there now. It's this old fuck named Daddy Bob."

Chubby did his famous laugh. Tullie said, "Daddy Bob. What the fuck do he smoke?" I said, "I don't know, but besides crack you know Sharon shoots up heroin?" Tullie said, "Really." I said, "Yeah I caught her ass doing it today. I opened up the bathroom door and there she was putting that needle in her arm. I told her. "Sharon, you shooting up? She hurried up and covered her arm up and hid the needle, then told me. 'Oh no, I don't do that.' I said, Well what the fuck is that? She had a plastic thing wrapped around her arm. She said, 'Oh,' when she looked at it. She knew she been caught so I just shut the door." Kevin said, "That's fucked up." I said, "Tan's sister Sharae smoke, Sharon smokes and I think Edward smokes but I'm not a 100 percent on that yet." Tullie said "Edward. Are we gonna ever have a problem out of that big ass nigga?"

I responded, "I don't think so. He don't want to get into it with one of us. Look at us, everybody strapped and we're 20 deep. What he gonna do? Bring in an army?" Chubby said, "Hell Naw, we run this bitch." Tullie said, "You got perfect timing. I'm glad you showed up." I said "What did I do? Did I win a prize or something?" Tullie said, "Shit you might have, depending upon what his man got in his house." I said, "What's in his house? Okay, I'm missing something. Fill me in." Tullie said "This man that stays in these apartments, his name is Mike. Do you know him?" I said, "Yeah he stay at the corner in Apartment. 10. When he see me he is very respectful. He says what's up, Marcus?" Tullie jumped in, "Ok right,but this Mexican owes us some money. We thought he had a good job, so Peanut been giving him credit." I said, "Peanut he hasn't given you dates and times when he's gonna pay you?" Peanut said, "Yeah but something always comes up. He be making excuses this happened or that happened. I told him alright. I'm a tell Tullie." Tullie said, "What's crazy about it is, he know how we get down. He see how we walk. We got all of Eden Roc geekin'. I'm not gonna let anybody fuck with our credibility!" I replied, "You 100% right Tullie. Is he there?" Tullie said, "Yeah he there. What the fuck are we talking about it for?" I said, "Well let's pay Mike a visit."

Everybody stands up. I continued talking and said, "Nobody kill this man unless we have to. We're gonna go see if we can recoup this money somehow. Let's go." The way everybody was so eager to go pay this man a visit, you would have thought we were heading to play in the State Basketball Championship. When we got to his apartment, it was dark inside the unit. Peanut said, "I saw him come home. His car is in the street." I said, "Okay." Tullie knocked real hard, but there was no response. Then Tullie said, "I hear something. He in there. Fuck this. He ain't gonna answer the door to us."

Just then Tullie took his right foot and kicked it as hard as he could. The door cracked and opened and we all rushed inside. Mike was in the hallway going to a room. I pulled my gun out in case he had one. He was shocked to see we kicked in his door. Peanut and Kevin grabbed him. Tullie yelled, "Bring his bitch ass here!" Tullie pulled a chair out for him in the living room. Tullie said, "So you wasn't gonna pay us, huh!" Tullie slapped the hell out of him.It was so hard I thought Mike might pass out. He let out a loud scream and said frantically, “Naw Tullie. I just need time.” Tullie yelled, “I wish I had some fuckin duct tape! But you ain’t going anywhere,is you? Put your muthafuckin hands behind the chair!” Chubby, Kevin, Omari and Peanut got slaps in on him as he was screaming. Tullie was telling him shut up! Peanut punched him. I was thinking how’s he gonna shut up when they keep beating him. I let the punching and slapping go on because Tullie was right. He deserved this. Our integrity was on the line here at Eden Roc. We can’t let one person say to anybody at Eden Roc, I never paid them. Then, what all we worked for would be in question. I stood directly in front of him, while at this time my boys were going through his house. I asked him, “Hey Mike, do you have any guns or weapons in here?” He said, “No Marcus,” with a look of devastation and defeat on his face. I continued, “They’re tearing up all your shit, Mike. Do you have anything valuable in here so they can quit fucking your shit up?” He replied, “A little jewelry but nothing fancy.” Then he started to cry and said, “Marcus please don’t let them kill me, please.” I responded, “Mike, this is what happens when you don’t pay killers. You look at us everyday Mike.You see how we walk around here. Do you think they’re a joke?”As I motioned to Kevin, Chubby and Omari. He said, “No,” as he was crying. Just then, Peanut came out of a room with a scarf wrapped around his neck and a black fedora and said, “Look Marcus. Do I look tight?” I looked up and said, “Oh shit. Peanut with the Pimp hat.” I looked at Mike and said, “Can Peanut have that hat?” Without waiting for Mike’s approval I looked up at Peanut and said, “Mike has no problem with you taking that hat Peanut.” I motioned for everybody to come on and said, “Mike, set up a payment plan with Peanut tomorrow, and if you don’t come up with some money, it will be much worse next time. I will have no control over that. Do you understand me?" He perked up as much as his condition would allow him and said, "Yes Marcus." I continued, "Mike, tomorrow you are gonna tell the office that you were drunk when you came home last night,and you got in a fight at a bar. That explains your condition. You're also gonna tell them you lost your apartment key. You didn't know what to do, so you kicked your apartment door in. Do you comprende, Mike?" He said, "Yes Marcus. Thank you." I said, "No, don't thank me, thank Tullie." He looked at Tullie and said, "Thank you, Tullie." Tullie didn't acknowledge him and said, "Let's go. We been here too fucking long." I saw Mike a few days later and he acknowledged me. He looked a lot better. He must have paid because I didn't get any feedback from the incident. I didn't sell to him. He was not part of my clientele. That was Tullie's geeker. A couple of months later, he did move out. Eden Roc was heaven for us. We could go into about 20 different units if we wanted to. We were more important than the property manager. Everybody respected and feared us. I walked around with my gun at all times. Sometimes when we left or arrived, I would fire my gun in the ground to let people know we were either coming or going. I was making a lot of money, I had the hottest girl there. It was like the wild-wild west and I was Doc Holliday and Wyatt Earp put together. Eden Roc was my Tombstone. Why would I ever leave?

CHAPTER EIGHTEEN

EDEN ROC DILEMMAS

AS TIME WENT on, everything was going good at Kenwood and in Eden Roc. Everybody was making money and getting their dicks sucked every day by either one of their bitches or a geeker that looked good. Crackhead women sometimes get a bad rap, as if they all look nasty. Some of them do, but some of them look good, have a job, kids, nice furniture and a car. For some reason, they get hooked on crack and they'd rather put their kids to sleep and fuck and suck you real good instead of giving you part or all of their electric bill or phone bill. We respect that, so we oblige them. I got in bad trouble for this reason with Tan, because I fucked her married older sister, Sharae, for a $20 piece of rock. It was an ordeal that lasted about a week. I thought that was gonna be the end of mine and Tan's relationship, but I have a way of talking and smoothing things over.

Edward, Sharae's husband, looked at me fucked up for a while after that, but what the fuck was his big ass gonna do? The way we roll, he would have been dead by fucking with me, and Sharae looks good but she ain't worth dying for. He understood that. One night, my boys Chubby and Kevin gave Sharae a hit of crack and after that she kept geekin and they fucked her all night. They kept meeting her at Ms. Mickey's house, another light-skinned black woman who everybody fucked but me. You would think Edward would know his wife is getting fucked by the homies every week. Tan left her house one day with her mother and me, and some of the homies played truth or dare with some of Tan's friends Toi, Antoinette and the white girl Carla, who lived at Eden Roc. As the game went along, somebody dared me to put my dick in Toi. I said, "Hell naw! I'm not getting in trouble again. Y'all got me fucked up." Well, for some reason, word spread and somebody told Tan that I did put my dick in Toi. Tan was already on edge about me and her sister. She just got a new tattoo with my name on it. It read MZ. VALDESPINO. She called upstairs and challenged Toi to a fight. With everybody in the courtyard outside, Tan yelled, "Come on down bitch! I know you a hoe and you fucked my man!"

Toi, upon hearing that, came out of her upstairs apartment and said, "What Bitch! You gonna call me out in front of everybody!" Toi came running down the stairs yelling, "Fuck your man, and fuck you bitch!" They both engaged and starting punching each other and pulling hair. This went on for about a minute of non-stop punching and yelling. They separated for a second, and were both out of breath. Then they collided again and I motioned to Vidal to get Toi and I grabbed Tan. Both bras came off and there was Vidal holding Toi's big tits. They were still yelling at each other, saying come on bitch! Fuck you bitch!

The crowd that gathered started laughing when they noticed Vidal clutching Toi's big breasts. We took them back to their house to cool off. Emotions run high, and that sometimes happens in the hood. The next day they were friends again. Vidal ended up fucking Toi later that night. A year later, I ended up fucking Toi as well. I also ended up fucking Tan's cousin, Antoinette, as did Carlton and Tullie. Ronald moved his friend from Kenwood, Dwayne, into his apartment. About three years ago, Dwayne who is homosexual used to be 6'0" 250 pounds of mostly muscle. Dwayne didn't take any shit from anybody. Now he has full blown AIDs, is hunched over on a walker and appears more like 5'9" 130 pounds and looks like the crypt keeper on the "Tales from the Crypt" TV show.

It was incredible to watch Dwayne's body deteriorate over the years. He couldn't hold liquid in his system very long. He had to piss in his special tub that was always in front of him. He also couldn't get around without his walker. He couldn't piss in the regular toilet for fear someone else would use it and acquire the disease. Once he pisses, Ronald(nobody else would volunteer) would have to empty the tub without spilling a drop.

One day, Ronald was gone and Dwayne had to piss, and he accidently kicked his tub away from him. He was screaming looking at all of us, "I gotta pee, I gotta pee!" We were in scramble mode trying to kick the tub back to him. Nobody wanted to touch it. He was yelling, "I'm gonna piss all over the floor!" I got the closest and put the tub in front of him so he could relieve himself. It's amazing to witness all of this, and still not be careful enough to start using condoms. What an eye opener, right in front of us. But some of us still put our dick on the crap table every night. Just then Ronald walked in, I told him of the ordeal that just transpired. Ronald said, "Lord have mercy Dwayne, you betta not piss on my carpet! I will move up out here with the French quickness!" Just then Chubby sat down right next to Dwayne, got in his face and real loudly did the Crypt Keeper laugh, hee-hee-hee-hee-hee-hee-hee-hee. Laughter erupted in the room. I said, "Chubby you can get away with that now, but a few years ago Dwayne would have jumped on you and started whipping your ass." Chubby replied, "Can't nobody whoop me, especially Dwayne." He got in Dwayne's ear again and did the Crypt Keeper laugh hee-hee-hee-hee. Ronald told Chubby, "You can't talk about nobody wit your funky feet. Them muthafuckas is through. They smell like something died and was dead for a while and then came back to life with dead feet!"

Laughter erupted! Ronald continued, "Those funky ass feet woke me up last night. I went to each one of y'all sleep here in the living room. I got to Chubby, grabbed a towel and started hitting him with it. I yelled, Chubby, Chubby! Get up with them nasty feet and get in there and take a bath!" Chubby said, "It's the shoes!" Ronald replied, "No it ain't. It's them dead feet. Go in that restroom and wash your feet in baking soda!" Everyone was laughing and Tullie said, "Chubby you is kinda funky. Go take a shower." Chubby replied, while laughing, "Fuck you Tullie. I don't smell that bad." Tullie responded, "Nigga, Chubby so funky sometimes he makes right guard turn left." Laughter erupted again.

I had my second child by Ericka. On December 28th, 1994 same day as Denzel Washington's birthday. Shawnelle Renae Valdespino was born at 12pm. That was the second greatest day of my crazy life. She was so beautiful. We knew she was going to be a girl by the sonogram and we couldn't wait. I thought of her name one day by watching the St. John's men's basketball team. Their starting center was named Shawnelle Scott, and I liked the way it was spelled. If I have a girl, that's going to be her name. But this still didn't stop me from running the streets. I had business to attend to.

One day, I looked out Ronald's window and saw Tan at the little washateria at Eden Roc. She looked aggravated like she was waiting on somebody to finish washing clothes. So, I went outside to see what my little momma was doing. I walked up and said, "What's up baby?" Tan replied angrily, "I'm waiting on this lady to dry her clothes. It seems like she's been here all fucking day!" I said, "Baby don't worry about her clothes. Look like they almost dry right now." Just then, this big black woman answered back loudly. "Excuse me! Look I'ma be through when I'm through. I don't care if this little girl gonna stand here all day and watch me. I'm not fin to rush for nobody! Especially her!" Tan jumped in, "Little girl, who you calling little girl?"

The woman responded, as she was getting her clothes out the dryer, "You a little girl, walking around here like you grown." Tan replied, "Bitch, who you think you talking to? I am grown!" The woman responded, "Who you calling bitch? You a little bitch? Fuck you!" Tan answered with, "Fuck you bitch!" I jumped in and grabbed Tan and said, "Say calm down! Go over there!" I addressed the woman. "Say woman! You need to take your ass back to your apartment and quit talking crazy!" She replied, "Fuck you Marcus! She started talking that shit first!" I thought wow, she knows who we are and we don't know her name. She got all her clothes and I responded, "See there you go talkin shit. Go up the stairs, bitch! Get in your apartment!" At this point, Tan and I were following her up the stairs. Tan said, "Fuck you ole bitch!" She responded, "Y'all gonna see Marcus! Walking around here like King Tut and Cleo fucking Patra! Y'all gonna see Marcus! Fuck both of y'all!" I said, "Yeah, yeah bitch, go inside."

She slammed her apartment door. I looked at Tan and said, "Who was that?" Tan replied, "Her name is Rhonda, shit I don't know." I told Tan, "Man, go wash your clothes." Tan said, "I need to dry them." I said, "Yeah dry em and quit starting shit. Ga-Dam." Two weeks later, me and Vidal were at Tan's apartment watching BET Videos. Then, all of a sudden out of the blue we heard a loud yell. A strong male's voice yelled "Marcus!" Me and Vidal looked at each other, then looked at Tan. Vidal said, "Who the Fuck is that?" I said, "It can't be Tullie and dem. They know where we at. They would just knock at the door." Then we heard it again twice, very loud, "Marcus! Marcus!" I said "What the Fuck!"

I was thinking who wants a piece of me? I'm like Henry Hill from Good Fellas. Who would call me out like that? Just then, Tan ran to the window, looked out the blind and said, "Oh my God, Who is that?" Me and Vidal looked at each other and hurried up and got to the window and saw this giant black man, 6'5" 280 pounds, that was all muscle. He looked like an African God. He looked like you could strike a match off him. He had an 8 pack. He was chiseled. He was wearing a do-rag on his head. He had no shirt and he was wearing warm ups with some Chuck Taylor shoes.

He was shadow boxing, looking like he was getting ready to take the winner between Tyson-Holyfield. Vidal said, "Ga-Dam! That nigga look like he could bend a crow bar. De-Bow might be in trouble with this nigga. Marcus who the Fuck is that?" I said, "I don't know and what the fuck do he want with me?" Just then Tan said, "Oh I know who that probably is." Vidal and I looked at Tan very intently. It just dawned on her. "Oh, I didn't tell you?" I looked at Tan very sternly, "No Tan! You didn't tell us. Enlighten us please!" Tan said, "That's what's her name's husband? Who just got out the pen. Ah, Rhonda, the bitch we got into it wit at the laundry mat and you called her a bitch."

Just then, Vidal's eyes were on me like what? I said, "I didn't know Rhonda had a husband, and I'm damn sure I didn't know he was in the penitentiary. Tan said, “I found out from Donna and dem he was getting out.” I replied, “Thank's for letting me know baby. Good heads up there. That's a monster outside.” Tan said, “I'm sorry baby!” Vidal jumped in and said “Damn, Marcus, you gotta pick this big gorilla ass looking nigga to fuck with? I replied, “Shit, I didn't know. Vidal we gotta go out there. I can't have this man call me out and not go. I'ma try and squash this shit and see where his heart is. It's two of us. We can't lose two on one. I don't care how big he is. If we let one person beat us, we can't show our face in the hood again. Look, we gonna go out there and I'm gonna try and talk to him. If you see that don't work I'ma hit him with everything I have, and then you jump on him from the side. I have my 38 with me in my back, if it goes bad I'ma just shoot him.” Vidal responded, “I'm all in wit you. I ain't never ran from no nigga and ain't finto to start now.” I said, “Neither have I, let's go.” Tan jumped up, “Oooh, my baby fixin to fight.” I said angrily, “Shit. Get back and just stay out of the way!”

I opened the door and all three of us went around the corner. He was still shadowing boxing, bobbing and weaving. I was like fuck. This muthafucka ain't playing. I yelled to him, “I'm Marcus what's up?” He responded “You Marcus nigga!” I replied “Yeah, nigga that's what I just said. What's up dawg! You makin' a big spectacle out of this. You got the whole apartment looking out their windows.” He said, very loudly, “You was calling my wife a bitch, Nigga!” Trying to defuse the situation I said, “Look man, you got it all wrong. Your girl got into it with my girl about the laundry mat. I was just protecting your girl and my girl from anything getting crazy. I didn't want your wife to go to jail. It was over some dumb shit. Look dawg. You just got out the penitentiary right?” He interrupted me and said, “Mind your business nigga. I don't give a fuck about that shit. I'll go back if I have to!”

I said, "Well what's up then? This is some dumb shit about the fucking laundry mat. I got bigger things to do than worry bout two females arguing at the laundry mat!"

He started walking closer towards me and said loudly, "You called my wife a bitch! Now you got's to pay!" I held my left arm out to stop him and put my right arm behind me where my gun was and I said, "Look, I don't remember calling her a bitch but if I did, I apologize. She was calling me out by my name and I was just standing my ground. You would have done the same shit." He responded, "We fin to handle this then. I'ma whip both of y'all niggaz, You about to test my penitentiary squabbles."

Just then I looked at Vidal and he was ready. Then I thought what if during the fight I'm on the ground and the gun goes off in my back. I was just about to hand Tan my gun when out the corner of my eye I see dark shadows coming up the side of the building and low and behold it's Tullie, Carlton, Chubby and Stix. Stix is 6'9", Tullie is 6'6", Carlton is 6'5" and Chubby is 6'1". As they are walking up, I could hear a sense of relief come out of Vidal. Vidal said, "UUUHWEE. Thank you." I was relieved too. I don't know if I'd ever been happier to see Tullie.

Tullie sensed something was wrong and walked right up to the man and said, "Marcus, everything alright? I heard some yelling from the car." Right then and there I could have set everything off and said, yeah this nigga fucking wit us. He up here starting shit. Let's fuck this nigga up. But I didn't do that. I said, "Naw Tullie, everything cool he was just defending his girl. He thought I called her a bitch when her and Tan got into it. But that's some old shit, it's squashed." I looked right at him and said, "Right?"

Tullie looked at him and said, "Is that true nigga?" This man's demeanor completely changed. It was an amazing 180 degree turnaround. He replied, "Oh yeah, I was just checking to see what happened. My wife be trippin. I get out the penitentiary and gotta hear this shit." Tullie looked at both of us and replied, "So it's over?" I said, "Hell yeah, it's all good."

The man nodded his head at Tullie in agreement. Then, Carlton jumped with his usually happy self and went straight to the man and said, "Well say nigga, now that this bullshit is all over, we havin' a little get together, a little party at the crib." He motioned to Ronald's apartment. "I know you been locked up. You can get your drink on and everything fool." Chubby did his laugh. The man responded, "Hell yeah nigga. I'll be there." Then we all split up and walked away. It's crazy how the hood is sometimes. It went from this man could have killed me or me and Vidal could have killed him and then I defuse the situation or he would have possibly been killed or fucked up by the rest of my boys.

Flash forward to five hours later and this man is in our kitchen getting full of beer, still dressed in the same attire. I walked up to him and said, "You having a good time?" He responded, "Yeah, dawg, everything good player." I said, "There's some hoes in here. I think they looking at you." He replied, "Shit! I ain't that drunk. My wife will walk down here and see me with one of these hoes and she will shut down this whole place." I said, "Hell yeah, you betta stay clear away from these females. You know what I'm saying? I know how she is." We gave each other some dap and I walked back to Tan's. As I was walking back, I was thinking what Ice Cube said in that movie is right. When a day goes by in the hood and you don't have to kill someone, it's always a good day.

CHAPTER NINETEEN

DEVLIN'S LAST PIECE OF ASS

I HAD GOTTEN back from North Star Mall when I pulled up to Eden Roc and there was Vidal and Chubby standing in the courtyard. They saw I had a bag in my hand. Vidal said, "What did you get?" I was just about to answer him when I saw Tan come out of her house. I yelled, "Tan!" Then I looked at Vidal and said, "You'll see what I got." Tan came running to me to give me a hug and said, "What daddy?" I said, "Look baby girl I just got you that new Monica tape." Tan very delighted said, "Oh the one with" and she started singing, "Don't take it personal. I just wanna be alone." I replied, "Yeah that one mama." She hugged and kissed me and said, "Thank you baby. You are so good to me."

I glanced at Vidal and Chubby and they had the look of oh brother whatever. Vidal blurted out, "Y'all got all kind of names for each other right?" Chubby did his laugh. Tan said, "Daddy I'm going to the store with wit my mama I be back in a little while, ok?" I said, "Alright mama, here goes 20 dollars. Buy yourself something there alright?" Tan replied, "Thank you, baby," with another big hug and then walked back to her apartment. Vidal said, "GA-DAM can I get a tape or 20 dollars or something? I done did more for you than she have. I done been wit you 5 years she going on 5 months!" Chubby laughed and said, "That's true Vidal but you ain't giving Marcus that good young black pussy." I replied, "Y'all Crazy!" Look there goes Tullie. Just then Tullie and Kevin walked around the corner with a cute Mexican girl. Tullie motioned and said, "Come on if y'all want some." I said, "Damn who is that? Looks like they fin to fuck." Vidal said, "I wish I could go in there but duty calls. I got this new hoe I'm fin to pick up right now and knock down(have sex with)." Chubby said, "Well Marcus, I'm about to go fuck. The question is are you gonna follow me?" I replied, "Shit! I don't know what I'ma do."

Then at that moment Tan listening to our whole conversation upstairs on her balcony said very aggressively, "Vidal you can go on and fuck your new hoe. Chubby you dismissed. You can go be third and fuck that tired looking Mexican bitch behind Kevin and Tullie. And Mr. I don't know what I'm gonna do? You gonna march your ass in my house!" I replied, "Well gentlemen good luck. I gotta go. Tell me how everything went tomorrow." Vidal and Chubby both laughed and we went our separate ways. I went upstairs with Tan to her balcony. She said angrily, "You was gonna go fuck that bitch right!" I said, "Hell naw baby, I was just telling them that. You know what I'm saying. Why would I do that and you right here. That don't make no sense." Tan replied, "Because you done did it before! Oooh Marcus I swear to God if you fuck another bitch Ooh I'ma fuck you up!" I replied hugging her, "Hell naw baby girl. All I want is you." She replied, "Okay." Then we kissed.

About thirty minutes later Tan was in the bathroom and I was still on the balcony. Tullie came out of one of the units. He didn't see me. I yelled, "Tullie what happened?" Tullie said, "Shit, we all fucked her." I replied, "Who talked to her first." Tullie replied, "Kevin had to hit her to get it going." I said, "Damn. She alright?" Tullie said, "Yeah, she going good now. We fin to take her to Kenwood and keep her ass all night. Let some of the other homies fuck. You coming?" I said, "I'll be there." Just then Tan came out, "Be where?" I'm a go to Kenwood for a while. She replied, "Ok daddy. I'm leaving with my mama to the store." I said, "Alright baby I'll holla at you in a little while."

It was not surprising at all when Tullie said Kevin hit her to get her going. You see Kevin Wallace is a woman beater, and has always been. Chubby told me the other day, Kevin raped this girl and just as they were about to leave. She was still very upset and yelled, "I'ma tell my brother!" Chubby said, "Oh Lord! What did she say that for?" Kevin turned around and beat her ass some more. So Chubby finished fucking the new Mexican girl. When she walked outside. I said, "What's up girl? You alright!" Looking at me like she was relieved to see a familiar face, meaning I was not black. She said, "I'm ok. Are you with them?" I said, "Yeah. What did they tell you that supposed to go happen after this?" She replied, "I think I'm supposed to with you all somewhere else and stay the night." I said, "Okay. You can ride with me. What's your name?" She said, "Melissa." I yelled to Tullie, "I'ma take her!" Tullie said, "Alright I'll be there in a few." When I pulled up at Tullie's house.

There was about thirty of the homies in the street. She said, "Oh wow there's a lot of them. Are they all with us?" I said, "Yes ma'am, come on let's go." I told her to go sit down in Tullie's yard at the bench. I asked Peanut, "Your mama and sister ain't there. They still out of town right?" He replied, "Yeah, they still gone." I said, "Say I think she gonna fuck everybody. Let's take her over there." Peanut responded, "Hell yeah let's go!" I motioned for Melissa to come on. I said, "Melissa, we gonna go to this other house." As I put my arm around her I said, "Are you down to fuck some other black men?" She replied, "I guess. Are you gonna be with me?" I said, "Yes I'ma be with you the whole time. I won't leave your site." She responded looking at me with a little puppy dog look. She said, "Good I don't want you to leave me." She was probably thinking about Kevin slapping her I said, "I don't blame you." We got to Peanuts and Omari's house. I told her to sit in the living room.

I went back outside and told Devlin Jefferson AKA Baby Tyson, "Are you ready to get some ass?" Devlin said, "Hell yeah, Nigga!" I replied, "Come on." We went in the house I told Devlin, "I'll be right back." I told Melissa to come on." I took her in Peanuts sister's room, told her to get naked and I slapped on a rubber and had sex with her for about 5 minutes. I told her when I was having sex with her that I wasn't gonna let anyone hurt her. At first I wasn't gonna fuck but when I saw how clinging she was to me, I had to get some. When I finished I took her into Peanut and Omari's room,

Devlin started getting naked and he grabbed Melissa laid her down and started fuckin. Omari and Peanut and I were watching and Phat Cheez and Tony came in. After five minutes Devlin bent her over and continued to fuck. Then he took out his gun from his shorts and put the gun on her back, while he was fuckin. Everybody thought it was funny. Devlin fucking this girl from behind with a gun fully loaded gun on her back. My boys, started chanting, "Go Devlin, Go Devlin, Go Devlin." I went down to Melissa's face and said, "Hey you alright?" She responded moaning loudly, "Yes."

CHAPTER TWENTY

JAIL TIME?

PEANUT AND OMARI'S sister and mom were still out of town, and I'm sitting over there at their house with Devlin, Scarface, Dongi, Peanut, and Omari (Murder 1). Tullie left to the Eastside to go steal cars with Chris Kelly and one of Chris'girls Danielle Armwood, better known as Lady D. That was one of Tullie's hobbies. He liked the adventure of stealing cars with Chris and I didn't quite understand that. That would never be one of my things. That sounds crazy to me. It was about 9pm and very dark outside. All of the sudden, Tony came running up with Phat Cheez right behind him and yells "Say Marcus these white boys playing basketball at the park and one of them called me a nigger!"

Devlin and I looked at each other with puzzled looks on our faces. I responded "What!" very angrily. Tony said "Yeah! We was on the basketball court and he called me a nigger!" At this point, all I saw was red. I got up and everybody followed me, Dongi, Scarface, Peanut, Omari, PhatCheez and Tony. We got to th e basketball park at Kenwood and sure enough there were three white guys playing basketball. There was a fourth one watching at the car they came in. We had never seen these white guys before in our life.

I was thinking, what are these white guys doing in Kenwood? It's not that if you are white you can't move to Kenwood. It's that we knew everybody in Kenwood. At this time, Kenwood is about a half-black and half-Hispanic neighborhood and we knew these guys were strangers. I quickly ran up to all three of them as they were standing underneath the basket. I yelled, "Which one of you called my nephew a nigger!" Looking completely stunned, all three of them simultaneously answered, "No it wasn't me."

At that point, I lost control and snapped. I didn't care what they had to say. I hit the first one that was directly in front of me. He fell to the ground. He had a look of horror on his face like if I was Jason Voohrees from the Friday the 13th movies. The other two looked like they were gonna crap in their pants. I yelled, "That's why you got knocked out bitch!"

Then suddenly, Devlin raised a 12-gauge shotgun in the air and hit one of them in the neck and I saw blood squirt out of him like a horror movie. He must have hit an artery. I've never seen blood come out like that. I didn't realize Devlin brought the shotgun to the park. I had a gun on me as usual, but I didn't feel enough of a threat from these guys to use it. They were very shocked and stunned like is this really happening to me? The next thing I saw was Peanut and Omari fly on the third man and the one I first hit and they started beating their ass. Devlin continued to beat the life out of them with the shotgun. I thought to myself this is bad, and they don't need me anymore. Those guys are gonna look like they had been attacked by a werewolf. So, I started running back to Peanut's house where my car was.

Phat Cheez and Tony followed me. As I was running, I thought I'm going to put Phat Cheez and Tony in my car and drive outta here and stay away from Kenwood for a while. Just as I was thinking that, an Olmos park police officer almost hit me with his patrol vehicle as I was running across Dora Street. After that, I changed my thinking. I thought he would see me get into my vehicle and then we would be on a high speed chase. So, I thought, better just run into Peanut's house and stay for a while.

What fucked up timing that a cop would be passing by and almost hit me at the exact moment I'm running from the scene of a crime. That is some bad luck. Me, Phat Cheez and Tony made it to Peanut's house, and right before I went inside, I tossed my gun on the roof. I didn't want another charge on me just in case they found us. About five minutes later, here came Scarface, Dongi, Devlin. Peanut, and Omari running in into the house. Devlin brought back the bloody shotgun. I yelled, "Why you bring back that fuckin gun man! Get rid of it!" Devlin looked at me strange, but he knew I was right. He replied "I'ma throw it out back!" I said, "Good. Get that muthafucka outta here!" Peanut blurted out, "Damn Marcus should we leave?" I responded "Fuck Peanut.

I thought about that, but if we leave now and get into a car they will see us and S.A.P.D. probably swarming the streets now! Shit did y'all see that Olmos Park Police? He almost hit me with his car nigga! Everybody just stay put, keep all the lights out like if nobody ain't here. Everybody just be quiet like we going to sleep or something." About five minutes later, there was a knock at the door.

A loud voice said "This is the police department. Open up!" They kept knocking and repeating the same thing. They were shining their flashlights through each window. I whispered to

Peanut, "They probably gonna get a search warrant and kick the door in, or they will set up surveillance and wait us out all day and night tomorrow. Go to the door and pretend you was asleep. Tell them you woke me up. What do y'all want? Sound agitated like you bothering me. Then shut the door and tell them, you going back to sleep." Peanut said, "Alright." He went to the front door, opened it and the S.A.P.D officer said, "Anyone else in there with you?" Peanut said just like he was told, "Naw I was trying to sleep y'all woke me up. What's the deal?" S.A.P.D officer said "Are your parents here?" Peanut said, "Naw, my mom out of town. I'm watching the house til she get back."

Under the circumstances, Peanut held his ground and did well for a fifteen year-old under police pressure. When the police asked him, "Is anyone else in here with you.?", I wish he would have said, "Yeah, my mom worked all day. She sleep, and I'm not waking her up for you.", and then just shut the door. But that didn't happen. They barged their way through the door and put Peanut in handcuffs. They came in like gangbusters, guns drawn, yelling "It's the police. Everyone come out with your hands up!"

They marched us outside, one by one, in handcuffs. They sat us down on the porch. They had a S.A.P.D. car with the spotlight on and the victim's relative or friend inside the squad car, the guy who didn't jump in and help. He just stood at the car and watched the beat down. I am surprised Devlin, Omari, or Peanut didn't go get him and beat his ass too. They probably saw the police and took off running. One by one, they lined us up in front of the spotlight on the street in front of the house and the hoe ass bitch, I mean, the fourth one who didn't help would say yes or no if we were involved in the assault. He said yes about me,Devlin,Phat Cheez, Tony, Omari, and Peanut. He said no about Scarface and Dongi. They walked home, but Tony and Phat Cheez didn't touch the victims. I only knocked one down with a punch, but all of us were taken in for two counts of aggravated assault with a deadly weapon. That shotgun Devlin beat them with, did us all in.

They searched all around the house and found the shotgun. Devlin was very upset. They made me and him ride in the same police car down to the magistrate office to get booked in. I looked at Devlin and the only thing I said to him the whole way was, "Damn, dawg we might be in the penitentiary for some years." Devlin looked at me with a disgusted look and just shook his head in disbelief. They took all six of us to where we had to talk to the detectives to figure out what happened and who did what and what we would ultimately be charged with.

We were standing there and the arresting officer handcuffed all six of us together like we were a chain gang. As we were standing there, waiting on the detectives to finish going over witness statements to be better equipped to ask us questions. The two arresting S.A.P.D officers were laughing and talking. One of them said "What was on these white guy's minds being from out of state, showing up playing basketball in Kenwood? I mean I guess they didn't know where they were at." The other officer said, "Shouldn't you find out where you are at before you start playing?" He continued laughing and the other one said, "I mean look at these guys. I bet they shit a brick when they saw them coming, especially this one," motioning to Devlin. Devlin is 6 feet tall and 240 pounds of solid muscle. He looks like he could compete for the heavyweight championship.

One of the officers said, "Why didn't you guys just beat their ass? You didn't have to use any weapons." I looked at them in amazement and said, "What!" The officer replied, "We would have found three white guys beat up, being in the wrong neighborhood. We would have just called EMS and told those guys they shouldn't have been here. This a bad place. The only reason it was a must to pursue you is because there was a weapon involved." The other officer said, "If that shotgun hadn't been used, you guys would not be here right now." After they said that, I looked at Devlin and said "Fuck."

Devlin looked up at me shook his head and then put it back down. Just then, two detectives came out. They unhooked us and put us in six different rooms. This is the strategy for them. They separate you and see if you will tell on your friends. It's a smart concept. Nobody wants to be locked up for a long time. I was put in a room and stayed in there for about 30 minutes. It was the longest 30 minutes of my life. That's another thing they do to you. They want you to marinate in there by yourself for a while and think about extended jail time.

The detective walks in. He is a very angular Hispanic man with a mustache. He had his gun and badge on his waist so I could see it. I could tell by his demeanor, he was going to be very direct and to the point. Looking at this man and the environment I was in I can see where this might be very intimidating to a person who has never seen someone dressing this properly and speaking properly, with a college degree backing them up. I knew none of my homeboys had seen this before, but you have to understand something about me. I come from a highly intelligent family.

The ten brothers and sisters that I attained through adoption are all very direct and speak very properly, and most of them have more college degrees than this man standing in front of me. So I was not about to be intimidated whatsoever. He sat down and said, "Well it's just like I figured. All your so-called boys said you fucked these people up. Why would you do something like that?" I responded very clearly, "My boys would never say anything like that because it's not true. You are going to have to show me on tape them saying that, and then I will believe you." He replied very sternly, "Look they said they will testify against you. Everyone saw what you did. Don't waste my time and your time with this. Tell me how these people ended up in the hospital?" I replied, "First off, my boys wouldn't tell on me. Okay.so now let me tell you what happened.

My nephew, which is Tony, came running up to me real excited and said this white man called me a nigger down at the park. So, I ran down there walked up to them and said which one of you called my nephew a nigger? They all denied it of course, but at this point I was so upset that one of them would say that so I hit the first one that was in front of me. He fell to the ground. I yelled at him, you got knocked out then I ran off. I figured my work was done." He looked at me with a perturbed look and said, "You didn't hit anybody with a shotgun tonight?" I replied, "No, why would I do that? My hands are sufficient enough for people like that." He replied, "Did you see Devlin Jefferson hit them with the shotgun? I responded, "No I hit the first one, then I ran. My work was done. I don't know what happened after that." He said, "You know they're in the hospital. They were beaten up badly." I said, acting surprised, "Wow, I don't know anything about that. I hit one of them and ran and that's all I am going to say."While I was saying that, I knew I was lying. I was picturing the blood squirting out of one of them when Devlin popped his ass with the shotgun.

The detective, with an ugly look on his face, got up and left. About forty-five minutes later, I was being processed in the Bexar County Jail with two counts of Aggravated Assault with a deadly weapon. Two counts? That told me two people got fucked up real bad. I saw Devlin afterwards when we were putting on our nice, beautiful orange pajamas, courtesy of the San Antonio Bexar County Jail. I asked him, "What did you say?" He said, "I told them I didn't do shit." I replied, "Me too. I told them the same shit. I didn't do shit and I didn't see shit." Reality sets in when you are in this environment. I was thinking, well this is how I'm going out. I've done a lot of dirt over the past 6 years. I guess this is my reap what you sow moment. I've got a wife, a son and a daughter.

All of the sudden, it hit me like a ton of bricks. I may not ever see my son's future basketball or football games. I won't see who my daughter goes out with. Fuck! My wife might get with someone else who raises my kids. Who knows who that is going to be. After being processed in, I called the same person who came to get me from the Bexar county jail in 1977 when I was four and a half years old, the time my parents got arrested for marijuana and cocaine possession. I called my brother through adoption, Edward Valdespino. He was my uncle in 1977, prior to adoption. This twenty year old uncle of mine, who picked me up when my Dad had gotten arrested and taken me to see the movie Sinbad, had now become an attorney, and here he was again, eighteen years later to the month, trying to save me again, but this time it was for something I had done.

Edward was great. He figured everything out and told me, "First of all we're going to get you out of here on a P.R. bond. Secondly, we're going to see if you can get probation. It's going to be difficult because the charge is severe. Two counts of aggravated assault with a deadly weapon is rough." I looked at him with tears welling up in my eyes and said, "My kids can't grow up without me. Get me out of here." He replied, "I will. Just sit tight. I will be back in a while." I said, "I didn't hit anybody with a gun. I just used my fist." He said, "That may not matter because you were with the people that did. Just sit back and wait. I'll see you in a little while." I said, "Okay."

About eight hours later, I was released to my brother Edward Valdespino. I ended up getting ten years' probation, which for my extreme charge is the maximum you can receive. The street term for getting put on probation is called I got put on paper. The terms of probation was that if I got arrested and found guilty for anything in the next 10 years, not only would I get prison time for the new charge but on top of that, I would get the 2 counts of 2-20 years for the aggravated assault with the deadly weapon. To my boys, probation is a set up.

When I told Vidal I got 10 years of probation, he said "They put you on paper 10 years? That ain't nothing but a nigga set-up!" They know you gonna fuck up in those 10 years so you get double the time." I understand what Vidal is talking about, but I agree more with my brother. I could be in the penitentiary right now. The system is giving me a second chance not to fuck up. Devlin Jefferson didn't get the same fate. While the rest of us got probation, Devlin got both counts of 2-20 years. Devlin and I had to pay for all the medical expenses for the victims and the restitution. It got put on me and Devlin because we were the adults, and the other homies were juveniles.

One of the homies later told me that those people were beaten within an inch of their life. Devlin caught the chain, and landed in a Texas state penitentiary. In 1998, Devlin beat up a prison guard and got more time. I feel for you Devlin. Hang in there, dawg. How the police knew we were in Peanut's house is that a lady trying to be a good Samaritan told police she saw a couple of us running into a house. I was surprised someone told on us, but it was probably a lady who wanted Kenwood cleaned up. The crazy thing is this didn't change me. I went home for a couple of days and then I was back in Kenwood. I loved being around my homeboys too much. I loved the camaraderie. You can't fabricate that feeling anywhere else. I was drunk with that feeling, and consumed by it. I was more upset about being caught. I made a decision, right then and there, that I was never going to get caught again.

CHAPTER TWENTY ONE

WICKEDNESS

A FEW DAYS later, I was at Chubby's house on Pine Street on the Eastside with Kevin. Tullie was out at some hoe's house, being Captain Save a Hoe again. I was standing in front of Chubby's house when I saw a nice dark-skinned black woman, very skinny and fit, walking by. I motioned for her to come here. I wanted to get her phone number and maybe she will go out with me tomorrow, I thought. I said, "Say girl what's your name?" She said, "Carla." I said, "Why don't you give me your phone number; maybe we can go out tomorrow?" She said, "Look, I don't have no phone number or no phone. I'm real busy. I got a lot going on in my life right now. I appreciate the offer and everything. You are cute. I love the color of your eyes. Maybe if I would have met you two years ago it would have been different. But I can do something for you right now."

Then it just dawned on me; she is a prostitute. She didn't look like it. She looked like a regular black girl walking to the store. Then I thought, wow I could just fuck her for 20 or 40 dollars and I don't have to take her out. I said, "What do you mean help me out?" She said, "Look don't play stupid with me. I don't have time." She started to walk away. I said, "No mama! Wait. I got 20 dollars. We can go back to my boy's house." She said, "Alright but give me the 20 dollars first." I said, "Ok, mama," as I reached in my pocket and pulled out a 20 dollar bill. We turned around and started walking to the back and I noticed Chubby and Kevin had watched and listened to our whole conversation. It was very dark; she didn't see them. I told her, "Go around back and wait for me. I will be there in a minute." Chubby and Kevin walked up to me and Kevin said, "Say Marcus, tell her you got two homies that want to fuck too and then we'll give her the money. We'll fuck her, then take her money and she can get the fuck on." Chubby said, "Yeah! You can get your money back too." I said, "Look y'all can do what y'all want. I paid this girl and I'm fin to go fuck."

I walked to the back. Chubby had a room back there. She got undressed. I had sex with her for about 10 minutes, and when I finished I hurried up and put my clothes on and told her, "I got two homies that want to fuck." Just as I said that, they came in the room. It was a glass door, so they had been watching me fuck and when I finished my sentence they didn't give her time to answer about whether or not she wanted to fuck them. Chubby said, "I'm the man of the house. I need some ass, girl. Don't be greedy." She responded, "Y'all got some money?!" Chubby said, "Yeah woman! We got money for both of us," meaning him and Kevin. She said, "Y'all need to hurry the fuck up. I got things to do."

I quickly left, shut the door and walked outside, turned around and watched through the glass window. I could see they were negotiating, but I think she gave in because Kevin Wallace, our resident rapist, wasn't gonna have any dialogue and began taking off his clothes. I watched through the window as they had sex with her for about 15 minutes, putting her through all kinds of positions. I was thinking, damn this girl trusted me and now she is gonna walk home with no money and a busted pussy. I think she started to realize near the end of the fucking that she wasn't getting any money because she started crying.

After Chubby finished, Kevin reached in her pants pocket and took out some money. I watched through the window as she was crying and putting her clothes back on. Then, she got upset and reacted violently and emotionally. She tried to get her money back, as she lunged at Kevin. Kevin threw her back down and slapped her real good. Just then, Chubby opened the door and I heard Kevin say, "Get outta here bitch! You ain't shit anyway!" Chubby did his usual laugh, then she ran at Chubby at the door and got in his face and said, "Y'all wrong for this! I got bills to pay! I got kids!" Chubby said, "We all do bitch," and he pushed her and said, "Now get the fuck on!"

As she ran by me crying hysterically she didn't notice me. It was so dark outside. There was only one light in the room. I'm glad she didn't make eye contact with me. She trusted me and I got her into this mess. I remember thinking well, this is the life she chose. She knows better than anybody if she keeps living this way she could die any minute. As she was running back home, she was probably thinking fuck I did all that fucking today and have nothing to show for it! I hope those muthafuckas die a slow death. But she probably happy to just be alive. Because as bad as my boys are, there are men out there that will fuck her and take her money then kill her.

I am happy she didn't have a knife, most of these street walkers carry a knife. If she would have had one and used it, she would have died and we would have all been in a world of shit. Just then Chubby handed me my 20 dollars back and said laughing, "I told you, you would get your money back." She had 32 dollars plus your 20, me and Kevin each got 16." Kevin said, "You made more money than we did and you didn't do shit!" I replied, "Technically that's not true. All I did was get my own money back. Y'all didn't put no money in and got a free 16 dollars each." Chubby did his laugh. I really didn't want to be there anymore. I said, "I'm going back to Eden Roc. I'ma holla at y'all tomorrow." They said, "Alright Holla!"

The next day even though I was still with Tan, I would occasionally take Ericka out. I picked up Ericka and we went to Jones barbeque on East Commerce Street. We got our food, we sat down to eat and were talking about our children. Just then I cannot believe it but the woman from last night at Chubby's house just walked in the restaurant with her son. I couldn't believe my eyes. Jones barbeque was a very small place. Where is she going to sit? Is she gonna notice me? I was talking to Ericka, but very distracted. She ordered her food and sat down with her son. She didn't notice or didn't recognize me in the daytime. When she got her order it was one sausage sandwich and a water. She gave the sausage sandwich to her son and watched him eat while she was talking to him about being a good boy. I had never felt so worse in my life.

All the shit I've done to people in my past, at that moment paled in comparison to watching a prostitute mother trying to provide for her child and I was part responsible for taking money away from her. She didn't have enough money for herself to eat or bring her other children if she had any. Part of me wanted to die in that restaurant. What do I do? Do I act like I don't know her and give her some money so she can eat and buy a big family meal for her kids to take home. What if I walk up to her and she recognizes me and yells rape and says, "Him and his friends took my money!" What if she was so angry, she tried to stab me with one of the steak knives in the restaurant. How could I explain that anyway?

I couldn't eat anymore. I felt like shit! Ericka finished eating. We left and she didn't notice me. I never told anyone this story. I was too ashamed. I wish I could find her today. If she is alive and talk to her, apologize and show her children a good time. I owe her at least that. To my boys at the time, she was sub human. A piece of meat. To me, she was a real person living breathing flesh. Just trying to get by in this crazy life. Later on that night, I was driving with Tullie and Vidal on Walters street having just crossed the bridge. We were by the Wheatley Courts and I saw this beautiful light skinned black girl walking on the street. I quickly turned in to talk to her and Vidal said, "What the fuck is you doing?" Tullie said, "What up? Marcus?" I replied, "Do you see that girl walking?" They both replied, "Yeah! So." I said, "Yeah so! She is off the chain. I gotta holla at her." I was waiting for their reactions because normally they would be just like me saying how fine she is and they wanna fuck.

They had no reaction at all. I looked at them and said, "Wait a minute y'all already fucked her right?" Tullie started laughing and said, "Hell yeah, She got some good pussy too!" I said, "Fuck that shit y'all hit it, I gotta hit now too." Vidal said, "All right turnaround and then pull in that first drive way." Tullie said, "Boy, Marcus ain't fin to miss no pussy right?" I replied, "Y'all hit already. Quit being stingy." We walked around the corner in the Wheatley Courts housing project and knocked on this door. This older black man answered and said "Ah shit Vidal"

I thought, you was crystal. I was ready. Vidal replied, "What's up unc? You doing your usual huh." He said, "Hell yeah, she out there?" Vidal said, "Yeah as good as she look she'll have somebody in a minute. Say unc you remember Tullie?"Vidal's uncle responded "How could I forget shit! He taller than Neckbone. What's up boy?" Vidal said "And this is my White homeboy Marcus." I said, "How you doing? Sir" He said, "I'm gonna be doing good in a minute when she get here. Shit Y'all can help me!"

I didn't know what he meant and I didn't ask. It was like they were all in on something but me. About two minutes went by and Vidal and his Uncle were talking then a knock at the door. Vidal's Uncle jumped up and told Vidal and Tullie, "Come On!" He opened the door and there she was Crystal as beautiful as she could be and right behind her a tall blond haired blue eyed White guy. I made eye contact with him and at first he was smiling. Tullie and Vidal were on each side of the door out of his line of site.

Then it just dawned on me something bad was about to go down. Just then Tullie and Vidal emerged and when the white guy saw them. His smiling face turned into the look of Oh Shit! What am I doing here? Vidal's Uncle shut the door and locked it and yelled, "Oh you thought you was gonna get some black pussy huh!" Then he hit the White boy from the back as hard as he could. He almost fell but he caught himself on a chair.

Then Vidal hit him very hard in the face and yelled, "What you doing out here peckerwood!" Then Tullie slapped the hell outta him. While he was on the ground. Vidal's Uncle said angrily, "Where's the money you were gonna give her?" Then he slapped the white man and reached in his pockets and took all his money. About $100 dollars. Then took his wallet, took out his driver's license so he couldn't see it and said, "Now I know you ain't stupid enough to go to the cops, but if you do. We gonna pay you a visit and have a repeat performance if not worse. You got that white boy!" He was a little disoriented and said, "Yeah I got it!" Vidal's Uncle said, "Now take your bitch ass on!"

He opened the door and let the man out and shut the door. After that he turned and he started laughing and Vidal and Tullie joined in on the laughter. I started laughing just to laugh. I didn't really care one way or another. I did think it was a little humorous that he was thinking he was about to have sex with this fine ass black girl and in return got his ass beat and his money taken. He knew what side of town he is on. I didn't think he was going to the cops, his face of terror suggested that. He was just gonna have to cut his losses and go home and thank God he was still alive.

About three minutes later, I looked at Vidal and said, "We gotta go Vidal, I still wanna fuck. Y'all beatin people up and shit." Vidal replied, "Oh yeah, I forget shit. That's why we're here isn't it?" Vidal went upstairs to talk to Crystal. About one minute later he called me from upstairs and said, "Come on she ready." He had went up there to tell her to fuck me. We passed each other on the stairs Vidal said, "Have fun" I replied, "You know it." I went into the room and she had her clothes off already. I took mine off. She took out a rubber and started sucking my dick while putting it on. I started fucking and about 10 minutes into it, I looked at the bedroom door and there was Tullie and Vidal looking at me have sex. I didn't mind though. That was us. We were real close.

I watched them fuck and they watched me. I've seen all my homies fuck a hundred times and they have seen me fuck a hundred times. Nobody gives a shit. Some of us are more shy than others, but that comes with the territory. You hang with the homies, you will eventually get watched having sex. The only time it's not cool is when your with the person you lay your head with every night. I'm the only one with a Wife (Ericka). They're not gonna watch me fuck Ericka. Vidal is with Nena Clayton.

I'm not gonna follow him home and watch him and Nena go at it. My homeboys may not have a Wife, but they have someone close to them, so in case they get locked up. There is a person they will be leaning on and calling and writing from jail. For example, we all went to Shiliterbahn for a couple of days. That was for Wife's or close girlfriends and family. Carlton took his girlfriend, Tullie took his girlfriend and I took Ericka and my children.

We left the other girlfriends and hoes at home. That vacation was for family. So there you have it, in a span of 48 hours I watched two human beings who thought they were getting one thing, then got something entirely different and both got a beat down because of it. I felt like horse shit, about one and the other one not so much. Another day of being in the hood with Lunatics, I love and I am one of them. Go figure?

CHAPTER TWENTY TWO

MAFIA

A FEW DAYS later everyone was in Kenwood chillin' and talking as usual. Chris Kelly was even there. I found out that he wasn't even Vidal's younger brother; they just pretended for a long time and everybody believed it because they looked alike. Chris hardly made it out to Kenwood. We went to Wheatley Courts or Blue Bonnet Street more than Big Tyme Playas made it to Kenwood. I had Tan over at Tullie's house. I took her to Tullie's room to make love to her, like I did daily. We had been in there about twenty minutes fucking real good when I started to hear some whispering. I played it off like I didn't hear anything. I was hoping Tan didn't hear it.

When I turned my head, I saw Chris and Vidal at Tullie's window watching. I heard Chris say, "Marcus be fucking good and he know all the positions, but he don't be fucking like a nigga, though." I looked back and said, "Come on Vidal, Chris. Give me some privacy, man." Vidal said, "Damn Chris, you got louder n shit." Tan replied, "Naw y'all can stay. You just need some popcorn." I laughed; they left. I told Tan sorry for that baby.

She said, "You don't have to apologize for them. I know how niggaz is." After I finished, we went outside. Chris and Vidal were leaving. I told Chris, "I probably come through tonight." Vidal said, "I won't be there. Im' a fuck this new bitch tonight." I replied, "When don't you fuck a new bitch?"

Everybody laughed and got in Chris's ride and left. I took Tan home. Tullie went to score some dope from Ramon, our connection in Kenwood. He always got 2 or 3 ounces of cocaine. Me and Tullie weren't Nikki Barnes, but it was enough to maintain our lifestyle and not be wanting for anything. I was hoping Tullie would be there when I got back. I never scored from Ramon. That was Tullie's connection in Kenwood. Tullie was scoring for the both of us. He must have taken some of the homies with him because when I got back I didn't see too many of us at Tullie's. About five minutes later, Tullie pulled up with Peanut and Omari. Tullie got out of the car in a bad mood. He slammed the car door and said, "I got some bad news."

I was thinking, what could be bad? We running shit, we making money, fucking hoes, doing whatever we want. What could possibly be bad news? I replied, "What happened?" Tullie replied, "Ramon is taking our money and scoring from the Mexican Mafia. That's his connection." I said, "Let me stop you. How does Ramon know the Mexican Mafia?" Tullie responded very excited, "Shit I don't know, probably his cousin or something. He must know them. Somehow he's getting dope from them!" I said, "Ok go on." Tullie replied, "Ramon said that the Mexican Mafia said that we moving too much weight in Kenwood and they want a piece of our action. I don't think they know about Eden Roc. They just know about Kenwood."

I replied, "What! That is bad news. Is Ramon lying to you, trying to extort money from us?" Tullie responded, "Hell naw!

Ramon knows I'll split his wig. He knows we get down; we not to be fucked with! You know Danny up the street? Ramon told him the same shit. They want 15% or else." I said, "Or else what?" Tullie said, "Shit, Nigga, figure it out. They will kill you!" I said, "What's Danny going to do?" Tullie said, "Shit, I don't know. But if I was him I would pay. He only one person; he lives with his family. Fuck that!" I said, "Well you just ruined my fuckin day." Tullie said, "Shit, mines too!"

I said, "That's some crazy ass shit. I can just hear Vidal now, what the fuck are we in Harlem Nights or something? Is Bugsy Calhoun about to pull up? Do I look like Eddie Murphy or old ass Richard Pryor? Look Tullie, you can go back and tell Ramon that we not giving anybody no 15 percent. They got us fucked up! I don't know what the fuck they gonna do with Danny, but that don't have shit to do with us! We not giving any portion to any organization, Mexican Mafia or whoever! I don't give a fuck who they are! Tell Ramon go back and tell his Mexican Mafia connection, Fuck You! You not getting shit, but the money we use to score the 2 or 3 ounces. Tell him we make it into crack cocaine. This is the black man's drug. We sell to old black people. They are the best customers. We don't sell to Mexicans, if this is a race thing. Even though I'm lying, we have Mexicans we sell to. But we make this drug ourselves. We cook this shit and it's potent. This ain't got nothing to do with the Mexican Mafia. We buy our two ounces and that's it with them."

Tullie responded, "I'm thinking the same shit. If they wanna go to war, fuck'em! It's like the Geto Boys said Nigga! If you wanna go to war I'll take you to war!" I replied, "Let's not get crazy, Tullie. This is the Mexican Mafia we're talking about. They probably can take us out. But we not going out like Willie lump-lump and dem. Tell Ramon, if they send anybody in here to kill us, tell him they better send people in here they don't like, because those mutha-fuckas will die! If you think about it Tullie, in order to kill all of us they would have to send an army in here. Now tell Ramon to tell them. Is it worth going to war with 25 gang bangers that are all armed, ready to die for their hood? Is it worth losing people in their organization for 15 percent on three ounces?" Tullie said, "Shit I don't know what they are capable of. But I know this, if one of us die over this shit, their first casualty will be Ramon and maybe his family. I will walk over there and kill Ramon and anybody that look like Ramon." I responded, "I'll go one step further. If any of us don't make it, we will kidnap Ramon and he will take us to his connection. Then people will surely die, starting with Ramon and his connection. Does anyone else know about this besides you and Peanut and Omari?"

Tullie said, "Nope." I replied, "We need to let everyone know. Tell Carlton and Chubby especially, because they walking or driving around Kenwood. I don't want them caught off guard with this shit." I didn't envy Ramon's position. He is caught in the middle, between Mexican Mafia vs. Kenwood dope dealers and gang bangers. We had to stand our ground. Maybe they're just trying to strong arm us and see if we would give in. That's not going to work. I don't know one punk in Kenwood.

Me and Tullie left Kenwood and went to the Eastside and picked up Chris, Vidal and Charlie. We were in the drive thru at Jack-n-the Crack and we told them our situation. Just as I thought, Chris and Charlie are a little more crazy and gung ho than Vidal. Chris said, "Man, fuck them Mexicans, Nigga. They bleed like we do. We got guns too, Nigga!" Then Charlie, who still hasn't found anybody he wouldn't rob said, "Say Marcus, call Ramon." I stopped him dead in his tracks. I said, "Tell Tullie call him. I don't deal with Ramon." He said, "Ok! Tullie call

Ramon. Tell him we gonna buy five ounces. Wait. How much do you score from him?" Tullie said, "Two ounces, sometimes three." Charlie said, "Ok, then I'm right. Tell Ramon you want five Ounces, then we'll rob his bitch ass of that dope and send a message to that Mexican Mafia."

I said, "Wait a minute, Charlie. That sounds all good with being ruthless and shit, but they know where we live in Kenwood. They will go right to Tullie's house and to Dongi's house. You wouldn't be just robbing Ramon. You would be robbing the Mexican Mafia. You would guarantee a war then. I don't want to rob the Mexican Mafia. We're just not gonna give them a cut of our hard earned hustling." Charlie sounded upset. "Well fuck it then. I don't know what to tell you."

I don't think Charlie has ever met a person he would not rob. That was his solution to everything. After we got our food, we went back to Bluebonnet St. and hung out for a while. I knew if we needed them (Big Tyme Playas) they would be there for us, as crazy as they are. We were always there for them most of the time. When they was into it with them New Life Village niggaz, Melvin called Tullie to walk over there. I remember they needed Tullie at the skating rink because they had some big niggaz. Me and Adrian were sitting out there selling dope, waiting on X and dem. We sat out there on any part of the Eastside a lot. Anything could have popped off and we would have been down to help.

When Tullie and I got back I told him, "You see how Chris and Charlie are? They shoot first and ask questions later; they too hot-headed. They don't think things through. It reminds me a little bit of the Adrian days. That fool. I loved him to death, but that nigga had me shootin at people and beating people I didn't know." Tullie said, "That nigga Adrian would have already been at Ramon's house jackin' his ass up and startin' a war." I replied, "Those days are over. We got to be smarter than that. Tullie what's your motto? Don't." Tullie jumped in. "Don't start none, and it won't be none." I replied, "That's right, I live by that now. You can tell all that shit we talked about today to Ramon when you see him tomorrow." Tullie responded, "Yeah that's all good. I got these hoes. Let's go get some pussy." I responded, "Suddenly my day just got better."

The next day Tullie told Ramon everything he needed to tell him and later on that night two hit men knocked on Danny's door and shot him a bunch of times right at his front door. I was told his kids were walking around his shot up body. When I got to Kenwood, Tullie asked me if I wanted to see his body. I said, "No it's probably a fuckin' dead body."

I told Tullie to get everyone together. "We need to have a meeting." They did this for two reasons. First, to kill Danny because Danny probably said fuck them I'm not paying you any percentage. Second, was to send us a message to see if we would be willing to go to war or just cave in and give the 15%. If Tullie told Ramon everything that we talked about, then they knew we were not going to succumb to their scare tactics. If they came after us, they would see everybody got heart. I went to my house real quick and got every gun I had and brought them back to Tullie's. We had a fully Automatic- Mac11, an SKS, 38 special, a couple of nine millimeters, two shotguns, three 25s, a 32 caliber and a 357

Tullie had his own personal 9mm Beretta with 2 clips on him. Everybody got together at Tullie's. They all knew the situation we were in and they just found out what happened to Danny. They were all on edge. I said, "We're gonna stick together and everyone has a gun." They watched me, as I strategically placed guns around Tullie's house and at Dongi's house and backyard.

I placed a gun right behind Dongi's back fence. I remember a couple of years ago, running from the police and getting away by jumping that fence. It's a great place for a gun because as you jump the fence, you can turn around, grab the gun and shoot the people chasing you.

As I was explaining this to my boys, you would have thought we were in the movie Outlaw Josey Wales waiting on the Commanches. We had lots of anxious moments that night and for the next couple of days. I walked around the neighborhood at night with my SKS. I did not go to bed for 48 hours. I stopped a couple of suspicious looking cars that I hadn't seen before with my SKS. Those people were scared as hell, but nobody called the police. After about 4 or 5 days, everything died down. It was back to normal. I guess they figured it was not worth going to war with gang bangers for purchasing a few of ounces of cocaine from time to time. Or we were just plain lucky and they had something else going on. With all the craziness going on, we had not been at Eden Roc in a few days. That explains why some of the geekers from Eden Roc were coming in Kenwood to buy dope and asking us why the hell we hadn't been back there? I let them know we would be back to take care of our business. We just had a minor setback.

CHAPTER TWENTY THREE

FUCK YOU! PAY ME!

A COUPLE OF days later, I was sitting at Ronald's apartment. Tullie was in the bathroom. Everybody else was either in a different apartment or back at Kenwood. Kevin, Chubby and Vidal might have been at that white family's unit. They would all fuck this fine 16 -year old white girl, named Cara. I think her mom would also get fucked too on occasions. This was an exciting time of year for me and Tullie, because everybody was getting their income tax checks and this was year 5 of me and Tullie getting the crack smokers' income tax money. I'd say over 5 years we have collected almost all the money from about 30 tax returns. People get their checks, they buy a little dope and keep coming back and back til their money was gone. We serve them dope(crack) with love at first, and then when they start geekin (getting high), we crum their ass because at that point they want the crack so bad they will just take whatever we give them. Ronald walked in the door, didn't say hi or anything and calmly asked me, "Marcus, let me see your gun." Keep in mind, Ronald deals with knives all throughout his apartment. He puts them in various places, in case his paranoid ass might have to use one. I have never, in seven years, seen Ronald handle a gun. I replied, "Ronald, why do you need to see my gun?" He responded, "Marcus, I just want to see it. I wanna see what it looks like!" I took my gun out, the one I was carrying at the time was a .38 caliber. I said, "Ronald I'ma show you what it looks like, see look!" Ronald said, "No, I wanna hold and see it. Marcus don't play with me. Have I ever asked you in all these years to let me see your gun?" I replied, "That's why I'm worried about it!"

I handed him my gun, so he would quit bugging me about it. He got the gun in his hand and said, "Thank you, I'll be right back!" As he turned around and walked out the front door, I was stunned that he left with my gun. Tullie walked out of the bathroom and said, "Who was that?" I said, "That was Ronald." Tullie said, "Why did he leave?" I replied, "I don't know, he asked me for my gun and left." Tullie responded, "And you gave it to him!" I replied, "Yeah, he ain't never asked me for anything like that before." Tullie said, "Shit, fuck that. Only God knows what he's gonna do with that gun!" Just as Tullie finished his sentence, we heard two loud bangs coming from outside. Pow!-Pow! Tullie and I looked at each other shocked, and ran outside. We saw Ronald point the gun at this older black man who we didn't recognize saying, "You keep fucking with me and your ass gonna get something you don't want!" I said, "Ronald! What the fuck are you doing? Give me the gun!" I took the gun from Ronald's hands and said, "Go inside, Ronald!"

The man had his hands in the air yelling, "Don't kill me! Don't kill me!" I was escorting Ronald into his apartment. Tullie laughing said, "Damn Ronald! What did he do?" Ronald replied, "OOH, I'm so mad right now, I don't want to talk about it! I shoulda killed his ass!" I went outside and saw the man walking away. I yelled, "Hey! Ronald said he was sorry and he didn't mean to do that, you alright sir?" He responded, "He's crazy. He's crazy," and kept walking. Of course, I was lying about Ronald saying he was sorry. I was just trying to smooth the situation over. The last thing we needed was the heat from cops coming into Eden Roc for an attempted murder. Later on that night, Vidal came over and I could see he was sitting on aggravated. I asked him, "What happened. Somebody die or something?" Vidal replied, "I don't even want to talk about it." That peaked my interest even more. I said, "Naw, tell me what happened?" He responded, "Chris snitched on me!" I said, "What! Chris… Chris Kelly?" Vidal responded angrily. "Yeah, Chris! What other Chris we know?" I said, "Damn! What happened?" Vidal said, "Phat Cheez was with him too, so they gave the police my name!" I said, "That's fucked up, but that's more of an indictment on Chris than Phat Cheez. Chris know betta than that shit. Phat Cheez is young than a muthafucka!" Vidal said, "I don't care! I'm not talking to them no more. I told you I don't want to talk about it." I said, "Alright!" Vidal said, "That just goes to show you that the hardest niggaz will crack when that police in a suit come talking to your ass, right? It don't matter how hard you are. Some niggaz can't handle that shit. That's pressure."

I replied, "I feel what you saying. I done already been through that bullshit. I didn't tell them detectives shit. They didn't get shit from me! It's just like in the moment of truth, when you're supposed to pull that trigger. Some niggaz be scared and that gun gets more heavy and it starts wobbling in your hand. I done seen that. I be like, I thought you was hard, Fool!" We're both laughing at this point. Just then, Tullie came outside laughing. "Say Vidal, Willie in there! Don't that fool owe you 80 dollars?" Vidal said,

"Hell yeah. He got it?" Tullie laughed. "I hope he do because he in there buying right now!" I thought to myself, Uh-Oh when you give a geeker credit and they haven't paid you and they're buying more dope from another nigga, that's a major problem. We all went inside. Vidal found Willie. Vidal said, "Can I get my money?" Willie replied, "I'ma have it tonight Vidal. I'll be back." He started walking to the door. Vidal, already aggravated said, "Hell Naw! You getting new shit? You ain't coming back tonight. You ain't fin to pull no geeker move on me. Who you think I am!" Willie said, "Alright, Vidal. Just calm down." Tullie said, "Watch it! Vidal. Willie be havin' a knife."

Just then Tullie turned up the music as if he knew what was about to go down. Tullie knew the music would drown out Willie screaming. Vidal took out a gun. I couldn't see what kind it was, and said, "You don't even plan on giving me my money right!" Vidal hit him with the back of the gun as hard as he could. Willie began putting up his hands in a defensive position but that was not gonna stop Vidal. Vidal yelled as he was hitting him, "You not just gonna steal from me and get away with it!" Tullie was laughing. Willie looked in pain and sick like the whole world was over. I went outside very quickly to make sure no one else could hear what was taking place inside. After it was over, Vidal went back to the Eastside. Willie looked like he was unconscious but arose to his feet and left after a while. Blood was everywhere. I hope he learned a lesson from that beating. A few days later this man, who shall remain nameless, owed me and Tullie 300 hundred dollars. We gave him a deadline and when it passed with no payment, me and Tullie went to his house and Tullie kicked the door in. I have never seen a door that Tullie did not mind kicking in. We went in with guns drawn and found nobody there.

We noticed he had a 60 inch TV, so we picked it up and loaded it on one of my trucks and took off. We all had big screen TVs so we took the TV to my father's house, and he loved it. I told my father exactly how we got it and he did not mind at all. Remember, he used to be in the game as well. The bottom line is we are going to recoup our money somehow, if not more than what you owe us. The next day I was outside at Eden Roc with Tan. It was a Saturday and all these little kids were outside playing. I had seen Vidal go in Ronald's apartment and I knew nobody was there. Then I had seen Ms. Mickey go in Ronald's apartment. I didn't think too much of it at the time, because I was talking to Tan about going to (Six Flags) Fiesta Texas. Then, all of a sudden, about two minutes later these little boys and girls came up to me and Tan and one of them said, "Vidal's fucking Ms. Mickey!" Me and Tan looked at each other with astonished looks on our faces and I said, "How do you know?" One of them said, "Come on Marcus, look." All these little kids ranging from 4yrs old to 14 went around the corner and looked in Ronald's bedroom through a window, and sure enough you could see Vidal on top of Ms. Mickey thrusting his dick in and out of her. Ms. Mickey looked like she was in a tremendous amount of pain. I was thinking shit! They couldn't put the blinds down? Tan was laughing.

Then I saw about eight kids, girls and boys standing with their head pressed against the window, watching in amazement. I said, "Hey! Y'all get away from the window. That's what adults do! Get away!" One of them comes back to me and said, "I told you Marcus!" I said, "I know. Thanks for telling me!" This little Mexican kid about 8 years old was still watching. I said, "Hey! You did hear me? Move it!" He said, "Man!" He was upset he had to quit watching and move but he left. Tan looked at me and said, "Does that give you any ideas?" I said, "No, what you talking about?" She said, "I wanna do it right know!" I said, "Oh that. Not right now, mama. I need to take care of some business right quick." She replied, very disappointed, "Okay." Tan went into her house, just as this Mexican kid named Nino came walking out.

He said, "What's up Marcus?" I replied, "Nothing, just chillin'. Where your brother Vito at?" He responded, "Inside watching TV. Man Marcus, you are lucky." I said smiling, "Why you say that Nino?" He replied, "You and Tullie and Vidal get to be with all these girls and then you get to fuck Tan. She's the best looking girl in my class." I replied, "Nino your time will come. You ain't ugly dawg! There's gonna be a lot of girls gonna wanna fuck you. And with the Tan shit, it not like if I didn't want her she would fuck somebody at your school. She a bopper. She going for much older guys and more money and power." Nino said, "I know Marcus. I just wanted to tell you how lucky you were and how you shoot the basketball so good?" I replied, "Hours and hours of practice, Nino. Remember my record, Nino? 38 college 3-pointers in a row. You think you gonna break that one day?" Nino replied, "Hell no Marcus. That's crazy!" Just then Vidal came out sweating. I said, "You know everybody was watching you right? All the kids through the window." Vidal replied, "For real! That's some crazy ass shit." Just then Ronald passed us by on the way to his apartment and said, "It's hotta than four prostitutes' pussy on Cherry Street at 3am!"

Vidal and I started laughing. I replied, "GA-DAM Ronald, that's hot than a muthafucka!" A couple of hours later, Tullie and Vidal were at Ronald's along with a couple of geekers that were guests of Ronald's, one named Toney and a white guy we called Wild Bill Irwin because he had long hair and a mustache. I left to go to Tan's house briefly, to see what was going on over there and as I was leaving White Boy Andy passed me by. I said, "What's up Andy? What you need?" He replied, "I just need to talk to Ronald!" I said, "Alright! They in there. Go ahead and open the door." I didn't think much of it. I thought maybe his mom wanted to borrow milk or sugar from Ronald. About 30 minutes later, I emerged from Tan's and saw everyone outside. I saw Tullie and Vidal laughing but Ronald looked upset, but also at any second he looked like he could laugh.

I heard Ronald say, "I'm a cut that nigga too short to shit and his socks won't fit!" I thought about it for a second. I said, "Damn, Ronald, that's pretty Mutha-Fuckin short." Vidal said, "Hell yeah Ronald, you cutting from the torso. That's a whole lotta cutting." Everyone's laughing at this point. Just then White Boy Andy came out of Ronald's apartment. Tullie said, "Damn Andy, I forgot your ass was in there!" Andy walked by and said, "See you later." We went back inside and Vidal went straight to the table and said, "Where my $40 dollars?" Tullie said, "Shit, you left $40 dollars on the table with a house full of smokers?" Vidal replied, very upset, "I don't give a fuck about that. Nobody fin to steal from me!" I said, "What other geekers were in the house in the last 30 minutes?"

Tullie said, "Naw, they had already left and Vidal was counting his money and then we went outside real quick because we thought we heard something." I said, "Vidal all you had was $40 dollars?" He said, "Naw! I got 800, I was on 760 when we ran outside real quick! I didn't think anybody would take my $40 dollars." Tullie said, "Andy was the only one in here and saw that."

Just as Tullie said that, Vidal bolted toward the door with Tullie right behind him. I thought to myself. Oh God, another person about to get destroyed. I walked outside and I could see Tullie banging on the door. I jogged over there, and just as I got there Tullie kicked in the door. Tullie wears a size 16 shoe and is 300 pounds. The door came completely off the hinges. That's when I realized Andy was guilty. He would have opened the door if he didn't steal any money. He probably stole the money to support his marijuana habit. I'm hoping nobody else is in there with him, because they will get fucked up too. The look on Andy's face was pure shock. As Tullie started talking, it turned to petrified. Tullie yelled, "You wanna put yourself in a grown man's position? You gonna be dealt with like a grown man! Simple as that! You shouldn't have stolen no money!" Vidal began to punch Andy over and over.

Vidal caved his face with his fist. Andy started to run. He went from the living room to his room. Vidal began body slamming him. The only time I felt a little bad for him was when Vidal picked up this board with legs. It looked like something you make for your mother when you're in grade school. Vidal put the board up against his face and hit him with the palm of his hand, full force. As it cracked in Andy's face, he let out a loud scream and was crying. I said, "Let's go Vidal. He learned his lesson!" Ronald walked in and saw Andy and said, "Y'all cold blooded!" and walked out. Tullie left. Tan walked in, because she heard the loud noises. Tan was looking at Andy in amazement.

Then Cara, Andy's fine ass older sister, who everybody was fuckin' but me, walked in and said, "Oh my God! What happened? What did he do?" I replied, "He stole some money from us." She replied franticly, "Oh my God! Leave him alone!" I remembered Cara and Andy were arguing real bad yesterday, but I guess when you see your brother beaten that bad, a petty argument goes out the window. I said very calmly, "Cara, just shut up. He fucked up! Don't make a big deal out of this before something else happens." Tan said, "I can't look at this anymore." I replied, "Then don't!

Go home." Tan left. Vidal got his $40 dollars and left. As I was about to leave, Andy's father showed up. He was not a small man. He was about 5'10 220 pounds the same as me. He said, "What happened?" I replied, "What the fuck you think just happened.? Your door just got kicked in!" He said a litter calmer, "Why?" I said, "Your son stole money." He replied, "Oh God!" and went to his son's room.

Andy's father knew how we get down and he knows his son is a fuck up. So I knew there wouldn't be any backlash. His dad knows the game. I remember thinking if that was my son, everybody would die. But that's the difference between me and Andy's father. I walked into Ronald's unit and the first thing out of his mouth is, "Marcus y'all cold blooded. I can't believe y'all did that boy like that." I replied, "Ronald he stole money. What did he need, a kiss?" Ronald did not respond with words, He just uttered, "Mm, mm, mm." I said, "Ronald, you worried about one kid who stole money and got dealt with. When we was watching the Oklahoma City bombing a couple of years ago, you wasn't worried about none of those people." Ronald replied, "That because the Murrah building sends me my check and if it blew up, my check blew up wit it."

I said, "See. You worried about a check and them people was fucked off." Ronald responded, "I don't know none of those people and it ain't my fault that white boy was thrown off his rocker and went crazy and blew everybody up! I need my check!" I replied, "See Ronald. You cold-blooded. Them people was dying and..." Ronald cut me off angrily and said, "I don't give a damn! I need my money! Can't nobody hold it betta than me. I got four pockets and socks and shoes I can put it in." Vidal and Tullie were laughing. Tullie said "Can't nobody hold it better than you, huh Ronald?" Ronald replied, "That's right. I hope them people are alright, but ain't nobody else gonna send me a check."

Well, there you have it. This world was about the haves and the have nots. Bottom line is, you need money. Whether it's big time corporations, people working regular jobs, people on food stamps, or even DOPE DEALERS like us. When it comes to people's money, everybody is thinking the same thing: FUCK YOU! PAY ME!

CHAPTER TWENTY FOUR

END OF EDEN ROC

MOST OF THE gang banging days for me and Tullie were over. The last time I saw Tullie, wanting to kill somebody for nothing was for these idiots giving him a good stare down, which we call mad-dogging. That was a year ago at a convenience store on the Eastside. I had to tackle him in the street with a gun in his hand as it went off, all for two bitch ass niggaz who are probably in the penitentiary right now. I had help from a friend of ours named Brett. Don't get it twisted now. If you cross us, that's bad news for you, but that would be if money was involved and not for something as stupid as mad-dogging. I still identified myself as a Blood but I quit wearing red exclusively.

It was all about making money and still fucking as many hoes as we could. If I was ever going to do a lot of penitentiary time, it would be for something I earned and I would do my time like a man. It wouldn't be a crazy situation that I got thrust into where I shot somebody for almost no reason, like the time Ronald called Tullie to come get these two niggaz who he said were threatening him. It was back in 1993, when Ronald lived on San Pedro near downtown. He was impatient, waiting on Tullie to bring him some dope, so he called another connection and he said they didn't give him enough dope for the money he paid. In our business, they call it crumming. They crummed him, so he called Tullie and because Tullie loves his brother so much, he would go defend him. Tullie never cared that Ronald was gay. Ronald was his brother. Tullie said, "Let's go Marcus. These niggaz is fucking with Ronald." I was in full gang mode at the time, and didn't care about anything but the task at hand. Tullie did the driving, and we went over there as quickly as possible. When we turned the corner by Ronald's apartments, I saw a bunch of guys on the corner where Ronald had just used the pay phone. I stuck my SKS machine gun out the window and said loudly, "Do y'all know Ronald!"

Three of them ran, five of them stopped dead in their tracks and didn't move. Tullie got out of the car and said, "Did y'all hear him! Who the fuck sold dope to my brother Ronald!" They were all scared and didn't say shit. I was in position, so that if any of them pulled a gun and tried to shoot Tullie, San Antonio would have another funeral on their hands, because I would chop them down. They saw my SKS, so I don't think they wanted any part of that. Tullie said, "I'm a go holla at my brother. If I ever hear about anybody selling dope to my brother, it's gonna be y'all ass!" I still had my gun pointing in their direction. I said, "What he just said. Put the word out! Now start walking!"

Tullie got back in the car and we went to Ronald's apartment, and he started yelling at Ronald not to be impatient and buy dope from those niggaz. He told him, "You don't know who they are." He said they could kill him if he starts trippin about the amount of dope he get and the only thing I said was, "If they kill you Ronald, then we'll have to go kill all of them." Ronald got the message but still said, "When I call for dope, bring it! Don't fool around."

You see, that's what I'm talking about? If one of those dope dealers got out of line and put me in a bad position, I would kill them and possibly be in the penitentiary for a long time and for what? Because Ronald got impatient over a $20 piece of crack cocaine. That's crazy. I am not doing that anymore. Tullie knows better as well. He used to tell me if he was in a courtroom and the judge said, "I now sentence Lawrence Bailey to Life in Prison." He said he would be speechless and probably fall out and be unconscious.

I told Tullie no more stupid crazy ass shit. We done already put in enough work. It's all about business. Tan's and my relationship was on its last legs. I still cared about her, but didn't love her anymore like I used to. The feeling was mutual. She moved to the North Eastside in the Glenn, off Montgomery and Walzem Road. I still did go over there and occasionally have sex with her. One night, I fucked her and her friend Ebony Washington. Guys, if you are listening I don't know if some of you ever gonna get the chance to do this or not, but I found out the easy way you can tell if you still have feelings for a girl. I put my dick in Tan and it was hard. I then put my dick in Ebony and it started to become flaccid. When I put it back in Tan it became hard again. I had fun with this for about 30 minutes. This let me know I still had feelings for Tan.

A few days later I met this woman walking on Callaghan. Her name was Gina. She gave me her number and said I could call her later. About 4 hours later(it was about 8pm), I called her to see if I could get together with her later on. Gina was a nice looking, very thick black woman with three children. To this point in my life, I have slept with about 200 black women. I have never gone up to any woman who wasn't black and tried to get a phone number. I have never had sex with a white woman and the only Mexican girls I had sex with were because they were with all the homies.

I think white women are beautiful but I never have had the urge to walk up and talk to them. I don't feel any connection with them. From 1988 to 1996, the last nine years of my life, I've had a strong connection to black women. Gina told me to come over but her kids were still up. I said ok. I didn't mind. I love playing with children. When I got there, I sat on the couch and her kids came to me and started messing with me like all curious children do. I played with them for a while.

About 10pm, she told them to go to bed. Gina started telling me the children's dad stayed there for a while but quit respecting her and started taking her for granted. The last straw was he told her he wanted to do a ménage a trois, with a girl he just met. She said she was shocked at first, but because she loved him so much she conceded to do it. The day before it was supposed to happen, she got cold feet and told him no. He was furious and left, and she hadn't seen him since. She said they probably shacked up somewhere. She saw how intently I was listening and I told her he was crazy, and if you have never done anything bad to him before like cheat on him, then he shouldn't act like that.

We were sitting on the couch together and then I reached for her stomach and put my head on her chest. I started pulling her shirt up and she told me no. Then I started to kiss her and she started to like that and she said, "Damn, you are persistent." I stood up, grabbed her off the couch and took her straight into her room. I undressed her and took off my clothes. Her black skin and body looked so good. At that moment I was thinking, who would put children in this beautiful body and treat it so bad and leave it? I knew if her husband had not treated her with such distain, I wouldn't be here.

After about 15 minutes when I was engaging in sex with her, I thought I heard a noise behind me. Gina didn't hear it because she was hollering and in another world. I turned my head around while I was still having sex, and saw her 7-year old son looking at us. The door must have come open or he opened it. He either wasn't asleep yet, or he heard his mom making loud noises and woke up to see if she was alright. The whole house was very dark. All the lights were off, and the only light was from the apartment lights outside. Her son was very dark-skinned and all I could see was his white eyeballs staring me down. I should have stopped and told Gina, but it was feeling so good I didn't.

For the next 10 minutes, I was trying to concentrate on Gina but was also thinking what her son might be thinking. For instance: "What is this naked white man doing on top of my momma and looking like he is hurting her?" I was going to start switching to a different position but I thought naw, let me hurry up and finish so her son can stop watching us. About five minutes later, I finished and got up. I turned and looked at him. He glanced at his momma, who still didn't see him. She just stayed on the bed with her naked body exposed. Her son's eyes stayed on me. He was watching my naked body as I was putting on my clothes. After I had them on, I was gonna walk by him and let him know everything was okay, when he ran from the door and jumped on his momma as if she had just been brutally attacked. He wanted to make sure she was okay, and that everything was all good. Gina told her son, "It's okay baby. Momma alright." She was hugging him tightly. Then they both started laughing and kissing each other.

I was very glad she wasn't mad, and I was happy he didn't go get a kitchen knife and try to stab me in the back while I was on top of his momma, thinking I was killing her or something. That's got to fuck with his mind a little bit, watching his naked mother have sex and it's not his father and on top of that it's a white man. I said, "Hey Gina, I'm outta here so you can take care of your son. I will come back tomorrow." She replied, "I'll make you a key." I said, "Hell yeah. Ok. See you later. Get up and lock the door. I don't want nobody coming in and messing with my stuff." She laughed and said, "You crazy."

I came over the next day to surprise her and before I knocked on the door, I heard a man's voice. I looked in the window and there was the kids' father, a big black man who was hugging his son and Gina. Even though I was upset, it looked great. Daddy's home. As I walked to my car I thought to myself, I hope it works out for them. I thought she might have felt guilty for having sex with me and called him and said, "Hey, I'm talking to this white guy, who likes me for me, so you wanna come home or you want me to pursue the new guy?" He probably got bored with the other girl and said fuck that. Nobody fucking my wife, especially in my house. I'm coming home.

It was too late for that. I fucked her real good, but what he doesn't know won't hurt him. I know I used her for sex, but she used me as well. She was upset that her husband was fucking someone else. Plus, I gave her attention he didn't. She needed that and I was happy to oblige her and go our separate ways. We never spoke to each other again.

I got to Eden Roc and saw Vidal and Tullie laughing outside. Ronald was also outside standing there with three crack smokers. As I was walking towards them, I felt footsteps coming behind me at a rapid rate. Then I heard in a high pitched voice, "What up nigga! What up Nigga! Nigga shit, Nigga shit!" I thought, "Oh no, it's crack head White Boy John who looks like Vanilla Ice but skinnier. A Vanilla Ice on crack. Tullie said, "Oh shit, there he goes." Tullie yelled, "What up nigga!" trying to copy White Boy John, in that high pitched voice. Tullie said, "I told you Marcus. This fool is nuts, dawg. Say it again, John."

John looked at Tullie puzzled, then quickly figured out what Tullie was talking about. John said, "What? Oh." Then yelled, "What up nigga!" Ronald jumped in with a stern voice and said, "White Boy John, you need to hush up. I ain't gonna be hearing too many more of your niggas." Everyone was laughing. White Boy John, oblivious to Ronald's advice said, "Oh Ronald, it ain't that serious! Hey, Tullie. I told you I had a black hoe," John continued very proudly. "You seen her last night, right?" Tullie replied "Yeah we all seen your black hoe. She about 400 pounds. She look like Kamala, the Ugandan giant!" Everyone was still laughing. It was getting pretty late and I noticed Chubby, Peanut, Omari and Kevin going into a vacant unit by Tan's house with a bunch of guns. I immediately walked over there to see what was up, while Vidal and Tullie went in Ronald's house with all the crack smokers.

As I walked up I said, "What's up with y'all? Y'all doing alright?" They all responded to me, everything is good. Peanut said, "Yeah, we just came from Kenwood." I said, "Y'all mutha-fuckas look scary comin in here with all them guns. Y'all look like war about to happen." Peanut said, "That's how we roll baby," as he cocked his 12 gauge (shotgun) back. I walked up to Omari and said, "I'm a little worried about you guys staying here in this vacant unit. It's so close to the street, somebody that don't live here could see y'all from the other apartment or their house and call the police." Kevin said, "Naw we gonna be alright man." Omari said, "Yeah Marcus, ain't nothing going to happen."

Then Chubby jumped in laughing, "What you think they look like Marcus? The little niggaz from Home Alone?" Everyone started laughing. I said, "Yeah I guess if someone come inside here, instead of a bucket thrown at their head, it will be a bullet in the head. Alright. I guess y'all good shit I'm a holla at y'all tomorrow. Y'all going to be anywhere later?" Peanut said, "Yeah probably to get something to eat." I said, "Alright holla."

As I left I was a little worried about maybe the police getting a hold of them, and arresting them for the guns. They might tell them if they don't give up me or Tullie or Vidal for selling drugs they will do the maximum time for the guns. The other part of me said Hell naw. They would never tell on me, Vidal or Tullie. They much better than that. I thought more the latter, which was that they would not give up Vidal and Tullie, so I had to get that crazy thought out of my head. The next day I woke up early in the morning and the first thing I did was walk over to the vacant unit to see if they were awake.

As I was about to turn the corner, I saw a police paddy wagon and all four of them were in handcuffs going into the back of it. Tan's old unit was vacant but her sliding door was still open, so I went in it and went to the balcony to get a better look. When I got up there, I saw about eight SAPD Officers going in and out of the unit, probably looking for crack cocaine. I was hoping there was no weed in the unit because Chubby sold it and usually had some for everybody. I stayed up there until they drove off. A couple of days later, they all posted bond and got out and when they got back to Kenwood Peanut said, "Damn Marcus, it was fucked up.

I went to sleep with my shotgun by my side and when I woke up this fucking policeman had my own gun pointed right at me." I said, "Damn that must be a fucked up feeling to wake up and the first thing you see is your own gun pointed right at you by the police." They were all laughing about it. I was glad we were leaving Eden Roc. I was sure we were being watched by the police. You can't sell dope at a place for too long because it gets too hot and we had been at Eden Roc for two years. That's actually too long to sell dope at one place, but we got away with it because we were in and out of too many units there. They could not concentrate on one place. They would have had to do a clean sweep. Who knows? They could have been close to doing that!

It didn't matter anyway because Ronald was moving out and Ericka and I were getting our own place on the Northwest side. Me, Vidal and Tullie used to talk about anybody can sell dope in the ghetto. There is death, despair and destruction in the ghetto. Nobody cares if someone sells dope in there or people are getting high in there. Plus there are too many dope dealers in the ghetto. Police can't keep track of all of them. If you could sell crack cocaine successfully on the Northside of San Antonio, that would be something. Can you thrive selling dope where it's about 60-70 percent Caucasian? Being Black on the Northside, all my homies are gonna stick out like a sore thumb in that environment. But we didn't care, we thought we were the shit and invincible. With my move to Wurzbach street on the Northwest side, we were about to find out how much weight we could move successfully without getting caught.

CHAPTER TWENTY FIVE

760 THE TICKET

I **HAD JUST** picked up Ericka and my children from Wurzbach Manor, the new apartments we were moving to and I had the radio on in the car. I was listening to a sports talk show. I almost always turned it on sports radio, unless I was listening to a cassette tape of something I liked, like Snoop or the late, great Tupac. It was 760 The Ticket. As I was listening, they were playing a segment called the fake Barry and Jerry Show. They were mocking the current head coach of the Dallas Cowboys, Barry Switzer, and the owner of the Dallas Cowboys, Jerry Jones. At the point in the show I was listening to, they were making fun of the fact that some student athletes on the Oklahoma football team(Barry's former team) were getting caught with machine guns at school. They were implying that Barry Switzer knew about this, and encouraged and allowed it. Barry Switzer, the enabler. Just win football games, baby!

That in and of itself was stupid, and not funny. That a college coach would allow his players to walk around with guns is preposterous, but that is not what I was most perturbed about.

The people putting on this segment of the radio show on 760 the Ticket have no idea what it is like for probably most of the Oklahoma players growing up in violent and desperate environments. The talk show made the college student athletes sound subhuman. For these people to make fun of some of the Oklahoma players who might still act out what they either used to do, or witnessed at some point, in their lives shows either a lack of compassion or their own idiocy. Maybe, it's a little of both.

I come from a school of thought that says we should be praising some of these kids who come out of ghetto environments and have made it to college with their brains and athletic prowess. It's not their fault. Some of them were born into a cycle of shit! Lift them up! Don't make fun of their misguided actions. After I heard the fake Barry and Jerry segment, I was truly upset about it and called the station right away. Now if I was to say what was on my mind and what I really thought, they would not understand me and think I was some black militant and would probably have hang up on me. So to get them to quit talking about a subject they knew nothing about, I had to go a different route and say, "My kids are in the car and they don't need to hear about a college kid shooting a gun on campus and the head coach allowing it to happen." When I called the receptionist, she dispatched me to the Sports Department and the Voice of the Spurs, Jay Howard, answered.

I really didn't give it any thought that I was talking to the great Jay Howard. I said, "My name is Marcus Valdespino. Are you listening to what's on your radio station right now?" He replied, "Yes, I always listen. I'm the sports director." I replied, "I have my kids in the car, and I thought we would be listening to actual sports talk. Instead, we're hearing that Oklahoma football players have machine guns and the coach thinks it is okay? Can you let whoever is on the radio know that that is not okay, and we wanna hear some real sports topics?" Jay responded, "Okay I understand what you're saying and I appreciate your comments. By the way, do you have any interest in being in sports at all?"

I replied, "Sure! I was born loving sports, especially football and basketball." He replied, "Great! Why don't you come down here tomorrow. We are in need of a few interns and you sound like a guy that is concerned and that we might need." I replied, "Okay, What time do I come down?" He replied, "Come down about 9:30 or 10 tomorrow morning. I will be here to go over what you need to do." I said, "Okay Jay, Thanks for listening. I will see you tomorrow." He said, "You said your name is Marcus?" I replied "Yes." Jay said, "Okay, Marcus. See you tomorrow."

As I hung up my cell phone, I was thinking, "Was he just bullshitting me so I would shut up and not complain anymore or so I wouldn't call somebody else and go higher than him? Or do they really need people, like he said. I guess I will find out tomorrow. When I showed up at the radio station the next day, I met Jay Howard, Tim Merriman, Bob Guthrie, Laura Green, Stan Kelly (a hardcore Notre Dame fan), Charlie Parker, Jim Forsythe, Andy Everett, Bill Rohde and the program Director, Andrew Ashwood.

Everybody was very nice to me. I was thinking, wow they get paid to be here at a radio station. I wish I could do this for a living. The following day, I was told I could sit in on the Charlie Parker show at 7am. I met John, his producer, and I was watching Charlie Parker do promos and take calls from callers to his show. About thirty minutes in, I was partially paying attention to John and how John was running the show, but I was more intrigued with the content of what Charlie and his audience were talking about. They were talking about NFL Football, one of my favorite topics. To get paid to do this is amazing. Charlie's show was entertaining and fun, but there wasn't a lot of substance on football. I was thinking I could enhance that problem immeasurably.

After the show I talked to Charlie for a minute, but he was in a hurry to leave. Then, Andrew Ashwood came flying down the hall. Everybody at the radio station called Andrew, "The Gorilla." It was funny to me. I said to myself, "The Gorilla!" I didn't make the immediate connection, but then as you got a good look at him, 6'1 and about a 300 pound white guy with kind of long blonde hair, I thought maybe he does look like a Gorilla. As he came in the room he said, "Hey Marcus, how'd you like the show?" I replied, "It was good and fun." He replied, "Yeah babe. You got to listen to the great Charlie Parker." I said, "Yeah, Charlie's great!"

I replied as he was about to walk out, shaking his head in agreement. I said, "Andrew!" I was not comfortable calling him Gorilla. "Who is your favorite football team?" He replied, "The best team in the history of pro football, the Green Bay Packers and they're on top of the mountain now and about to become the new dynasty now." I said, "Wait a minute. They're on top now, but they're not going to become a dynasty. They have a quarterback who is too much of a gunslinger. He is not careful with the football; he takes too many chances." Andrew answered, "You kidding? When it's all said and done, Brett Favre will become one of the best quarterbacks ever to play."

I interrupted him and said, "Troy Aikman is a Hall of Famer, Favre isn't and will never be. I will be willing to bet, by the time his career is over he will break your heart every year and he will only have that one Super Bowl. I don't even know if this is possible, but he might mess around and end up with more interceptions than touchdowns." Andrew said, "Troy's great, but he has got more talent around him than Brett." I replied, "Troy has got great talent around him. The evidence is those three Super Bowls, but don't get it twisted now.

Brett Favre's got talent too. Mark Chmura, Robert Brooks, Andre Rison, Antonio Freeman, Dorsey Levens. Those guys didn't just fall out the sky. Those are good football players." Andrew said, "It doesn't sound like you just fell out of the sky either. You going to be here tomorrow?" I said, "Yes." He said, "Great! I'll see you tomorrow!" I said, "Ok." A week went by of talking to Andrew Ashwood and one day he asked me, "How would you like to be on the radio?" I said, "Hell yeah. That would be great." I tried not to sound so enthusiastic, like if I had been there before. He replied, "You're going to be on with Charlie Parker in the mornings."

I said, "Great! Is he ok with this?" Andrew said, "He is fine with it. You start tomorrow morning." I said, "Ok. I will be here." As Andrew left, I was thinking damn. I sell crack cocaine till about 5 am sometimes. I either won't sleep or I will have to change my crack selling times. As it turned out, over the years he and I were both right about Brett Favre. Andrew was right. Brett went on to have a Hall of fame career and become the most durable quarterback in NFL history. I was right as well. The Packers did not become a dynasty. After Brett Favre won his only Super Bowl for the next 12 seasons, you could count on three things: death, taxes and Brett Favre ending the Packers or Viking's season on a bone headed interception. Besides throwing for more touchdowns than any quarterback in NFL history, he also threw more interceptions than any quarterback in NFL history. I always knew no matter what team Favre would play for, he would always end the season for his team with his brain or lack thereof, no matter what the situation was. It didn't work out for his teams for 19 of his 20 seasons. He also had a (1-8) record against the Dallas Cowboys.

When I got home, I told Ericka I was gonna be on the radio in the mornings. She was very excited, but she also asked what any woman would ask. She said, "Are they gonna pay you since you gonna be on the air?" I replied, "No, I'm still an intern, but to go from intern to being on the air? I don't know if that has ever been done here. I just have to take advantage of this opportunity." I told some of my boys I was gonna be on the air. Tullie and Vidal were happy for me, but they didn't think much of it because they knew I know my stuff when it comes to sports. Now, everybody else will. I overheard Tullie tell people. "I knew my boy could make it wit his sports knowledge." Unfortunately, my homeboys weren't gonna hear me on the radio, anyway.

By the time the 7 a.m. Charlie Parker show comes on, they will have gone to sleep. They usually get to sleep about 4 or 5 a.m. That's the way it is when you sell dope. Most of the time, you stay down all night. I know there are gonna be some nights when I go into the radio station at 6:30 a.m. and I will have not been to sleep yet. But like I've said before, this is the life I've chosen. This is the only life I know how to live, and I will keep living this way until someone else hands me a nice check for my services. I was hopeful that this radio station gig was my opportunity!

CHAPTER TWENTY SIX

THE CAUCASIAN MAJORITY

A COUPLE OF months went by and I was doing well being the co-host on the Charlie Parker morning show. It was Charlie's show, but they wanted me to have a nickname, so in the intro they could say Charlie Parker and the blank show. I thought about it for a minute in order to come up with a name and I thought, who else knows the roster for the University of Illinois Football team or most Big Ten rosters and lives in Texas? The answer is nobody. I'm like a Freak of nature when it comes to sports history or current sports events. I have a photographic memory. I can remember everything. So they started calling me the, "Sports Freak." Every morning I got to work at 6 or 6:30 am, I would see Bob Guthrie and Stan Kelly about to go on the air on 1200 WOAI. Stan Kelly, a great Notre Dame fan would always tell me, "What up, Freak?"

I like Stan Kelly. He is a great guy. After the show one morning, Charlie had already left and I walked into one of the rooms at the station. I came upon a conversation Laura Green and Charlie Parker's producer, John, were having. John was saying,

"God, every other sentence is, you know what I'm saying, you know what I'm saying. You get sick of hearing it over and over. Don't they know how to speak? Didn't they go to college?" Laura replied laughing, "Oh I know. It's like every time they say it, I'm thinking yes I know what you are saying. You just said it." I easily got what they were describing: the inability of some black athletes that have difficulty putting words together without following up their story by saying, "You know what I'm saying." This might be a fundamental flaw in their speech. It might be the way they grew up and the fact that everyone around them might have said that phrase in their household and schools. I was thinking, "Right, like these two know so many black people that they can't stand the phrase anymore." It was as though this bothered them so deeply that they were disgusted by it. I had only been there a couple of months, but I remembered something I had always heard Laura say.

I looked at both of them and said, "They may not know how to speak properly, but that's probably due to their upbringing for so many years. Four years of college might not cure zero to eighteen years of talking like that, and Laura, I have heard you say plenty of times after some of your sentences, 'You know what I mean.' There is not much difference in you saying that and them saying, 'you know what I'm saying,' except for the tone."

As I finished talking, they were looking at me with their mouths dropped and their eyes wide open for about ten seconds of complete silence, which seemed like an eternity. The expressions on their face were saying, "Who the fuck are you to question us about what we're laughing about? How dare you?" I think I now understood how the white majority felt about black people with regard to the phrase, "You know what I'm saying?" and how they perceived it as ignorant. I quickly shut the door and forgot what

I originally came in there for. I didn't earn any points for doing that. It would have been better if I would have just come in and said, "Hey, my name is Marcus. "Fuck You! I'm going home," and then added, "You know what I'm saying?"

`It would have been really easy just to agree with them and make friends, but that's not me. I'm going to tell people if I think they're saying something wrong. They didn't know what the hell they were talking about. The next few months were fun for me, working on the Charlie Parker show. Charlie was a really good guy. He knew the radio business very well. He never really had any slip-ups on the air. He was a cool customer. We got along fairly well. Tim Merriman, who was the producer of all the on-air shows, was a smooth character as well. Andy Everett was a salesman and on-air talent. Andy was a real square, but he and I got along great. Jay Howard and I got along okay. I got the feeling he didn't want me on the air, though. He looked at me one day before I went on the air and said, "You can't be a successful radio personality without having a favorite team and favorite player. That's what should drive you every day. It gives you your passion."

I told him, "I see your point. I've got favorite players and teams in each of the three major sports," but I still felt the need to call it like I saw it and not be a complete "homer" who just sided with the teams he liked. Laura Green was a little hottie. She booked most guests for a lot of the shows. She was also on-air talent. She and I had a few run-ins. I don't think she liked me very much. I didn't ever dislike Laura or like her. I just didn't care about our relationship, if it was good or not.

One day I messed up with something, editing-wise, something a producer is supposed to do, and she came in the office and scolded me in front of Jay, Charlie and Andy. I let her finish because I was in the wrong. I did screw up, but a few minutes later I pulled her aside and said, "I don't mind you telling me if I screw up, but don't do it in front of a group of people. Pull me aside and tell me what I did." She looked at me even more upset, but didn't say anything. I loved Bill Rhode. Every time he had extra tickets, he would give them to me. Needless to say, Ericka and I would be at every Spurs game. I got along pretty well with Andrew Ashwood (The Gorilla), our program director. He would always leave for the weekend and head to either California or wherever the Green Bay Packers were playing. When he would come back on Mondays, he always had me in his office to discuss what transpired with sports over the weekend and talk about some of his sexual conquests. He was very fond of the daughter of former head coach of the Oakland Raiders, Tom Flores. He would talk to me about how he was the first one to discover Jimmy Kimmel.

I would ask him at least once a month, when I would stop being an intern and start getting paid. I thought this was my ticket to stop selling crack cocaine. I wish I could have told Andrew this is what I was doing and I don't want to do it anymore, but I figured if I would have said that, he would have fired me immediately. He would always tell me to hang in there, "We're going to pay you soon." So I hung in there. I believed him. One time in one of our Monday meetings, he was just telling me how great JT the Brick is at being on-air talent. I told him, "I listened to JT quite a bit and he is really good," but here is another example of how I can't keep my mouth shut and just agree with the Caucasian majority. I told Andrew, "You know JT likes to call some of the black players in the NBA thugs. I got news for JT. There are no thugs in the NBA. Each one of these players JT says are thugs, like Rasheed Wallace, are millionaires. They're not in any gang, they're not terrorizing anybody, and they're not selling drugs.

The money these guys make is incredible. They're like their own corporation. Rasheed yells at the referees. Big fucking deal. That doesn't make him a thug. Rasheed Wallace is no more of a thug than you are. JT doesn't know what the hell a thug is, and when I see him I will tell him."

Andrew looked at me with his mouth wide open, like how could I talk about the great JT like that. He didn't disagree or agree with me. His only response was, "I don't think telling JT that would be a good idea, bub." He turned around to his computer and said, "Hey, I gotta get back to work. Go ahead and get ready for the show." As I left Andrew's office I thought, "Oh man, Marcus. You did it again. You went against the Caucasian majority. Did I just cook my own goose? Now Andrew seems like he's disappointed in me." I could have just agreed with Andrew and said, "Oh yeah, JT's calling them how he sees them. Some of those NBA players are thugs." It would have been a lot better for me if I would have done that, but that's not how I'm made. I call bullshit when I see it, and calling Rasheed and some of the NBA players thugs is bullshit.

When J.T. was down here for the 1999 NBA Finals, I avoided a scenario in which Andrew would have to introduce us. I was afraid I wouldn't keep my mouth shut. I did see WOAI's Randy Beamer trying to get J.T.'s attention, and J.T. ignored him. The look on Randy's face was like, "Fuck him." I had lots of run-ins with what I thought were these smart but weird people. It always seemed like I was the only one with my own point of view, and that none of these people agreed with me. It was sometimes hard dealing with them, even though in my heart I knew I was right. I had a couple of on-air and off-air arguments with Andrew Ashwood and Laura Green about Tiger Woods versus Jim Brown, about who does more for the black community.

I tried to convey to them, "Yes, you are right that Tiger has more money than Jim Brown and he throws lots of money into certain programs that help, but Jim Brown is actually in the ghettos of America, walking around mentoring black youths about not being involved with guns, gangs and drugs. Jim Brown is in the trenches with these children and young adults, trying to make a difference. He is making an emotional and physical impact on some of the sadness and madness of the black community." Jim Brown, while he has had run-ins with the law, is still making a huge difference with the limited resources and money he has. He has been there through the Civil Rights Movement and through the gang activity in the 1980s and 90s. Black people will walk with Jim Brown any day of the week before they walk with Tiger Woods, who they consider a sellout, because on the Oprah Winfrey Show, Tiger had a hard time convincing black America he was one of them. My thinking, again, did not resonate with the Caucasian majority. Their response was that Tiger puts lots of money, much more than Jim Brown, into programs that help black youth.

All the callers agreed with them. No one was on my side, and it was like they were in a bubble and I could not penetrate with facts. They are set in their ways and that's that. They didn't even have the nuance to agree with me partially, and say that Jim Brown does lots of good for the community. They just wanted to say that I was wrong and they were right. Then, off the air, Andrew looked at me and began sticking up for Tiger's Oprah performance and said, "Marcus, you know Earl Woods, Tiger's father is only half black so Tiger is only ¼ quarter black, so he was right on Oprah when he said he wasn't black." After he said that, I didn't want to talk about it anymore.

I looked at Andrew, like they were right when I knew they were all in a bubble that you can't penetrate, and that was that. I knew Earl Woods wasn't half black and Andrew was full of shit, but if I would have said that it would have made things worse for me. There were days when I left the radio station knowing my days were numbered. When you don't agree with the Caucasian majority and your half-Caucasian yourself, you get looked at like you're a pariah. I knew I was gonna go down one day and get fired, but I wasn't ever going down without standing up for what I believed.

CHAPTER TWENTY SEVEN

END OF RADIO STATION

THINGS WERE GOING okay for me at the radio station. I still sometimes felt like an outcast. That being said, I was still expected to know everything when the lights came on for the sports shows. That's why I was there. I loved the challenge. If a caller called in to the show and said something like, "What do you guys think of Nebraska's defense?" everyone would look at me as if to say, "Well, answer the question." That's why the powers that be tried to come up with silly local talk show questions for their local listeners. For instance, who do you hate the most in sports today? They didn't want specific questions. If they got them, everyone but me would be toast. I'll give you a hypothetical. If all of the sudden Andrew Ashwood ran in the room and said, "Hey power is down in California, and our show has to go National." Everybody would have been fucked but me. I would have said, "Bring it on."

We had a draft party at Retama Park for the 1998 NFL Draft and I couldn't wait. I grew up watching Mel Kiper, the NFL Draft expert on ESPN. I got a chance to channel my inner Mel

Kiper. “Fantastic! Bring it on!” It was at night and Tullie, my brother Martin, my wife and kids showed up. Pick after pick, I described player’s strengths and weaknesses. When it got to the Raiders pick, the guy in California abruptly hung up. Before he did, he said the Oakland Raiders would take Mo Collins. When he hung up everybody had looks on their faces like, “Who the fuck is Mo Collins?” especially Charlie Parker. I didn’t have any notes, and never got on a computer. People think I’m some kind of savant, because I remember everything. Charlie looked at me like he had Save Us written on his face. I gladly said, “Mo Collins is a 6’4, 330 pound guard out of the University of Florida. Tends to put on more weight than he needs to. He is a natural right or left guard. Some scouts think he can play tackle, but I don’t think so. He doesn’t have quick enough feet for defensive ends at the NFL level, but a solid pick here for the Oakland Raiders.”

Everybody looked relieved. The next day I got a lot of high fives from people at the radio station that I didn’t even know. They knew I could talk about any player in college or pro basketball and college or pro football. I can do a mock Draft and memorize the first four rounds of an NFL Draft and still can do this to this day.

Charlie Parker went back to 1200 AM WOAI, down the hall. Jay Howard, Laura Green and I were on Sports Talk San Antonio in the afternoon from 4pm-7pm. I still carried a gun wherever I went. I had it on me at all times, in and out of the building, in and out of the offices. They were remodeling the part of the building where we conducted the show, so we had to do the show from Jay Howard’s office. It sucked, but I never complained. Who am I to complain?

To them I’m still some nobody street kid, who went from intern to on the air with Charlie Parker and the Voice of the

Spurs, Jay Howard. I almost had a "heart attack" on the air once because of my gun. I was rocking my chair back by Jay Howard's desk, with Laura Green to the left of me and Jay Howard to the right of me. As I was rocking back and forth, we were on air and my gun, a .38 special, almost fell out of my pocket. I caught it both times and immediately looked up to see if they saw what happened. Thank God they didn't! A great sportscaster, Paul Alexander, came to do the show in Jay Howard's office. Paul Alexander was a fixture in San Antonio sports history, because he did sports on television on KSAT Channel 12.

I remembered I had to keep covering my gun so he wouldn't see it, by putting a folder or the sports page on my right leg. The butt of the gun kept sticking out. Imagine my dilemma, trying to outwit Paul Alexander on a radio show and also worrying that he might see my gun. Paul Alexander, to this day and in my opinion, is the only person in the world who knows more about the Dallas Cowboys than I do. I had one run in with Jay Howard off the air about what an NBA basketball player should have done in a certain situation. I told him he didn't know what he was talking about, that I had seen that move by the player up close so many times.

He fired back angrily, "I've watched over a thousand NBA games. I think I know what the hell I'm talking about!" After he said that, I didn't say anything. I let him maintain his authority. That went against who I am as a person. I wanted to let him have it but I knew if I did that I would never get paid by the radio station and I would be exclusively in the streets for good. I wanted to tell him, "Hey Fool! I've thrown many alley-oops to my homies. Have you done that! I can shoot and dribble better than anyone you know, except NBA players! And if a high school in San Antonio called and said, 'Marcus can you coach this team?' I would absolutely say yes! I know you couldn't, so shut the fuck up!" I would have been right out the door if I said that, which all is true. We went to a restaurant once in a while to do the show and Sean Elliott was going to be a guest. I was a little excited, but not as much as I thought. When Sean walked in, he remembered me. Just to give a little dig at Jay and Laura, I asked if he remembered 10 years ago, me beating him at horse and he said yes. The looks on Jay and Laura's face were priceless, but they feigned fake smiles and quickly changed the subject. That would qualify them as Haters. They would never want me to have success.

The radio station hired these two brothers named Jason and Rob Thompson. They were cool as hell. We shared this fantasy football show. I once told them that Jeff Garcia was going to be a good fantasy player because he makes all kind of throws from different angles and has weapons. They laughed at me. Jeff Garcia went on to make three Pro Bowls. Another on-air talent Chris Duel was a really good guy and very funny. They hired this new guy named Walter Pasacrita, from New York. When I first met him, he looked real unsure of himself. I gave him the benefit of the doubt. He is in a new city and has a new career. I'm not a hater. I try and get along with everybody.

A few days later, I walked into one of the sports rooms and Walter was running the board to a game on the radio. I introduced myself and he smiled and did the same. There was something not quite right with him and me at that moment. It was as if he heard my reputation about knowing everything about sports and was apprehensive to engage when talking to me. I noticed he was watching a Notre Dame game on the screen in the room, so I tried to lighten the mood. I said, "You know Jarius Jackson, the Notre Dame quarterback? He's waited a long time for his opportunity to get his chance to play. I hope he makes the most of it." I got no response. He looked at me like a deer in the headlights. I continued, "I think Arnaz Battle is a better athlete though. I wanna see him get an opportunity as well." He responded, "To tell you the truth, I don't pay much attention to Notre Dame Football." I said, "Oh ok," and I walked out.

I left thinking, man he will never get on the air. You either have it or you don't, and he didn't know anything at the time. One guy I met while I was there who I thought would have a long career was Jeff Vexler. I walked up to him one time to see what he knew. I said, "Have you seen Elton Brand play? He is an undersized power forward at 6'8 that is a tenacious rebounder and has great touch around the basket and runs the floor with the best of them." Jeff responded, "Yes, can shoot from 18 feet. I agree with your assessment. He reminds me of Karl Malone, just an inch shorter." I thought, wow. This guy is the only one here who can break down player's games besides me.

One day, Andrew Ashwood called me in his office and said, "Hey I got good news. We're going to start paying you." I replied, "Hell yeah! Thanks Andrew." I was very excited, I had been waiting a year and a half. He said, "Calm down, calm down. Don't tell anybody, especially Laura." I said, "Okay! I won't say anything." I left the office very happy. It was hard for me to contain my emotion. I never graduated from high school. I was a gang member for 10 years. I had been selling crack cocaine for the last nine years and the radio station is going to pay me for talking on the air? I would like to see anybody walk in my shoes and contain their emotion.

When I got back down the hall, Andy Everett knew I had been summoned by Andrew because he was with me at the time. Andy noticed I was happy and said, "Andrew said they are gonna start paying you, didn't he?" I smiled a little more and Andy said, "I knew it! I knew why he called you in his office. You been here long enough. It's about time." Andy was not a hater. He was smiling when he was talking to me. He didn't care if I got paid. What I didn't know was that he would eventually tell Laura. Then it dawned on me that Laura Green didn't get paid. I didn't know that. I thought I was the only one. They decided to pay me before Laura. No wonder Andrew said, "Don't tell Laura." I didn't think Andy would tell her.

Upon hearing that Andy told Laura, Andrew was pissed. Now he had to pay Laura. I dug myself a deeper hole with Andrew, with my naivete. The one person at the station you can't do that with is Andrew Ashwood. A few days later, Jay, Laura and I were on the radio and a caller called in and made a comment about Bernie Mac and Beyonce, Laura and Jay didn't know who they were. I said on the air, "Y'all don't know who Bernie Mac and Beyonce are?"

They both looked puzzled and said, "No!" and Jay said, "Are we supposed to?" I thought they were kidding. I thought everyone knew who they were. I let the Beyonce thing go because Destiny's Child was in the early stages, but Bernie Mac? I couldn't let that one ride. I said, "Yeah, you should know who Bernie Mac is. He is one of the best comedians going right now." They both looked puzzled and Jay motioned for Laura to go look up Bernie Mac on the computer. I said, "Boy you guys aren't very hip, are you?" After I said that, the looks on their faces was of one embarrassment.

Their white faces were turning red. I probably shouldn't have done that, but at first I thought they were joking. A few months later, Bernie Mac was on the Kings of Comedy tour. Just chalk this up as another day closer to me leaving the radio station.

I embarrassed the Caucasian majority. You can't do that at the local radio station. Your days will be numbered. You must go along with them on stuff like that. A few weeks later I got a chance to go to Dallas Cowboys training camp through the radio station. I rode in the car with Andy Everett and Charlie Parker's nephew, Jason Penney. It was a unique experience for me. I got to meet people in the Cowboy organization that I had been watching on TV throughout the 90s.

There was a funny story on the way to and on the way back from the long drive to Wichita Falls. When I got back, I ran Charlie Parker down in the hallway and said, "Hey Charlie, before we left to Cowboy Camp, we stopped at Andy Everett's house and his wife comes outside and says, "Now Marcus, I've heard about your reputation. You make sure Andy comes back in one piece. Don't do anything stupid over there and then y'all get in trouble." I looked at her and said, "Yes Ma'am." On the way back from camp, Andy is doing over 100mph and a cop pulls him over and makes him get out of the car and takes him and puts him in the back of the police car. I told your nephew, Jason, "Now there's some fuckin' irony for you. Andy's wife is worried about me getting him in trouble and he is the back of a police car and it don't have shit to do with me!" Charlie laughed his ass off. Also at Cowboy Camp, I had to explain to Jason Penney what the Dixie Flag meant to black people. He didn't think the flag was a big deal. He thought of it as a representation of white pride in the South and not demeaning to blacks. Jason Penney is NOT a racist, by any means, but I just had to let him know that the flag is a disturbing image to most black people who understand their history of slavery and segregation in this country.

Near the end of the year 2000, I was called into Andrew Ashwood's office and he told me we had to part ways. I got a little emotional, because there was a lot of stuff in my personal life going on. I told Andrew I could be the Howard Stern of sports here in San Antonio. He said, "We don't want or need that." That told me they are a billion dollar corporation and can get anybody to come fill a role. They don't want you to rock any boat. I wish I could have told Andrew about my life growing up, my last 10 years of selling crack cocaine and gang bangin. Then I thought if I tell him all of that, he'll still let me go. I think I would have lost it, and I had too much respect for him to do that. When I look back at what he was right about, I didn't see it at the time but it was that I didn't work hard enough. I didn't want to come in at 5 a.m. on some mornings and do news spots and stuff like that. I thought I had arrived and thought that was too petty for me.

I had lots of stuff going on outside the radio station that I know nobody here could have survived. My only regret at the radio station is after we interviewed Tex Schramm in 2000, the former General Manager and President of the Dallas Cowboys about the death of Tom Landry. I said after the interview on air, "He sounds like he is close to the grave as well." That was very insensitive on my part. He died in 2003. Some years later, when I heard Andrew Ashwood died, I felt bad. Even though he fired me, he discovered me as well. He was a good guy. RIP Andrew Ashwood (Gorilla).

CHAPTER TWENTY EIGHT

WURZBACH MANOR (THE TAKE OVER)

I HAD JUST pulled up at Kenwood in my brand new 1997 Nissan Sentra I had just recently bought, when I saw Tullie and Carlton standing by the back of a Cadillac Eldorado. I noticed Gilbert, a Hispanic man, one of Ronald's friends in the driver's seat. It looked like Tullie and Carlton had just scored and had already turned the cocaine into crack. I was there to talk to Tullie about how he wanted to handle my new spot at Wurzbach Manor. I knew the goal was to turn Wurzbach Manor into The Carter from New Jack City, just like we did Eden Roc but I just wanted to see where his head was at. All of the sudden, Gilbert became impatient and started to drive off with Tullie still cutting dope on the back of the Cadillac. Carlton yelled, "Woe-Woe! Gilbert where the fuck you going?" Carlton was trying to save the dope that fell off the car.

Tullie ran to the driver's side and yelled at Gilbert, then began slapping him ferociously, "Gilbert you dumb bitch! We got dope on the car!" Gilbert looked completely panicked. He probably was high as a kite. Tullie was trying to yank him out of the car.

Gilbert ended up driving off. I didn't blame Gilbert for driving off, Tullie was gonna beat the hell out of him. I just wondered why he drove off in the first place. When Gilbert drove off, Tullie lost most of the dope because Tullie had cut it into rocks and was about to make 50 packs. As you would expect, Tullie was pretty hot. "I'ma kill that bitch when I see him! Shit we almost lost all the dope!" A couple of days later Arthur, Nikki's husband, beat the shit out of Gilbert. I don't think that ass whoopin was due to him driving off. They had their own feud going.

In the end, Gilbert was a bloody mess and got what was deserved. A few weeks later, just as anticipated, Wurzbach Manor was a gold mine. My house was the spot. You had to have a special knock to get in. You had to rock a beat. If you knocked with a regular knock or knocked hard like the police, you either wouldn't get in or would get yelled at. All the homies made it their home. Tullie started messing with this beautiful black woman named Kenny, she had a cute little boy named Tony, Anthony Bernard Woods. Carlton started messing with this girl named Shelia Tripplet, who had a bunch of sisters that stayed there in the complex. Their names were Prissy, Tammy and their little twelve year-old cousin named Chicken(Laqueesha).

Every time you saw Chicken, she was always roller skating around the complex. There were Jackie and Sherita Miller. Sherita pretty much stayed to herself at her unit. Jackie was always roaming the apartments with her old friend Alisha. There was this thick black girl named Rochelle with her two daughters, named Kitty and Desiree. Rochelle's real name was Ka'Chna Lewis. Everybody wanted to fuck Rochelle. Her ass and titties were second to none, but she was with some dumb thug nigga who liked to rob people and was always around his crew. They didn't fuck with us at all. They kept their distance. That was a good move for them. I didn't think they wanted to die. The main thing was they did not sell dope or that might have been a problem for them. They were basically just robbers. That's how they made a living. When they found a good lick, they hit it and moved on to the next one. That thinking was way too stupid and dangerous for me. One false move and they're on a fast pace for the penitentiary. Ericka's and my neighbors across the hall were a family of seven, Moses and Debbie Avila. Moses smoked dope and Debbie didn't.

I knew, eventually, that relationship was headed for disaster. You can't have one parent be one way, and the other the complete opposite. That never works. You can't have one person in the relationship a dope fiend or an alcoholic, and the other doesn't smoke dope or drink at all. They either both have to be alcoholics, or both don't drink. One of the keys to me and Tullie's takeover of any apartment complex was developing a relationship with most of the moms with little children. It's so much easier roaming the apartments with impunity when you have a rapport with most of the parents. In low income housing projects, about 90% percent of the people occupying the complex are usually single women with children and older residents who don't want any trouble. Most of the mothers are on welfare and there are absolutely no fathers or husbands to these mothers and children, respectively.

There are many examples of this. Let me give you a couple. When the ice cream man comes along, Tullie and I would buy all the kids that showed up at the ice cream truck an ice cream. That would usually cost Tullie and me about $50 dollars daily. Neither one of us worried about that. We always had about 1000 to 2,000 dollars in our pockets at all times. Then sometimes when we were heading to the store and if a kid was outside we would tell the kid, "Hey go tell your mom Marcus or Tullie is going to the store.

Does she want anything?" The kid would be happy and run and tell his mom and usually it was yes, I need something, diapers, soap, etc. These mothers usually had food stamps, so they usually wanted to purchase non-food items. If a mother was outside, we would just ask her directly.

This would also be a benefit sometimes, sexually. Tullie or any of our crew would have sex with some of these mothers with no man or husband around. After that, basically their house would become our house. At this point in my life I didn't partake in all the sex I could have at Wurzbach Manor. The difference being that Ericka and my children were living there. It would have been too close to home. One day while everybody was at the Manor, I saw them just sitting and moping around. I thought to myself , I don't play a lot of games but I'm gonna teach these guys baseball. I got everybody together and brought a chair from inside my unit.

The chair was the imaginary catcher. When I pitched to each one of the guys, if the ball hits the chair that was a strike. The first one to ten base hits wins the game. The guys took to the game very well, and were having fun with it. When 15 yr. old Omari's turn came up, he hit the ball real hard and it was a base hit. As Omari was running to first base, his gun fell out of his pants. It was a deuce-five. He stopped at first base, and everybody was either laughing or just in amazement. I said, "Omari put your gun up dawg or secure it better!" He replied, "Sorry Marcus," as he was laughing. He was trying to put the gun back in his pants and he was having trouble with the process. I yelled, "Omari, just put the gun down over there. Chubby and Kevin are right there. They ain't gonna let anything happen to it." Omari laid the gun down, and Kevin retrieved it.

A couple of moments later I thought to myself, that's some crazy shit. You know that comedian (Jeff Foxworthy) who says you know you might be a redneck if? Well, I thought damn. You know you are in a housing project if while playing baseball one of the kids can't make it to first base without dropping his gun on the pavement. We also had to stop the game if a crack smoker (geeker) came by. We had a nice little crack cocaine empire going on. Our operation was sound. There were a few of us that sold crack, so we had to take turns getting sales. This white lady we called Wacky Cathy would come by quite frequently. This old rich Mexican guy would be there at least three times a day, buying at 200 dollars a pop. He went by the alias of Tommy Hilfiger. He was pretty funny. I checked him out; he was not an informant.

We did not sell dope to anybody we didn't check out or know. Chubby sold strictly weed (marijuana) and Me, Tullie, Shawn, Carlton and Phat Cheez and sometimes Vidal (when he dropped by) sold crack, and we spread the wealth around and made good money. If only one of us made that all that money, that person would be driving a Bentley. Wurbach Manor was twice the size of Eden Roc. We had 90% of Eden Roc geekin'. We eventually had 50% of Wurzbach Manor geekin. Later on that night, we got a disturbing call from Tawanda. Tawanda was Tullie's sister-in-law. Tullie's brother Albert and she had separated at the time. Tawanda called crying and upset that some nigga named Michael wouldn't leave her house. I could hear Tullie tell Tawanda, "Calm down, we'll be right there! Don't tell that nigga to leave no more. We on our way!" Tullie turned to us and said, "Let's go!" Just four of us went. It was just one nigga. We didn't need everybody to go. I thought for sure when we got there, the idiot would have left. Did he not know who we were? When we got there, we barged straight through the door and there he was right there, waiting like a dummy. He was a tall black guy with a du-rag on his head. Tullie went straight to him and slapped the hell out of him and yelled, "Didn't she tell you to move around! What the fuck is you still doing here?"

Chubby grabbed him and held him for Tullie. He didn't put up put up any fight. He was scared to death. He said, "Naw man, I was leaving. Tawanda just be trippin!" Tawanda yelled, "Shut the Fuck up! Don't be lying on me!" Tullie said, "Yeah, you gonna be leaving, alright! It just depends if you gonna be leaving in one piece or not! What do you think Marcus? Should we ride his ass off?" I knew what Tullie meant, put him in the car and he would never be seen again or heard from again. I thought hell no, for what, just refusing to leave Tawanda's apartment?

I wanted to scare him so we never have to deal with him again. I replied, "Hell, Yeah! Ride his bitch ass off! We got a couple of holes dug up on the Northside! Throw his hoe ass in one of them!" The look on the man's face was unbelievable. His eyes were wide open in disbelief, like this may be his last breath on earth. Then, Tullie looked at me puzzled. Holes dug? Then he just played along and said, "Alright good idea. Chubby throw his ass in the car!" Chubby is strong than a muthafucka. That man tried to get away, but Chubby corralled his ass so he couldn't move anymore. As Tullie passed by I whispered, "You know I was just bull shittin. Just drop his ass off somewhere on the Eastside and tell him how lucky he is." Tullie looked at me and said, "I know. I'll meet you back at The Manor." As they left, me and Tawanda laughed for a minute. Then I left.

Tawanda was a light-skinned black woman and kind of fine. I always respected her because even though she smoked crack, she never gave any of the homies pussy. I didn't have sex with Tawanda until several years later. That was a good time in my life. I was making money through the drug trade even though I didn't really want to, but that's what I had to do to survive. I was talking sports on the radio. I talked sports all the time with my homeboys. I may as well expand to another audience. The best thing about my life was that I could live with and take care of my family, while having my homeboys around me all the time. Before 1997, I couldn't do that. I had to commute back and forth from home to the hood. What I didn't know was that I was about to experience something that would hurt me forever that I absolutely did not see coming.

CHAPTER TWENTY NINE

THE ULTIMATE BETRAYAL

ONE MORNING I woke to the sound of loud hip-hop music. It was shaking the windows. I looked over at the clock and it was 8:38 am. Then I saw Tullie almost ready and dressed to go. He was putting lotion on his face, then splashing himself with powder. We made eye contact and Tullie said, "Get up Marcus. We gotta go." I said, "Man Tullie, it's early! Where the fuck we gotta go!" He replied, "We gotta pick up this black hoe from Edison, talking about she ain't never been with black dick before. Man, I'm fin to tear that pussy up. Plus we gotta score from this nigga named Rob." That's a funny name because I was thinking one of these days we might have to "rob" his ass. I replied, "All right, let me get up and brush my teeth. Fuck! Dam, I can't get no pussy or she don't have a friend?" He replied, "Shit nigga, you know I already asked. She missing school for me and none of her friends would miss. Stix ain't getting no pussy either."

Just then Eric Twyman who is 6'9 and 190 pounds, better known as Stix because he is so skinny, emerged from the room and said, "If I would have known we were getting up this early, I would have stayed home." Tullie replied, "That's why I didn't tell you! While I'm breaking this bitch down, you gonna score dope with Marcus." Stix replied, "And what do I get for going?" Tullie said, "A slap to the mouth if you don't shut the fuck up!" Tullie liked to get up in the morning to Slick Rick's rap song, "Children's Story." Tullie began playing it over and over. Ronald came out of his room and went over to the stereo and turned Slick Rick off and started playing Earth Wind and Fire. Ronald said, "Uh- Uh! It's too early in the morning for that shit! I need something nice and easy to listen to." Tullie shouted back, "Say Ronald, this ain't the 70's. Put Slick Rick back on." Ronald said, "That sounded like some bullshit kid stuff." Tullie replied, "You got Slick Rick fucked up! That nigga's rhymes is on hit." Ronald responded, "That's why the nigga in jail right now because he can't rhyme."

Everybody started laughing. There was a knock at the door. Tullie said, "That's her!" Then, he handed me his half of the money for the cocaine. "I'll holla at y'all later. I'll be at the Skyline Motel on Austin Highway. Just come over there when you finish scoring." After scoring 3 ounces of cocaine from Rob, Stix and I pulled into the Skyline Motel. Tullie had called us and told us the room number. We pulled up right in front of the room. The room was upstairs. The hotel still had lots of people there from the previous night. Stix and I began talking about sports, when all of the sudden I stopped him and said, "Stix look down right here," as I moved my gun in the middle of us." Look at all that cocaine, and then here is my gun. Do you know how much time we would get if a police officer rolled up on us right now? For the dope and gun?"

Street value of this cocaine once we rock it up and turn into crack is about 3,000 dollars if served correct. Stix replied, "Shit. I don't know, but probably a lotta time." I said, "Yeah that's a good assessment, probably a lot and we're just sitting here like fools waiting on somebody to get suspicious and call the police." Stix replied, "Fuck that! Let's go up there and get him or wait for him up there." I replied, "You took the words right out of my mouth. He's taking too long. Let's go!" As we got to the door, you could hear somebody screaming in the room. I gave the beat knock like we always give. We have a rule about knocking. The police knock on doors hard. You can't knock like the police. You have to have a rap beat or nobody answers the door.

The screaming stopped and Tullie answered the door sweating. "What nigga!" I said, "Tullie let us in dawg! We not fin to stay out there with all this dope. Let us in!" Tullie said. "Alright come on. Shit I was almost finished. I looked at the girl's face. She was in pain. Tullie cut the lights back off, then started to fuck again. The girl began screaming at the top of her lungs again and after one minute I cut the lights back on and said, "Say, Tullie, she gonna have to stop screaming. Somebody gonna think a bitch is getting murdered or raped and call the police." Tullie pulled his dick out and looked like an innocent participant and turned to us with a hard dick and said, "Look nigga, I can't help it. That's just the way it is!"

Seeing I would get no help from Tullie, I looked at her with a stern stare and said, "Can you keep it down!" She said reluctantly, "Ok!" Then Tullie started again. She didn't scream as loud, and the ordeal was over in two minutes. As Tullie was putting his clothes on he said, "Boy y'all caught a nigga off guard. I didn't think you was gonna knock." I replied, "Shit! We wasn't fin to sit outside with all that dope. Let's go!" When we got back to

Wurzbach Manor, everyone was there and awake. Standing outside was Carlton, Chubby, Kevin, Shawn, Tony, Phat Cheez, Omari, and Peanut. When we got out of the car Kevin came up to us and said, "Did y'all see that black man leaving the apartments?" We all said, "Yes!" I said, "Why! Who was that?" Kevin said, "That was the fucking police. Nobody ever seen him before and nobody knows who that was." Tullie, very intrigued said, "What did he want?" Kevin said, "He asked where he could get dope from and he had heard from one of his friend's that this is where you could buy the best dope." I replied, "What the fuck did you say!" Kevin responded, "I told him. Don't nobody sell dope in here and whoever told you that lied to you." And then he started talking about some other bullshit that I wasn't trying to hear and I walked away." Tullie said, "I'm glad you did that. Them muthafuckas getting bold." I said, "He looked like a geeker too. They dressed him good. Damn, Tullie. They want us!" Tullie said, "Fuck'em. Let's cook this dope," as he went straight for my apartment. Then Kevin called me over on the side of my unit and said, "Marcus, look at that office building. They might be looking at us from in there." There was an office building adjacent to the apartment complex, separated by fifty feet and a fence. I replied, "Good looking out with that informant, and you possibly could be right on that office building. I'ma walk over there later and see for myself." A few days later, I was watching a movie with Kevin and Ericka in the living room.

The movie got kind of silly, so I left outside with a couple of the homies. Ericka was on the couch and Kevin was sitting on the chair. I went in periodically to check in on my children. About an hour later Me, Ericka and Tullie were in the living room with everybody else outside and Tullie blurted out, "Boy you like watching movies with Kevin, huh?" Ericka smiled and said, "No!" I thought it was a big joke and I said, "Uh oh, you gonna leave me for Kevin?" Tullie, Ericka and I were laughing. I said, "Kevin ain't got no ride. What y'all gonna be, one of those couples at the bus stop." Tullie said, "Kevin and Ericka sitting in a tree. When he take you to the movies he gonna have to pick you up from the bus stop." I said, "And he ain't got no money, so you gonna have to pay." Tullie and I were laughing very hard. Ericka was only smiling.

About two days later, the whole apartment complex was outside laughing and talking. My real father made an appearance to pick up my kids and take them out to eat. My front door was left wide open, and Ericka was getting the kids ready to go. Kevin was sitting in a chair in the living room and my father was waiting on the couch. Tullie had called me to the side of the building with a very serious look and said something I would never expect to hear in a million years. Tullie said "You know Kevin fucked Ericka, right?" Upon hearing that I felt like somebody hit me in the stomach with a shovel. It took about thirty seconds to respond. I said, "No I didn't know that!" Then I started walking very fast towards my unit. Tullie ran and got in front of me and said, "What are you gonna do, kill'em? Your dad in there. Calm down and just go in there and tell Kevin I want to see him." I didn't respond and I walked into my unit. Tullie was probably praying he didn't hear a gunshot and was hoping to see Kevin come out. When I walked inside, I saw a baseball bat in the living room.

All of my body and mind said pick that up and bash his brains in, but suddenly my father looked at me and said, "The kids ready?" I said, "Yeah dad, let me check." I looked at Kevin and said, "Say Kevin. Tullie wants to holla at you." My impulse was to kill him and my father asking me about my kids made me lose that train of thought. After Kevin walked out of my unit, I went to the door to see where he was going. I could see Kevin met Tullie about thirty feet away from the top of the steps leading to the parking lot. Tullie did all the talking for about two minutes.

Then, I saw Kevin walk away. He walked toward the exit of the complex. Tullie told him he would have to move around. If he stayed here, something bad might happen. Tullie was protecting our friendship but he was also protecting our operation. If I killed Kevin, business would stall for a long while if not for good. Tullie wasn't going to let anything get in the way of our little empire, especially infidelity.

After my father left with my children, I sat on the couch for a few minutes to process what just happened. How could she be so weak, as to do that with a 19 year-old kid, one of my homeboys no doubt? Not only was he not big time, he didn't have a pot to piss in. He had no car, no money. The only thing he brought to the table was muscle. You can replace muscle. It's hard to replace intelligence. He didn't even have the intelligence to be an entrepreneur and sell dope! Tullie and I even told her a few days before that, when we were joking around. He didn't have anything. He was a step above a hanger on and you let him fuck you! To top that off, Kevin is a rapist. I know five girls that Kevin forced himself on. Chubby knows there's more. Little 15 year old Jackie, the other day, ran off when she saw Kevin. It didn't take a genius to figure out that Kevin forced himself on her. He didn't have to force himself on Ericka, my wife. You can't rape the willing. What made it worse is we just had a new baby born March 14, 1997, a little girl named Valerie Voshon Valdespino.

I walked outside and saw Tullie and said, "When did he fuck her and how many times?" Tullie replied, "Dawg! Do it matter? Just know they did!" I said, "Hell yeah it matters! Tullie, I want to know!" Tullie said, "From what I know it was only once and it was early in the morning, after you left to go to your radio show." No wonder Tullie didn't want to tell me. It felt like I got hit in the gut again with a shovel. While I'm trying to make a life for her and my children by going to the radio station, so that one glorious day we wouldn't have to rely on selling crack cocaine for a living, she goes and fucks my 19 year old homeboy, a rapist and a nobody! She got me fucked up.

I charged in the house and went to our room where she was. I shut the door behind me. I looked at her with a very pissed off look and said, "You fucked Kevin?" She looked shocked but also had a look like she knew she been caught. She didn't have words to respond. It looked like she was about to say something, but I didn't let her get it out and I slapped her very hard with my right hand on the left side of her face. I yelled, "You fucked my little 19 year old homeboy that don't have shit!" She started crying and said, "But Marcus!" Again I didn't let her get words out. I slapped her again. Just then, Tullie walked in. I yelled, "Me and Tullie told you the other day he didn't have shit! He's a fuckin rapist. Did you know that! I thought I didn't have to tell you that! I didn't think you were that stupid!" I slapped her again. She was screaming and crying and I slapped her for the fifth time. Then Tullie intervened and said, "Say Marcus, I think she's had enough, dawg. You made your point."

At that point, I walked out and Tullie walked out behind me and shut the door. After that, I didn't care about anything. I was in a daze for a couple of days. I don't know how I functioned on the radio. The next day I was yelling at Ericka and she started crying and called her mother, Mary Wilson. She was on the phone in the kitchen and I was in the living room. She started to tell her Mother she wanted to kill herself and then I heard her grabbing at metal utensils. I walked in the kitchen and Ericka's sobbing on the phone. She had a big butcher knife in her hand and was telling her Mom she wanted to die. Ericka started sinking to the floor with the phone in her left hand and the knife in the other.

I immediately went in there and grabbed the knife and phone. I put the knife back and put the phone to my ear. Mrs. Wilson, who still thought she was talking to her daughter said, "You can't kill yourself over no man. What's wrong with you!" I answered, "Mary she ain't gonna kill herself. I got the knife. She gonna be fine. We just need to talk. Don't worry," and I hung up the phone. About a week later, there was no Kevin in sight. Tullie banned him for a while. Everything went back to normal. The unfortunate thing, though, was that I drowned my sorrows in other women. The next few months I had sex with Jackie's friend, this black woman named Alisha a few times and Carol (Leo's Wife from whom he was separated). Leo and Carol were separated because Leo, and I quote from Carol, "Leo left with that white Bitch!" Tullie told me, "Shit nigga you wanna feel good? Fuck Carol. That bitch will suck and lick you from head to toe."

Tullie wasn't lying. She did just that. Tullie and I also shared these other fine black girls named Angie Miller and Tavon. Tavon was Tionni's friend. Tionni was Chubby's woman. I have nothing bad to say about them. They were good women. They liked me and Tullie. The crazy thing is me and my wife's marital problems was third in the pecking order of my problems. At the radio station I had to know everything about each player in baseball, basketball and football. If I didn't, there would be a problem. That's my responsibility. I had to know everything, or I would look foolish on the air.

Then, the FEDs and SAPD were sending informants into our complex. It was evident they were watching us. We couldn't make a mistake. One mistake by me on the radio, and I would look like an idiot, and my future earnings and credibility and maybe me getting out the dope game was on the line. One mistake by me and Tullie selling dope and we could be in the penitentiary for years. My wife will have to get through what she's done on her own. I have bigger fish to fry.

CHAPTER THIRTY

WHITE GIRLS—TAKE 'EM OR LEAVE 'EM?

IT WAS A nice Saturday afternoon at the Manor, and everybody was kickin it as usual. Most everybody was outside, except for me and Tullie, Phat Cheez and Peanut. The kids and Ericka were gone with Ericka's sisters, Monica and Samantha Thomas. My front door was wide open. This little Mexican man, named Rudy, knocked on the door. I said, "Hey Rudy, come on in. What's cracking Rudy?" Tullie said, "Your wife let you out the house, Rudy?" Rudy offended replied, "Shit, she's with her mom. I can do what I want." We all started laughing. Then it got quiet for a few seconds and Rudy said, "Marcus, I need to talk to you." I replied, "Rudy am I a mirage? I'm right here. Talk."

Rudy started looking around the room and then said, "Marcus, I need to talk to you alone." I replied, "Rudy, we're not close friends, so what you say to me is about business. You see these people in this room? I don't keep anything away from them. If I told them to leave, they might think something is wrong. So whatever you have to say, start spitting it out." Rudy looked puzzled for a moment and said, "I still owe you 20 dollars. Can I get another twenty (dope) and then I will owe 40 on Monday?" I responded, "Rudy, I usually… well, I'll speak for all of us. We usually don't give credit anymore because if muthafucka's don't pay us, we have to go hunt them down and hurt them and it's a big hassle, and sometimes we don't get our money anyway and it's an aggravation we don't need, but we make an exception in your case Rudy because you live here and I know you will pay because you love your pretty little wife and you don't want nothing to happen to her, correct?"

Rudy shook his head in agreement. I pulled out my plastic bag with my dope in it and handed one rock to Rudy and said, "So here, Rudy. I will see you Monday night." Rudy, shaking a little bit, took the rock and said, "Thanks, Marcus I'll be here Monday after my wife cashes her check, before 7pm." I said, "I know you will Rudy."

Later on that night I took my wife and kids to see the Godzilla movie with Matthew Broderick. I left the homies at my house watching the movie The Playa's Club. We had watched that movie so many times it had started to wear out in the VCR. When I got back, there was a cute white girl in the living room with Shawn, Carlton, Tullie, Chubby and Tony. Tullie said, "Marcus, let me holla at you for a minute." We walked outside. Tullie said, "Say we found this white girl and everybody hit already. She could barely take our dicks though. She was squirming and in pain, but she legit though. She ran away from home and she says she is 18. We don't have to worry about that statutory rape shit, and she doesn't want to go home for shit. We going to keep her a while and see what happen." I said,

"What's the girl's name?" Tullie responded, "I think it's Megan. Shit, do it matter?" I replied "All right. Shit it sounds good. Get her to clean our different apartments." Tullie said, "Shit, what you think I'm going to tell her to do." A couple of weeks went by and Tullie sang a different tune. Tullie came up to me and said, "Say, you going to that hotel on Fredericksburg because Mello wants a hundred, right?" I said, "Yeah, I need money too." Tullie said, "Well looka here, Mello and his crew of misfits want the white girl." I told him alright. The dope's a 100 dollars and I will throw the white girl in for 200 dollars, so get 300 from his ass and leave her ass there." I replied, "Do she wanna go with him?" Tullie got kinda angry and said, "Look, the girl doesn't want to go home. She likes to be around niggaz. Do it matter this nigga or that nigga?" I said, "Alright where's she at. Tell her let's go."

Mello was a nigga that used to strictly sell dope. Now we figured out, he started smoking it, getting high off his own supply. Smoke some, sell some. He tryin' to be a seller and a geeker at the same time. Eventually, that shit don't work. As we were riding to the motel, I asked her, "How come you don't want to go home?" She replied, very soft- spoken, "Because my mom hates me and my sister's a bitch." I said, "Why do you say that?" She said, "Because that's the way they are and I don't want to talk about it." I said "Okay."

It was only a seven minute ride from the apartments to the motel. We pulled up and got out of the car. I was familiar with Mello and he was familiar with me and my crew. I didn't think he would rob me and take the drugs and the girl, but I was strapped as usual just in case. Like I have said before, I will never be a victim again. I wouldn't let them take my gun and hold me hostage. I will go down shooting and make sure I kill at least one of them. One of Mello's associates answered the door, a big black, bald man. A very eager Mello said, "Hey Marcus my nigga. What's up?" I said, "Shit, I'm good." I didn't want to waste any time. I wasn't here for socializing. I continued, "Here go two 50-packs and they cut with love. You know Tullie. He ain't gonna do you wrong." He responded, "I know that's right. Ya'll some very fair ass gangster ass niggaz and that's rare." His attention turned to Megan. He said, "OOH. Shit, what have we got here? You look good mama. Make yourself at home. Here go 300, Marcus. I'll holla at you and Tullie tomorrow."

As I was leaving, it dawned on Megan. She wasn't coming back with me. She turned to me and grabbed my arm, didn't say anything and shook her head in fright. Mello noticed her frustration and said, "Marcus, I done already gave you the money, but I don't want no female here that don't want to be here." I said, "Let me talk to her outside." I grabbed her arm and opened the door and took her outside. I said, "What are you doing? Did you think you were just coming for a joy ride?" She replied, "I don't want to stay with them. I wanna stay with y'all. I like being wit you guys. Y'all are funny." I said, "Megan, they don't want you though. That's why you here. I would have taken you home and given Tullie 200 hundred dollars out of my own pocket, but you don't want to go home. You like being around niggaz right? Right. That's your thing isn't it?"

I got no response but a dazed look. I continued, "Well, this a new set of niggaz. Go in there in there and be nice. If it doesn't work out, you know where we at. You can come back. Got it?" She did not object and I didn't wait for a long response. I grabbed her by the arm and opened the door. Mello had a very anticipating look, and while rubbing his hands together said, "Marcus, are we good dawg?" I said "Yeah it's all good. She just didn't know she was comin over here. That's all." Mello replied, "Alright, I'll holla at y'all tomorrow." I shut the door and drove back. I never saw her or Mello again. I later head Mello went to Houston, and had to get rid of her. What does get rid of mean? He killed her? He sold her? It still fucks with me to this day.

A week later there was another white girl that showed up. I thought, "Is it raining white girls?" This one was more beautiful, a blonde, 5'10 and gorgeous. Look, we get our fair share of fine women, but what was she doing with us? She looked like a model. I guess she liked being with niggaz as usual. At this point in time, Tullie got his own place on Lockhill Selma. He bought a brand new, black 1999 Dodge Durango. He hired a guy to sometimes drive him around, Tullie's own chauffeur. Chubby, our resident weed seller, was usually with Tullie. He always kept two crack smokers, Gary and Leo, around to run his errands. I bought a new, black 1999 Nissan Sentra, two big screen TVs and new furniture. Our little empire was a huge success. The new white girl's name was Barbara, but she wanted to be called Barbie. She was great. She cooked and cleaned for everybody. She gave good head and fucked you when you wanted it. I went over to Tullie's one night. All the homies were playing dominoes. I came in and said, "Where's Barbie" Tullie said, "She's in the shower." I said, "Shit, I need some pussy, I'm gonna fuck her right quick." Everybody was oblivious except Tullie to what I was talking about. They were into the game. Tullie said, "Go right ahead." I went into Tullie's room and shut the door. Barbie came out of the bathroom. I had all the lights off. She didn't see me on the bed and was about to go into the living room in just a towel. I said, "Say girl, where you going?" She turned around very quickly and said "Oh my god Marcus, you scared me. I didn't see you." I removed the sheet I was under and had my clothes off and my dick was on hard already. She said, "Wow! You are ready." I told her, "Quit stallin'." She climbed on top of me and we had sex for about thirty minutes.

You could hear noise coming from the living room periodically. They were yelling to each other about the dominoes game, and I remember thinking, here she and I are in this crazy-ass world. I'm 100% sure we probably both had bad childhoods, or we wouldn't be exactly where we are at this point. Two twenty-something year old white kids having sex in a dark room while a bunch of black guys are in the living room playing dominoes. A few weeks went by and, this particular afternoon, Barbie was in the living room with Ericka watching Oprah. Everybody else was outside chillin' and talkin'. About a hundred feet away, I saw a motorcycle come into the complex. It pulled into the parking lot and most everybody was looking at it to see who this was.

After the individual got off the bike and pulled his helmet off, I could see it was a blond haired white man with a medium build. This man looks like he could outrun everybody. He was in great shape. He picked me out of the crowd, and made a straight line right towards me. It's funny because there are about 50 people outside, and I'm the only one that's white and he comes to me. The first thing out of his mouth was, "Hi my name is Mark. I'm looking for my little sister, Barbara. She is about my height. I'm 5'11. She is very cute, with blond hair and blue eyes. Has she been around here or have you seen her?"

I thought to myself, holy shit, he is talking about Barbie and she's in my living room. All the homies that heard him stayed stone faced, as did I. I replied, "No I haven't seen anybody that resembles that and I don't know a Barbara." He took his wallet out and showed me a picture, and the picture was easily her. I was praying she didn't come outside while he was here. I was trying to get him outta here. I took the picture, looked at it and said, "Naw Mark, I ain't seen her man. Have a good one."

He took the picture back with a disgusted look put it back in his wallet and went back to his motorcycle and drove off. I'm so glad I was there to intercept Mark from any of my homies. There are endless possibilities or scenarios that could have taken place, if I wasn't there. I looked at Tullie and said, "Let's get Barbie the fuck outta here. I don't want him coming back and back, driving through here. Then something bad might happen. We definitely don't need that, and he might be just the surface. Somebody else higher up than him might be looking for her." Tullie said, "Alright, what do you wanna do?" I replied, "I don't know. I didn't like the last situation we had like this. I don't want to sell her." Then Vidal said, "I'll take her off your hands. That bitch kind of fine. I'll take her ass with me."

Later on that night, Vidal took her to the Eastside. The next day Vidal returned and said, "Man, you ain't never gonna believe what happen." I was thinking, oh no please, tell me she is alive. Vidal continued, "We were driving in my car, right, and the police swooped up on us with the flashing lights. I had some dope on me, so I stopped on the highway and threw the dope. They didn't even see me throw the dope because there was a hill there. They caught me down the hill. I was running fast than a muthafucka, but you can't outrun vehicles. Niggaz always make that mistake. When I looked back, that white bitch was running too." Vidal was laughing as he was recounting the story. Vidal continued, "I bonded out today for reckless driving, evading police. Like I said, I ain't worried about it. They didn't see no dope. They never even asked me about the white girl. They must have just taken her home." Tullie said, "Shit nigga, you got lucky there was that hill, otherwise you would be stuck."

I was glad it was over and I didn't have to sell her or give her to a new crew. I hope she is at home with her sexy self. I give her brother some props. It takes a lot of nuts for a white guy to go into a housing project where there are a bunch of killers looking at him and ask about his sister. I'm pretty sure he was in the Army because of his tattoos. I bet he is telling her right now, "Don't do anything like that again."

Just as fate or luck would have it, another white girl showed up in Wurzbach Manor for Tullie. Tullie had sex with this Mexican girl and asked if she knew anyone that was down to fuck his homies. The Mexican girl gave him a number. He called and picked her up. Everybody fucked her for about two days. She even made dinner one night. This white girl was also legit. She did whatever we said, but after three days nobody wanted her around anymore. Tullie thought of a couple different crews to sell or give her to. I trusted my homie on many things such as the most important things in my life, my wife and my kids, but I didn't trust him with another human being like her and how he might handle the situation. Somehow, I thought if I left it to him, something would go wrong. She would be either raped or killed and it would get back to us. So if I wanted it to get done correctly, I had to do it and get rid of her myself. I put her in my ride to meet another set of niggaz we had set up. While we were driving, I was thinking, do I sell her or just give her away? Then I thought, hell naw. I will just give her away. I don't want money for another human being. What am I doing? This is twisted. We were driving on Eisenhauer Street when she asked me to stop at the store. I stopped at this little store on the corner of Eisenhauer and Corrine Street. She went inside, and I had a flashback of the white girl I sold to Mello.

I didn't want to have that happen again. I could not do this kind of thing again. While she was in the store, I put my car in reverse and drove off. I guarantee when she came out the store, she was mad I left her. What she doesn't realize is that it was the best thing for both of us. I left her there. She doesn't need to be used and abused by another crew, and I don't need that on my conscience anymore. What happens to most of these white girls is that they might come from a bad home or just want to get out of a situation they have at home. They might be fascinated by the allure of sleeping with black men and the excitement of a certain lifestyle. Once they get in with a crew, they get lazy and complacent. They feel they have arrived and they quit working, no more cooking and cleaning and that's when they wear out their welcome and the niggaz don't want them anymore.

Tullie and I got thrown for another loop.

While Kevin was banned from Wurzbach Manor, he and Chubby would hang out at Chubby's house on Pine Street. Chubby and Kevin grew up together and were very close. Kevin and Chubby got into it with some niggaz from Lock Wood. They did a drive by on Chubby's house one day and shot Chubby up pretty good. They used an AK-47. Chubby was very lucky to be alive. He stayed in the hospital awhile and had a few surgeries. He can't go to the bathroom anymore like the rest of us. He now has to use a shit bag and a piss bag. A funny story to this was a couple of months later, Chubby was trying to fuck this girl in Tullie's bathroom when his shit bag exploded and shit went everywhere in the bathroom. The girl was terrified. After it fills up, you must deposit your feces and put on a new bag. That had everyone rolling in laughter.

But on a serious note, Chubby getting shot really affected Tullie. That was like his little brother. Tullie said, "I'm telling you right now, that's starting to fuck with me. These niggaz think they can just shoot one of my homies and act like it ain't shit! Back in the day, a nigga would have paid all them hoes a visit!

But we got so much shit going on right now, I can't go back to that gang-banging shit! I don't know what the fuck Chubby and dem was doing with those niggaz!" I asked, "It was those niggaz from Lock Wood or what?" Tullie replied, "Man, I don't give a fuck if it was the hardest niggaz in Compton. About three years ago, they would have been dead. Shit nigga, about two years ago they would have been dead."

I responded, "I see what you saying, but no matter how painful it is, we have to keep our eyes on the prize. Ain't no one nigga getting into it with another crew worth fucking up our little empire. That would be like if Nikki Barnes just stop selling dope and became a serial killer. That sounds stupid as shit." Tullie replied, "Yeah, but I tell you what. If we ever, by coincidence, run into these niggaz, there's gonna be a serious problem." I replied, "You know the FEDs is looking at us right now. We gotta be on top of our game." Tullie responded, "Shit nigga, that was the point of the discussion, being on top of our game." With everything going on, I was literally surprised sometimes why my head didn't explode. That's why it was a relief to have sex with as many women as I did. I never drank and did not smoke or do drugs. The women were my DRUG.

CHAPTER THIRTY ONE

WURZBACH'S DILEMMAS

I WAS DRIVING by myself one day on the way to Wendy's, when I saw a beautiful light-skinned black girl sitting at the bus stop. She had on a Wendy's uniform. Her name was Netta. I maintained a sexual relationship with Netta for years, until one day I picked her up as usual, and we went to one of my many spots for such occasions. After ten minutes of really good sex, she began to cry. I stopped and wanted to know what was wrong. After a few minutes she finally told me that she was engaged to an Army guy and what we are doing was wrong. She said their wedding was a month away. I said fine, I didn't finish or pursue it any longer, and I took her home. That is not the first black woman that has cried with me during a sexual encounter. I have had sex with a few black women that have been molested and raped by a family member or a family friend.

It always goes one of two ways. After our clothes are off, I always begin to rub them all over and get them more in the mood, and to my liking. As I'm inserting my penis, they shut down emotionally and begin to cry. Then they tell me their story of what happened to them and who raped them as a child or as an adult. Sometimes it was repeatedly and sometimes once or twice. I had to comfort them and let them know that I'm not that person, and it was not their fault. If they don't want to do it, then we won't.

After I would listen for a while, they felt comfortable with me and began to open up to me. Then we would go on and have great sex. Other times we would already be engaging in hard core sex and about twenty minutes or so in, they would start shutting down and crying. After getting their frustration out and telling me, we would finish and have great sex. Again, I go back to some history with black women. They have endured more hardships than any race of woman in America. The incest, the rapes, being impregnated by men who leave, black children with no fathers at an alarming rate.

It is an endless cycle. After a few one night stands on Friday and Saturday nights, black women feel cheated that they're not getting back the love they put in. That's one of the reasons you see many of those same women at Church on Sunday. They feel JESUS is the only man that they can trust. I admire the ferociousness of black women because when that fighting spirit is channeled in a good way, that's when you have great black women lawyers, doctors and managers of companies.

I had a brief discussion with a white man one day at Walmart. We were at the magazine and book aisle. He was talking to his son about prison populations and that blacks only make up 12% of the country and more than half the population in the prison systems. I interrupted him because, if you know me I call bullshit when I see it and I said, "There are many reasons for that and I don't have time to talk to you about all of them, but don't blame black women who are raising all of these black children."

He had a mad look on his face and said, "Why can't I blame them? I don't agree with their discipline techniques. Every time I see them they're always yelling at their child or hitting them." I replied, "Well sir, with all due respect, you have not seen enough black women disciplining their kids for you to make that assessment. The discipline they employ on their kids is fine. The problem is that most of the time there is no black man there to help in the punishment phase. Black women have to become Mother and Father and that's very difficult, especially when you're dealing with black boys.

Most of these problems stem from the decline of the black man in black families and there are many reasons for that which I don't have time to educate you and your son about." He had a look on his face like who is this white-Hispanic guy trying to tell me and my son about anything? I walked away before he could respond. I got back to Wurzbach Manor and saw the Mormon guys I kicked out of the hood three weeks ago. As I pulled up, Tullie and Vidal were standing outside by Tullie's Dodge Durango. When I got outta the car Tullie said, "There go your boys, Marcus!" I replied, "Yeah I got this!" As I walked over there I heard Vidal say, "What's he gonna do?" Tullie laughing said, "Watch this shit!"

When I got to them they tried to tell me something but I cut that short and said, "Hey didn't I tell y'all not to come through here anymore?" One of the Mormons responded, "I don't think it was us two sir. Is there a problem I can help you with?" I replied, "Yes, there is a problem with one of your founding fathers of your made-up religion. Did you know Joseph Smith and Brigham Young said that if you had sex with a black person, you should be killed on site with no exceptions? "The Mormon kid responded,

"I don't know if they said that, but we definitely changed policy since then." I replied, "I don't care about your policy changes.

The two founding fathers of your religion are racist and disgusting people, so now, since supposedly you changed your policy down here, suddenly up in your fake Heaven those two got morals and changed with you?" They both had puzzled looks on their faces like they wanted to be anywhere else but here. I continued, "So let me get this straight. Your two leaders died with bad hearts thinking brown and black people were an abomination and they changed their filth in their hearts up there because you guys changed policy down here?" They didn't respond fast enough. I said, "Gimme a fuckin break! Ok, let's stay off the race thing. In your religion, you guys believe Adam and Eve were born in Missouri? Get the fuck outta here!"

They quickly turned around and got onto their awaiting bikes. I yelled at them from a distance, "And every time I see you talking to a black person, I'm going to stop and cut that conversation short!" When I was walking back, I heard Tullie laughing and telling Vidal, "I told you he was gonna make them hoes get up outta here." Vidal said, "Marcus you is crazy than a muthafucka. Well I'm up outta here." Tullie said, "They havin' a topless party at BJ's. I think it's Wednesday night?" Vidal replied, "If I have to walk backwards to that muthafucka, I'll be there." Tullie and I were laughing.

About twenty minutes later, the ice cream man pulled up and about thirty kids were standing outside knowing Tullie and I were gonna buy them ice cream. It takes about twenty minutes to get all these kids ice cream. This little fat Mexican kid named Paco was the first to get some ice cream and tried to fool Tullie and went up to the truck again and said, "Tullie, I didn't get one." Tullie said, "Alright hold on, I'll get you one." I noticed what was going on and yelled from a distance at Tullie, "Hey Tullie! Paco already got one, on the first go around." Tullie turned around and looked at Paco who had his shirt off, and noticed he had some ice cream on his body. Tullie said, "Say Paco, you ain't trying to fool nobody. Look at you. You got ice cream on your tittie boy. Get the hell outta here!" Just then this little twelve year-old black girl nicknamed Chicken, came up to the ice cream truck on her roller skates waiting on Tullie to notice her.

Tullie turned and looked at Chicken up and down and said, "You ain't gonna get pregnant before you're sixteen is you!" Chicken, with a disgusted look yelled, "Naw!" Tullie replied, "Okay what kind do you want?" Just then Tullie's girlfriend, Kenny, had walked up and said, "Hey, I didn't get pregnant before I was sixteen. Can I have one?" Tullie, looking at how fine Kenny is said, "Girl you can have whatever you want. You can have this whole ice cream truck if you wanted, as a matter of fact. How much is this truck with everything in it?"

Tullie turned and looked at the Hispanic man in the truck. The man stunned, responded, "I don't know." By then, I walked up and Tullie handed me his ice cream he had been eating and he and Kenny's lips embraced after a few seconds. I said, "Tullie, I will drop this shit right now!" Tullie said, "You can do what you want with it. I got business to attend to." As he and Kenny walked away, I threw his ice cream in the street and got Chicken her ice cream. Later on that night, Tullie's driver and I stayed outside all night selling dope till about 6 am in the morning. It was a Friday night, so I didn't have to go to the radio station the next day. Tullie's driver was selling dope for Tullie and each time a geeker would come in, we would take turns with each sale.

There were a couple of times Tullie's driver would leave and I would get multiple sales. I knew that since Tullie's driver was selling Tullie's dope for him, but had left several times, he wasn't doing his job right, so when he came back, I would give him the money I made on a sale and he would give me some of the dope he was holding for Tullie. This way Tullie wouldn't get cheated. His driver was being lazy and not doing his job and I was tryin to help make up for some of it, so Tullie wouldn't make less money that night. The next night, everybody was outside chillin'.

We were all talking and Tullie said, "I didn't make that much money last night! What happened?" I said, "Neither did I! It seemed like a lot of geekers were comin through but they didn't come with anything significant." Upon hearing that Tullie's driver said, "Shit if Marcus wasn't hogging all the sales last night Tullie, you might have made more." I thought to myself for a second. This silly ass nigga is gonna try and come between me and Tullie? It seems like we just met this fool the other day. I've known Tullie for ten years. Besides, he was lying anyway. I would never prohibit Tullie from making money. That's not in my DNA. Tullie knew that. I looked at this muthafucka and yelled, "Say DAWG! You got me fucked up! You need to stop bumping your gums and quit talking! I would never take any sales away from Tullie! You a dumb bitch!"

Everybody got quiet for a second. I was hot and I was not gonna let this ride. I calmly walked over to him and hit him with everything I had. I almost knocked him down as he staggered for a second. He reached up to his eye and yelled out a man scream and wiped blood away from his face. My mistake was I didn't jump on him right away and finish him off. He recovered somewhat, and started charging at me. He was the exact same size as me, 5'11, 230 pounds. We were both bald. To an observer watching a fight, we looked similar physically, except that he was black and I was white. I started hitting him and he ducked his head and I was hitting the top and back of his head. He almost went down after repeated blows. Then, I felt a pop in my hand. It hurt like hell. When I looked at my hand it was all mushy. I knew I broke something. When I looked down and was checking my hand, he punched me in the nuts. I went down to my knees with my hand throbbing and my nuts felt like they were in my stomach.

He got up and was about to hit me when my boys grabbed him and said, "Naw, not like that!" The next day I went to the doctor and found out I broke my metacarpal on this man's head. Tullie still kept him around as a driver. It didn't bother me though. Tullie knew where we stand with each other. Besides, business is business. We don't let anything get in the way. A couple of months went by and business was booming. Jackie, a girl who lived in the Manor and had just turned 16, somehow found out that once in a while or maybe just by pure luck, we kept dope sometimes in the cabinet.

With my door wide open, nobody noticed her little ass going in my unit to sneak some of Tullie's dope. Once we found it was missing, we conducted an investigation and found out it was Jackie. When we caught up to her a few days later, she got punished. Tullie slapped her a few times and fucked her. She knew better than that shit! She knew she was in the wrong too. She accepted her punishment like a woman. I was proud of her. Once you accept punishment and responsibility, you can still come around. I have never met anyone, and I mean anyone, that Tullie wouldn't slap.

Another month went by and we were making a few thousand dollars a day. Tullie was at my crib, when in comes Jackie and this old white lady, named Sandra. Sandra started talking to Tullie about a bunch of nonsense. She had her arms uncovered and she had all kind of sores all over her arm. There were sores on her mouth. She had blond hair and blue eyes, and was the most hideous thing you want to see. She looked like death. Tullie looked her up and down and said, "Say, a nigga about to eat! Jackie you wrong for this bringing her in here. Girl, look at your arms. It looks like they about to fall off. Get the fuck outta here, both of y'all!" Sandra said, "Oh big boy. It's okay! I don't bite unless you want me to?" Tullie said, "What!" I knew Tullie was hot. She replied, "Just kidding, damn! Here is a twenty, I need a hit or two or three." As she was laughing. Tullie took his dope out and gave her a rock and said, "Now get the fuck on!" Sandra said, "We'll be in touch, Tullie. Bye." Tullie was disgusted and said, "Did you see that shit! A nigga lost his appetite looking at that. Fuck!" I started to laugh and said, "She looked like she had everything from Hepatitis to AIDS. They need to warn us before she come. Damn Tullie, you can't even eat your enchilada plate. I ain't never seen that before." Tullie was shaking his head in agreement.

We were still kind of freaked out about this white man that kept looking at us while we were picking up our food from Nachito's Mexican Restaurant. We thought for sure he was with the FEDs or SAPD. About twenty minutes later, we were standing outside the apartments and we saw Rochelle's boyfriend and his crew running through the apartments. When we saw that, I knew these idiots did something fucked up. A few days prior, these idiots broke into a pawnshop and stole all the guns. They sold us a few of the guns, so I was happy about it. I let my homeboys know now, and a long time ago. You never rob the white man, meaning stores and businesses. They will never forget about it. They will hunt you down like a dog. You have to be smart enough to make your money some other kind of way. Even if you turned your life around 15 to 20 years later, they will knock on your door and take you away from your family forever. I knew these idiots were running to some vacant units.

Thirty seconds later, SAPD was swarming Wurzbach Manor. About fifty feet away from me, I saw two SAPD officers running, with guns drawn, and stopped Sheila's child named KT. I saw KT point and the officers went in the direction KT pointed. About five minutes later, they had all of them in handcuffs and marched them to the squad cars. I heard one of the niggaz in handcuffs yell, "How did you find us!" Then, before he got put in the car, I saw that he noticed one of the SAPD officers acknowledge KT, like he was saying you did a good job little buddy. I watched his demeanor before he got put in the car, and was shaking his head and real pissed off.

I walked up to one of the officers and said, "One of your guys was patting this little boy on the head before you took those fools away. Now they know who told on them when they ran. Now, I might have to protect this little boy!" The SAPD looked at me like, who in the fuck are you and how dare you talk to me about that. He replied, "Don't worry about it!" I didn't respond and walked KT back to Shelia. Shelia said, "What did KT do?" I said, "He told the police which way they went." Shelia looked at KT like he got in trouble at school and said, "KT why did you do that? You suppose to mind your business, boy!" I replied, "It's alright Shelia. He didn't know any better. He thought he was doing the right thing. I won't let nothing happen to him." I looked at KT and said, "Don't worry about it. It's over." A few minutes later, we found out that they robbed the Chinese restaurant Golden Wok, across the street. I told Tullie we might have to protect KT one day. Tullie said, "Yeah we will." KT was scared. He didn't know any better. Shawn and I were happy Rochelle's boyfriend got locked up. Now it was open season on who will get to fuck Rochelle first. The next day, Shawn and I scored a couple of ounces of cocaine and were driving a 1997 Chrysler Sebring convertible. We had just finished getting head at the same time from this Mexican girl. We were actually holding a conversation while she was sucking our dicks at the same time. As we were driving, the topic turned about Rochelle. Shawn said, "Damn I can't wait to put my dick in Rochelle. She got such a beautiful ass, perfect titties. The only problem is she so short. But fuck it. You can't have everything!" I responded. "I don't care if you hit it first. All I know is I'm gonna hit it eventually. Say Shawn, I think this SAPD car has been following us about a mile. Don't look back!" He replied, "What! You gonna have to speed up and turn the corner real quick so I can throw the dope in the bushes. I don't want to spend the next five years in the pen!" I listened to what Shawn said. I sped up a little bit, and went through a yellow light.

I looked through the rearview mirror and a car was in front of the cop car and he got caught at the red light. He quickly turned on his flashing lights and made the car in front of him move out of the way. There was no street for me to turn into quickly enough for Shawn to throw the two ounces of cocaine, so I turned right into a Kentucky Fried Chicken. There were these bushes surrounding the restaurant and Shawn quickly threw the dope in there, as the car was moving. There was an outdoor shopping mall attached to the Kentucky Fried chicken, and by the time I got to the end of it, two police cars boxed me in. They came out with guns drawn.

One of them said, "Get out of the vehicle with your hands up!" The other one said, "What are you running for?" I replied, "Runnin? I didn't see you comin after us at all. We were on our way to get some chicken, when I noticed they were closed." The cop said, "Shut up! Stand against the wall!" They had us against a wall, by the dumpster. Shawn didn't say anything. When you are young and black, that's probably the smartest thing to do. They, the police in America tend to whip up on the minorities if they speak up, no matter how right they are. Shawn had a look on his face like, I threw the dope at the bushes at Kentucky Fried Chicken. They will find the dope and I will be put away for a long time. They hemmed us up for about thirty minutes, meaning they searched the car, they searched all over the ground and ran our names to see if we had any warrants. They handed me my license and told me and Shaun, "Get the fuck outta here!"

We did what we were told. We got into the car and Shawn and I looked at each other and started laughing. Shawn said, "I can't believe they didn't look at Kentucky Fried Chicken! I replied, "You! I'm still in shock they didn't go over there, and that we're driving on our own right now!" Shawn replied, "I was hoping the dope gods were shining on us and Colonel Sanders came out of the restaurant and got the dope and held it for us!" I couldn't reply, I was laughing so hard I almost missed my turn for the apartments. Then it got quiet. Shawn said, "We gotta go back and get it!" I replied, "I was thinking the same thing! If we go back and tell Tullie what happen, he will march back to Kentucky Fried Chicken and get it himself." I went down a back street that led back to the restaurant. We thought, this could be a setup.

The cops leave the dope there and think we're stupid enough to go back and get it, then they apprehend us. They would have been right. We are that stupid. When I got back to Kentucky Fried Chicken, Shawn jumped out of the convertible, grabbed the dope in the bushes and we drove off! We were thinking at any second we would get pulled over. That was one of the longest three minutes of my life, riding back to the apartment. I think Shawn thinks the dope gods are smiling and he might be right, but the FEDs gods were onto us big time. The next day Tullie, and I were at Sonic. We got outside of our vehicle, sat down at the bench and started to order, when Tullie noticed the same white man that was at the Mexican restaurant the other day watching us. Tullie said, "Marcus that's the same white man that's been following us. Dawg, let's get the fuck outta here!" I replied, "Tullie are you sure? You know all white boys look alike sometimes." Tullie said, "Naw, nigga that's him! Let's go!" I said, "Alright!" I didn't want to look at him when Tullie first told me, but when I passed right by him going to the car, I glanced at him. Holy shit! Tullie was right. It was him.

When we got into my ride very casually, you could feel him staring at us. We pulled out of the Sonic and both of us looked through the mirror. I was looking in the rearview mirror, and Tullie the side mirror. To our amazement, we saw him get up and get into his little black car. He pulled out of the Sonic and turned in our direction and began to follow us, Tullie said, "You see that shit! Hurry up and go to the apartments. Fuck!" I said, "Damn Dawg, this is some serious shit!" When we got back to the apartments, we stayed outside awhile and the black car never came in. Tullie and I knew we had to be way high up on the list of wanted drug dealers in San Antonio. You're not going to put surveillance and that kind of manpower on the street for nothing. The crazy thing is, this didn't deter us. We knew we had to step up our game even more, and be careful. It was a race to see if they could catch us, or could we outsmart them and sell as much dope as we could. Usually they catch up to you.

The police had one big advantage over us and that was the element of surprise. We didn't know when they were coming to raid us. We didn't care though. We were having the time of our lives as stressful as it could sometimes be. Tullie and I thought we were invincible, and we were just about to find out how invincible we were.

CHAPTER THIRTY TWO

GETTING RAIDED

TULLIE WAS ON edge most of the time, and for good reason. Ever since the passing of his mother, it was easy to set him off. Now we knew the Feds were getting close. Most people would have felt the walls closing in, but to us it was business as usual. Tullie walked up and told me in a pissed off manner, "Say, I think either Gary or Leo stole some dope from me while I was asleep or fuckin. I'm leaning towards Leo. I don't think Gary is that stupid?" I replied, "I wouldn't put it past neither one of them. You're the one that keeps them around." Tullie said, "I don't want to hear that! Let's take them to my crib. I don't want to scare everybody here." I said, "Okay, let's take two cars." Tullie had his driver, Leo, Gary, and his nephew Tony with him. For some reason, Shawn's girlfriend Ma-Me and Tullie's girlfriend Kenny ended up in the car with me. When we got to Tullie's apartment, he told Leo and Gary to sit in the dining room. Kenny and Ma-Me stayed in the living room. They knew something was about to go down because I told them on the way. Tullie didn't waste any time. Tullie said, "Leo, why would you steal from me!" Leo, with a shocked look like he had been had said, "Tullie I didn't steal anything. What you talkin bout?" Tullie yelled, "Don't fuck wit me Leo! It's either you or Gary, and I don't think Gary is as stupid as you! Gary! Did you take some dope from me?" Gary said, "No, why would I do that? You occasionally gives us some." I said, "Exactly. That's why he's so upset. He keeps you all around and this is how one of you repays him." Leo jumped in, "That's what I'm talking about Marcus. I was thinking the same thing. We wouldn't steal from Tullie!" Tullie interrupted. "Shut the fuck up, Leo! Come here Marcus!"

Tullie proceeded to grab Leo's arms and put them behind his back. I knew this meant he wanted me to punch Leo. I didn't mind doing it. Leo had to learn a lesson, but I was apprehensive because I had just cut off my cast I had on from breaking my hand. I had the cast on for 2 months and the doctor wanted it on for four. When I got up, Leo knew what was coming. I hit Leo with about 75% of force right below his left eye. He was lucky I couldn't hit him with everything I had. I yelled, "That's what your bitch ass get! You know betta than that shit Leo!" Gary chimed in, "Tullie is this necessary?" Tullie yelled, "Gary you betta shut your bitch ass up and be thankful this ain't you. Fuck that! As a matter of fact, you next!"

I hit Leo a second and a third time with about the same amount of power. Leo was wincing in pain and began to yell. "This is fucked up!" My hand began to hurt, but I didn't show it. I was thinking fuck, if I break my hand again I'm gonna be pissed. I told Tullie, "Tullie, let me holla at you for a minute." We went in Tullie's room. I said, "Tullie I'm ready to go. I'ma take the girls back to the Manor. I think Gary and Leo got the message. You have to remember, they're crack heads. That dope is always gonna trump rational." Tullie yelled, "I don't give a fuck! They get free dope, and they get to chill and that's how they do me!" I couldn't tell who it was but either Tullie's driver or Tony said, "Oooh Tullie mad. Y'all fin to get it." Leo started to get up and Tony said, "Uh-Uh-Uh, you ain't going nowhere son."

After Tullie yelled, I didn't respond. I went back to the living room and told the girls, "Let's go!" I told Leo and Gary, "Well, Leo, it was nice knowing you, and Gary you not fin to be left as witness. On your grave it's going to read: Here lie Gary, wrong place at the wrong time!" As me and the girls walked out, they were laughing. Then Ma-Me said, "That would be fucked up if we heard gun shots." They both started laughing. I replied, "Yeah that would be bad!" I didn't think Tullie would kill them. He was just upset and wanted to make a point. I saw Gary and Leo the next day and said, "Well I guess Tullie let y'all make it, huh?" I got no response. They both had dejected but relieved looks on their faces. I went back out and Leo was holding my 4 year-old daughter, Shawnelle. When I walked up, Shawnelle noticed Leo's cut on his lip and she asked Leo, "What happened to your mouth?" Leo responded, "A bad man got me real good. See my eye?" Shawnelle said, "Ohhh, where's the bad man at?"

Leo looked up at me, and I gave him an awkward look and Leo replied to Shawnelle, "That man gone. He ain't comin back." Shawnelle, satisfied with Leo's answer said, "Ok!" and took off running. Tullie was much more caring to crack smokers (geekers) than me and Vidal. I wasn't belligerent towards them just because they smoked crack. I knew they all had former lives, before they fell off and got into this Hell. Gary had been an architect.

Leo and Earl were military men. They told us they were part of the team that got Noriega. Leo worked on Boeing 757s. That is why they were so interested when the U.S. started bombing Iraq in 1998. Tullie was sittin' on aggravated and pissed off as usual. Tommy (Hilfiger) was on the way and nobody had dope but Phat Cheez. Everybody went outside my apartment, but Tullie and me. I said, "Hilfiger comin' with 200." Tullie said, "Shit I know. I guess Phat Cheez gonna get the sale. Fuck, this nigga ain't answering." I knew the nigga he was talking about was our connection to score cocaine.

Just then, Moses walked in. "Hey Tullie. I need to talk to you!" I replied, "Moses, now is not a good time." Moses said, "I know, but I got a proposition for Tullie right? I told you." I said, "Moses. Not now. It's not a good time." At that moment, Tullie grabbed Moses and put a choke hold on him, almost lifting him off the ground. I started laughing, because Moses knew better than that. He saw in Tullie's face that he wasn't playing. I yelled, "Tullie! Tullie! Put him down. Take it easy." Tullie put him down and said, "Don't your muthafuckin' ass hear good! We told your ass. Not now!" Moses was getting his breathing back in order. I said, "Moses you alright? You need to move around and come back later." Moses didn't say anything and walked out. I told Tullie, "Calm down, Tullie. We gonna score in a little while." Tullie said, "I know. I just hate missing money when it come through."

Carlton popped his head in through the door and said, "Damn, what happen to Moses? Shit, anyway Hilfiger here. This fool just pulled up in this big giant pedophile van, nigga. It look like he'll snatch a bitch up and sell them hoes." I told Cheez his buddy was here. That was a joke because for some reason Phat Cheez and Hilfiger didn't get along. Nothing ever happened between them. It's just that Hilfiger likes to talk shit and play around. Phat Cheez is a no-nonsense person. Phat Cheez will play around, but it's not gonna be with a geeker like Hilfiger. Hilfiger walks up and looks at Tullie and says, "What's up Shaq? I got the money."

He was flashing two one hundred dollar bills. Tullie replied, "I don't have it, Tommy. Go to Phat Cheez." Hillfiger looked disgusted and walked over to Phat Cheez and yelled out loud, because he is a clown, "I'm the Hilfiger!" Phat Cheez looked at him and yelled back, "I don't give a fuck." Hilfiger replied, "Hey watch it."I quickly intervened and said,"Tommy what's going on. What's the problem?" Hilfiger said, "I don't like that guy, man. I only deal with Tullie." I interrupted him, "Tommy, let me tell you something. Maybe he doesn't like you either. You're not here to be Phat Cheez's friend. You're here to buy dope. Tullie don't have any right now, and neither do I. So if you want any, you have to get it from Phat Cheez." Hilfiger didn't say anything for about 10 seconds. He had a pissed-off look like he didn't want to go over to where Phat Cheez was. I continued, "What do you want me to do? Go over there and whoop his ass for you?" Hilfiger replied, "Yeah go over there and whip his fat ass!" Just then, it got quiet and Tullie upon hearing that, looked at the Hilfiger with a harsh look. Hilfiger noticed Tullie's disapproval about what he just said and responded, "Tullie, Shaq I don't mean no disrespect." Tullie yelled, "Tommy go over there and score from Phat Cheez or get the fuck up outta here!"

Hilfiger did what he was told right away. Phat Cheez was 200 dollars richer, and Hilfiger left in his white pedophile van. About thirty minutes later, there was breaking news on the television. There had been a school shooting in Colorado, a massacre in Littleton, Colorado, at Columbine High School. One of the reports Ericka had seen said that two white kids started shooting up everybody they came across in their school, and one of the shooting victims was a black kid. The report stated that one of the shooters madea derogatory comment towards the black kid and then shot him dead. I went outside and told Shawn about what had just transpired. He said, "Yeah, them white boys over there are crazy. They will shoot anybody for no reason at all." I replied, "That's true. Whenever you hear about a black or Mexican shooting at a school, he goes and shoots that one person he is having problems with. He don't shoot up all his classmates for nothing." Shortly after this, Sheila and Tammy had a knock-down dangerous fight. They tore up Sheila's whole apartment. It stemmed from years of pent-up frustration from family problems. I intervened, but when they started throwing knives at each other, I told them, "Y'all is fuckin' crazy! Y'all on your own!" and I got the hell up outta there. Later on that night, I stayed with my wife and kids, and Tullie and the whole crew left. About 9pm, two cars full of my homies pulled up. Tullie very hastily got out of the car and said, "Nigga! It was straight out of the movies nigga! They boxed us in! They just searched all the vehicles!" I replied, "Who!" Tullie said, "The Feds, nigga! Nigga, we couldn't go nowhere. I tried to push the gas and this car was in front of me and I couldn't move. I was about to get out of the car and go correct his ass, when all these white boys drew guns at us yelling get out of the car! Nigga, they searched the car, but they didn't find shit. They must have not known I've been dry for a minute."

Carlton jumped in, "Nigga they raided us before that!" Tullie jumped back in. "Oh yeah nigga, they want to catch us with cocaine bad! They left a pound of Chubby's weed on the couch. They went through my whole apartment." I said, "They left a pound of Chubby's weed?" Tullie replied, "Hell yeah! They want us wit dope bad. It's crazy. I'm glad I didn't score now or I might not be here. Thank god for that dry spell." Shawn said, "It's the dope gods." I laughed and said, "There you go again with the dope gods, but I hope you right. Damn, they want us bad than a bitch." Carlton said, "Say it was the Feds. They confiscated all the guns we had, including an SKS. If it was SAPD, we would have went down for them guns." I replied, "What the fuck. They didn't take you down for the guns either! That's some crazy-ass shit! Tullie, you still trying to score?" Tullie said, "Hell yeah! I'ma a little paranoid but a nigga still need to eat!" I wasn't surprised. What else are we all gonna do? Go get a job at McDonalds? Fuck that. They wouldn't take us anyway. We're all convicted criminals. People like us had very few choices or great job prospects lined up.

The next night, our favorite team, the San Antonio Spurs were about to win the NBA Championship. It was Game 5. Everybody was at my apartment. My apartment was filled with my homies. We were about 30 deep. Tullie and I scored 3 ounces each. The geekers were coming all day before the game, during the game and all night after the game. I was in a good mood because I thought I gave a great performance on the radio station, 760 The Ticket, handicapping the biggest game in the history of San Antonio.

It was a mad house at my apartment that night. My brother, Martin Valdespino, came by as well. At that time, I didn't know if my brother knew what was going on. He knew I worked at the radio station and he knew that my homies sold drugs, but I don't know if he knew how deep in I was. It was something we didn't talk about. He also didn't know this nor did anyone except for me and Ericka and my crew: There were so many guns at my house, it was crazy. You couldn't open a cabinet and not find one of my homie's guns there. Tullie and Vidal had a reminiscing moment about Vidal helping Tullie turn all that cocaine into crack. Vidal made the comment, "Good dope sells itself."

My door was wide open as usual. We were all watching the Spurs game vs. the New York Knicks. Moses barged right in. Not knowing the circumstances of the game, he went right up to the TV and blocked part of it and said very loud, "Oh shit, they're hanging in!" Tullie yelled, "Moses get the fuck out of the way!" Moses replied, "Oh shit, sorry." Vidal said, "You got to give it to Moses. He ain't scared of shit. You yell at him all the time and put him in a headlock, and he still come around." I replied, "It's that dope calling. Moses will run through the gates of hell to get a hit." Moses responded, "I'm the Spanish mechanic. I'm not afraid of shit." Tullie jumped in. "I'ma tell you right now. You done worked on your last car if you don't get somewhere else or sit your ass down somewhere." Moses said, "I got 20. That's what I came here for. I got 20." Tullie turned to Cheez. "Phat Cheez, you up." Moses got a rock from Cheez and left. I knew he would be back in a while. Despite all the turmoil with the Feds closing in on us, we had a great time that night. The Spurs won the NBA Championship and me, Tullie, Carlton, Phat Cheez, and Shawn made over 9000 dollars combined in total sharing sales.

The next day, I had a talk with Ericka, and she was a little skeptical about me selling dope when she heard about Tullie getting raided. She knew we were being watched. I couldn't blame her. I was worried too. She stayed by my side, because she knew I wouldn't let her down and lead her down the wrong path. She trusted me in that regard. Earlier in the day, Ericka and I took some guns I had to my father's house. Just in case we got raided and the police took all our guns, we would still have some guns left when I would get out of jail. We did not want to be without guns. My father's house was six miles away, and Ericka swore up and down there was a helicopter following us. I saw the helicopter at my father's house. I thought that it could be for us. That's crazy. Back at Wurzbach Manor, everybody was outside.

I walked down to the side of the apartments where everyone was. Ericka stayed outside by our apartment, talking to her friend Debbie, Moses's wife. When I walked up, Tullie was in the middle of a discussion. "I pay the cost to be the boss around here! Don't nobody do what I do! A nigga don't bar none! Ooh, shit except for that nigga on…what's that movie Marcus?" I knew what he was talking about. I said, "The Professional, that's Jean Reno." Tullie said, "Yeah that nigga. If he was after me Nigga, we really would have to be ready. Shit. Say, Marcus we just finished watching The Player's Club. Damn, Lisa Raye fine. That bitch Ronni might even be finer. It's just something about Lisa Raye, though. I wanna put my dick in her so bad. That's when you wanna get a bitch pregnant, if it's Lisa Raye. Normally you like, hell naw." Shawn jumped in. "Ga-damn Ronni is finer, but I want to put my dick in both them hoes. I'll walk to Africa to fuck Lisa Raye cause she more famous." Tullie said, "You ain't gotta go that far. She in Hollywood."

I changed the subject to our other favorite topic, as we were still feeling the thrill of the Spurs' NBA Championship win. "How bout them Spurs!" Tullie yelled, "Hell yeah! Best team in the NBA. Can't nobody fuck wit us!" I replied, "You know when we got Tim Duncan. I thought he was gonna be like our Kevin McCale for the next 10 to 15 years. I didn't know he was going to be better. He is the best player in the NBA. He is a cross between Hakeem Olajuwon and Kevin McHale." Carlton said, "Yeah that nigga dominant." Tullie reached in his pocket and pulled out a grip of money and with the rap group Cash Money Millionaires blaring from Tullie's car he said, "Look at this. I feel like them Cash Money Niggaz, richa than a muthafucka, but still street. I will never forget where I came from nigga!" At that moment, Tullie was standing on the bench, which made him go from 6'6 to 10 feet. He noticed a bunch of cars coming into the Manor that he had never seen before. Tullie yelled, "Look at all those cars coming in. They ain't supposed to be in here." I noticed the cars right when he said it. It looked like a funeral procession of nice cars, following each other. Tullie yelled, "It's the fucking police, Nigga!"

Everybody started scattering everywhere. I grabbed Tammy by the arm and said, "Tammy, pretend we're just a couple taking a nice walk outside." I couldn't believe how quick they came up on us. It was like they were behind us as well. Out of the corner of my eye, I could see the police making everybody get down. A police officer or federal agent, with a badge hooked to a chain around his neck, jumped out of his car and quickly got behind Tammy and me and said, "Stop! Are you Marcus Valdespino?" I thought about lying and giving a fake name, saying I was Tom James, but they would look at my ID. So I said, "Yes, what's the problem? I'm just taking a walk with my wife." He replied, "You're just the man I want to see, and that's not your wife."

He moved Tammy out of the way and put the handcuffs on me real fast. He took me to his car and put me in the back seat. He drove me to my apartment. I played dumb, like I was taught in the game a long time ago. I said, "What's going on? Why do you have me in the back of your car? This is bullshit." He replied, "Don't play stupid with me, Marcus. You know damn well what's going on." I said, "No I don't." He put the car in park, and walked me into my apartment. Everybody was in handcuffs outside.

It was a huge spectacle. The Feds told the people who were outside, "Go back in your house. We have this under control." I was thinking, Ga-Damn, all those guns in my house. There are about 10 guns in my house and I'm definitely going down for my SKS machine gun. When I walked inside my unit, the first thing I noticed was my kids looking worried, sitting on the couch with Phat Cheez. Ericka was in handcuffs on the other couch. There were 7 to 10 Feds in my house, going through everything and ransacking my house.

They were turning everything over. They didn't leave anything unturned. They even tore up my kid's rooms. The dogs were everywhere, jumping on stuff. Ericka heard themoverturning things and yelled, "Hey, that's our stuff! You are tearing it up!" One of the Feds responded with, "Ma'am, this stuff was probably bought with dope money, so settle down!" Ericka said, "No it isn't. I work!" Ericka was right. She worked at a daycare center with her mother. One Fed came up to the living room and let the dog jump on my 50 inch big screen TV and scratch it up. I yelled, "Say man!Your dog is fuckin up my TV!" He didn't respond. He just looked at me like who gives a fuck. One of the Feds yelled from my back room and said, "Uh oh, what do we have here?!" I yelled,"You don't have SHIT back there. Y'all are planting shit back there!" Don't be surprised about how I was talking to the Feds. I'm fighting for my life right here. This isn't like when you get pulled over by a police officer and you say yes sir, no sir. Fuck that. I've got to speak up.

There was one SAPD officer in uniform, standing outside my door. I said, "Say they're planting shit back there!" He turned to me and said, "Not my problem." I replied, "Well then, what are you doing here?" He said, "This is much bigger than me. I was just told to stand here and not let anybody in or out." I thought, damn this is big. I had to watch my parents go to jail 22 years ago, and now my kids are watching the same shit. I can't believe they haven't found all the guns in the house. I thought to myself, there is no way Ericka was fast enough to get the guns out of the house. I whispered to Ericka, "Where are all the guns?" She whispered back looking confident, "I got them outta here." I replied, "God, I Love You."

I was thinking, I sold my last 50 pack (crack) earlier so I knew I didn't have any dope left, but I knew Phat Cheez had dope on him. He couldn't have gotten rid of it that fast. They came up on us too quick. Phat Cheez looked calm, cool and collected, but I knew inside he was hyperventilating. The Feds must not know about him yet. He had Valerie, my two-year old daughter in his arms, and my other two children, Shawnelle and Marquis, were sitting next to him. He knows for a fact that if the police come up on you real quick and you can't run, you have to hide the dope and put it in your ass. I knew from that moment just by looking at him that Phat Cheez had a lot of dope in his ass.

He looked like a little overweight innocent- looking black kid, but he couldn't take sitting there anymore knowing he could go to jail for many years if discovered. He said to the SAPD officer, "Sir, I'm not involved in any of this. I don't know what's going on, but these kids don't need to see this. Can I take these kids outta here and get them something to drink please?" The SAPD officer pondered that for a couple of seconds and looked at me and Ericka and said, "Can he take your kids outta here?" Me and Ericka looked at each other and said, "Sure." He looked at Phat Cheez and said, "Come on," motioning him to leave. I thought to myself, Phat Cheez did it. He did his best Richard Pryor imitation and played the innocent victim. He was walking out of a raid where there is no dope in the house, and the only dope around is walking out the apartment in Phat Cheez's ass. Phat Cheez used my kids as a bridge to get the fuck outta there. It was pure genius. I don't blame him. I would have done the same thing.

About three minutes later, which seemed much longer than three minutes, the same federal agent that put the cuffs on me came out and said, "Hey, we got you on tape. This isn't going to go on too much longer." I replied, "If you have me on tape, let me see it." He looked at me and gave an evil smirk and said, "Uncuff them." They uncuffed Ericka and me, and as the last one left I said, "Hey, y'all fucked up all our shit. Do we get an apology?" He looked at me as he was walking outlike I was stupid and said, "It'll be in the mail."

Ericka and I looked at each other in great relief. We just dodged a major bullet. When the federal agent said,"Uh-oh, what have we got here. He had a baggy in his hand that had a white powder substance. Ericka as trouble swallowing pills, so she chops up aspirin into pieces that leave a powder substance and that is what the Feds were referring to. Ericka said, "Me and Debbie saw all those cars go to you all down there, and when they made everybody get down, we knew it was the cops so I ran and got all the guns as quickly as I could and put them in Debbie and Moses' house."

I replied, "Wow, that shit is fuckin' awesome, mama. You thought quick as fuck." The mistake the Feds made was that they saw all of us standing outside at a different part off the complex, and they concentrated their manpower on us and left Ericka alone for a couple of minutes. They mistakenly gave her enough time so she could get the guns out of my unit. They should have sent at least one federal agent to my unit where they had a warrant. If they had done that, I would have left with the Feds in handcuffs that day, and not come back for awhile.

About a minute later, I went outside and experienced a sense of relief and euphoria at the same time. The way some of my homies were acting, you would have thought we were heavily favored in a championship game and barely won. We could have just won the lottery, and it wouldn't be better than the Feds driving off and not having any of us in the car with them. I saw Tullie and yelled,

"Phat Cheez had all the dope in his ass and the fuckin' police let him go with my kids!" Tullie replied, "Nigga, they didn't find shit for a third time! Nigga, they even had search warrants for all our cars! While you was in there getting raided, they was going through about seven cars!"

Everybody was outside talking and having a good time. I knew it was party time tonight. Carlton said, "We survived again nigga. We survived again." Shawn had forgotten. He thought he left dope in his ride, and thought he was gonna go down for years. It turned out he left it in Kenwood. We had to pick him up and revive him. He was so relieved. He was as happy as you could get after awhile. Shawn later said, "I told you the dope gods are smiling on us." We did it! Nobody's going to the penitentiary. Tullie was more emboldened than ever.

After this, he thought he was untouchable. You couldn't blame him. One of the most powerful organizations in the United States is after us and they can't get us. I did feel somewhat emboldened, as Tullie did, but I wasn't as excited as he was on continuing in the dope game. I knew nobody else was thinking the same way I was. Everybody else was like, keep the party going. I respect the dope game very much, but the dope game don't respect anybody. I knew it was just a matter of time before I had to quit serving (selling dope). My kids witnessed the whole thing. Marquis was 7, Shawnelle was four, and Valerie was two and a half. I don't want them to ever see that again. I was the only one in that position, to have children present. I had seen it as a child. It wasn't a good feeling.

Sometimes, when people go through life-changing moments, they change their course in life. I have been through many such moments, and I knew this was a major one. I just had to figure out a way to tell Tullie I was out.

CHAPTER THIRTY THREE

FRIENDSHIP

GETTING "OUT the game" I would say, from an emotional impact, is going to be hard on me. I am going to miss being around my homeboys 24/7. From a financial standpoint, it is going to be a strain on me as well. I will now have to get a regular job and sometimes rely on my family for support. Who wants to hire a convicted felon? My total in calculations, for one year, among my homeboys and me from selling crack cocaine was a little over a million dollars in 1999, maybe close to 1.2 million that is a little over 3000 dollars a day. That's collectively split up between 5 and at some points 6 people sharing in total in dope sales. A multi-million dollar single crack cocaine dealer might say that's not a lot, but me and my homies never set out to be a bunch of Nino Browns. All we wanted was to have a couple of thousand dollars in our pockets at all times and our families to not want for anything. Mission accomplished. Remember dope money is not good money. You can't open up a bank account with it. What you do with your dope money is score with it and buy shit with it very quickly.

Dope money runs through your hands very fast. None of us were greedy. We all shared the wealth.

Tullie made more money than any of us but he usually picked up the check at restaurants. We all loved Tullie. I liken his generosity to what we hear about from NBA player, Shaquille O'Neal. I told Tullie one time. What if we did not share dope sales and one of us made all this money? Tullie responded, "Shit that nigga could fly to Cancun a few times and chill for a while." Tullie and I also connected on our love for black women. Tullie used to say, "Shit if I get a basketball scholarship to an all-black college, nigga it would be over for me. A nigga would be swimming. I would never be able to concentrate on my school work." I replied, "My sentiments exactly. Let's not find ourselves in an all-black college. We would be in big trouble talking to different sets of females."

I have known Tullie since high school began for him in September of 1989. We hit it off right from the beginning, and we have had a symbiotic relationship ever since. In the eleven years, I think we have only been upset with each other once. It was when this girl from the Wheatley Courts didn't want to give me any sex because she was on her period, and I thought she was lying. So I didn't want to take her and her friends home, and I left. It turned out, she was on her period. Tullie called and told me he that he found out she really was on her period, but not to worry about it because he found them a ride home. We never really argued. The only time we spent away from each other was when he went to Clarendon Junior College. I didn't like that time when he was away. I missed our camaraderie. I guess he didn't either because when he came back, he never returned back to college.

You can't fake that kind of friendship. It is something I cherish. Like for instance, I'm the only one who can tell him to be quiet in the movie theatre. It sounds like something small, but it's not. He gets on his cell phone at the movies and starts talking loud. There are people around him that want to tell him to be quiet, but they won't because Tullie is 6'6" and 300 pounds . I notice this and tell him to quiet down in a nice respectful way, and he complies for about 4 to 5 minutes. Then I have to tell him again, and this sometimes can happen for a whole movie until he walks out.

It's almost like we are a couple, and neither of us is going anywhere, unless we go the penitentiary or die out. This is not lost on me. It is very special. It seems like we're joined at the hip; we connect on a level most haven't seen. I wish everybody could have a friendship like that. I would have to say Vidal is pretty close to Tullie as well. It's just that he would drift to the Eastside, a little more than we did. I will never forget Tullie and I getting pulled over in my first car, a maroon Subaru, in 1990.

I had a gun in the car, and I hid it in the metal part where you move the seat back and forth. A news crew showed up for some reason. The police hemmed us up for thirty minutes. The cop felt all over where I put the gun, and didn't find it. Tullie and I looked at each other like what the fuck, he didn't find it? Unbelievable. Another time I picked him up from the Bexar County Jail house for serving time for tickets. We weren't a block away from the jail, when this big white guy with a beard walked right in front of my car, and I almost hit him. The guy got really pissed off and hit my car with his hand. Tullie got mad, and was about to get out of the car, when the white man yelled, "What are you gonna do, Nigger!" Tullie turned about as mean as I've ever seen him. Tullie yelled "What the fuck did you just say muthafucka!" Tullie was half way out of the car. I started to drive off, and at the same time with my right arm, I used every bit of my strength to keep Tullie in the car. I was yelling at him, "We can't beat that white man down, right here. We right in front of the jail! We'll be right back in that bitch, if we stop!"

He was yelling at me right back that he didn't give a fuck! I was real upset too. Anywhere else, that man would have been dead, but I knew I made the right decision. I will never forget in 1994 when we were driving on HWY IH-10 by Huebner, and this dark blue Mercedes or BMW or something cut in front of us, and we had to switch lanes real fast. Tullie yelled, "What the fuck! Catch up to that bitch!" Upon hearing that, I pulled up to the car real fast and Tullie was yelling and motioning for the man driving to pull over and get out! I looked over at who was driving, and it was NBA player Eric (Sleepy) Floyd, who was currently a San Antonio Spur. I yelled at Tullie, "Say that's Eric (Sleepy) Floyd!" Tullie responded as only he could, "He got the right name because that nigga gonna be sleepy in a minute when I catch up to his ass! I'm gonna put that nigga to sleep! Run that bitch off the road!" I tried to pull him in front of him, but when he saw we were trying to pull him over, he quickly used his V-8 engine to get away. Tullie was pissed. Good news for Eric (Sleepy) Floyd. He didn't get beat down.

Tullie also didn't like horror movies. When we had them on, he quickly went outside. He would say that Leather Face, Freddy, Jason and Michael Myers were trippin because they waste a lot of good pussy. He said that he wished they would let him fuck them first, before they got killed. He also loved Selena Quintanilla, the famous Latina singer who was shot and killed in 1995. He used to say because of Selena's big lips and big ass, that she had to have black ancestry in her past. One night, a few nights after we got raided, we were up 'til about 3 am in the morning(as usual) when Tullie said he was hungry. I told Tullie, "I got a motto now. I don't eat after 8 pm. It's bad for you." Tullie looked at me like I was crazy and replied, "Fuck that! I got a motto too. When you hungry, you EAT!" Everyone erupted in laughter. Tullie and I got thrown another curve ball we were not expecting. Tullie's older brother, Ronald Green, passed away in August of 1999. It was probably a combination of pill popping and smoking crack, who knows. The bottom line is he was taken away from us way too early.

I pulled Tullie aside one day at the beginning of the year 2000, and told him, "I can't do this anymore." He said, "What you talkin' about?" I said, "Sell dope and hang out with all the homies all the time. My kids saw what happened when we got raided. I can't put them in that situation ever again. Plus, we on the most wanted list. We've been at this shit for 10 years. I'm just tired of it all." Tullie took his time processing my words. He had the look like he had just lost a friend. I continued, "Shit, I ain't leaving the earth. We are moving to these duplexes off Grissom Rd. on 5220 Meadow Rise. You know we be cooking dinner every night; you can come over when you want." Tullie finally replied, "I guess you right. You the only one that got kids in this situation. You a grown ass man. You gotta do what you gotta do." I said, "Alright, I just wanted to let you know first."

When our conversation ended, I noticed a little frustration with Tullie, but it wasn't just about me. Tullie felt the walls closing in. He lost his brother Ronald, Phat Cheez went to go sell dope in the The Sticks on the eastside another one of San Antonio's Notorious Ghettos. Vidal went back to the Eastside for mostly gambling purposes. Chubby, after being shot up, was only half the man he used to be. Peanut (Roy) and Murder1 (Omari) went back to California. The two homies that stayed with Tullie were Carlton and Tullie's nephew, Tony. Carlton is a very competent individual that is college-educated. He just had a drinking problem. Tony was a hell of a fighter, but a hothead. Tony will beat your ass or shoot you. Then, he will not ask questions later, because he doesn't give a fuck about you.

The next few months, I spent more time with Vidal than Tullie. I didn't want to be caught up in any raid, where I wasn't responsible for the dope. Tullie took me up on my offer and would come and eat dinner with us from time to time. Once in a while, he would show me and Ericka six or seven thousand dollars and say, I had a decent couple of nights. Ericka and I would tell him leave some of your money here for us to hold for you just in case something happens. He could have money here in case he needed it.

He could come over, like we were his bank and get money when he needed it. God forbid, if he would get locked up, we would have had the money to bond him out, but he didn't take us up on this offer. He said, "Naw I got it; ain't nothing gonna happen." Carlton, Tony and Tullie would frequent the Northside a lot, selling dope at hotels on IH-10 by De Zavala. Carlton let Tullie know just what I thought. That side of town is predominantly Caucasian. Carlton told Tullie, "We stick out like easily, and it's not just cause we black. Tullie is 6'6 300 pounds, I'm 6'5 255, and Tony is 6'1." Carlton told me that Tullie thought a couple they knew might be informants. So, he had Tony bring them up to a hotel room, and he slapped the shit out of them. I thought, there Tullie go. He still has not met a person he wouldn't slap. I was thinking Fuck! It's just a matter of time before they get caught up.

I called Tullie on more than one occasion, and told him, you can't put no gun in Tony's hand. Tony is not responsible enough to carry around a pistol 24/7. The only time I would put a gun in Tony's hands, is if we were going to war with another crew, not to walk around with. Tullie didn't take my advice. He felt he needed Tony with a gun in case something went down. He thought he had no choice. I knew three different restaurants that Tony robbed. When you do stuff like that, you don't have the intellect or the patience it takes to sell dope successfully. Not everyone can sell dope. To do it correctly and not get caught is an art. Robbers and jackers usually don't have the patience, the hustle and, most of all, the intelligence to sell dope. It is a learned skill. Tony's brother, Phat Cheez, had these qualities. Had Phat Cheez put his mind to do something else other than sell dope, he would have been a big time success. Tony kind of took my place in two aspects. He would carry a gun with Tullie whenever, wherever he wants and he would help him sell dope. I thought these two things would be Tullie's undoing.

CHAPTER THIRTY FOUR

MURDER, AUGUST 2000

I GOT A call from Tullie on a late August night, and he sounded very worried. I have heard Tullie nervous before, but this was different. There was hint in his voice of him being shaken to his core. When I answered my phone, I knew it was Tullie because of the caller ID. I said "Hello." Tullie replied, "Say dawg, Tony done fucked up." I said, "What are you talkin about, he fucked up?" Tullie said, "I don't want to talk about it over the phone, but It's bad." When Tullie said he didn't want to talk about it over the phone, I knew it was either a murder or a robbery. I said, "How bad?" Tullie replied "It's about as bad as you can think." I TOLD HIM, "i CAN THink of some pretty bad shit. You said, Tony fucked up. Is he with you?" Tullie responded, "Hell naw, that nigga on the run!" I said, "Did whatever happen take place at Wurzbach Manor?" Tullie said, "Yes Fuck! I can't believe this shit!" I said, "Are you at the Manor?" d, Tullie replied, "Hell fuck to the naw!" I said, "Good. well I'm not gonna ask you where you at, but so far you told me Tony did something fucked up, and it happened at the Manor. You shouldn't have nothing to worry about. You not at the Manor and you didn't do anything. You said it was Tony. Stay away from the Manor and Tony for a while until we figure out what to do."

Tullie replied, "Alright, I'm a head to my girl's house. Fuckin Tony, dawg fuck! He shouldn't have done that shit!" I responded, "I know, I know. I'll holla at you tomorrow." When I hung up the phone, I knew from Tullie's voice that Tony didn't rob anybody. I knew Tony murdered somebody at Wurzbach Manor or he did both, robbed and killed somebody at the manor. It fucked with me all night. I didn't want to tell Tullie, I told you so. That wouldn't accomplish anything. When Tullie said he was going to his girlfriend's house, I knew it was Tanaporn. Tanaporn is a young pretty girl from Thailand, who Tullie been fuckin with for a few months. The next day I didn't hear from Tullie and when I called, it went to voicemail. Then there it was all over the nightly news and every channel. The newscaster kept repeating: "Suspect Lawrence Bailey, African American male, 6'6, 280 pounds, armed and extremely dangerous. on the run, suspected in a homicide at Wurzbach Manor. He's said to frequent the Medina Base area."

I knew when that message ran across the screen, it was bullshit. Tullie would never lie to me about that. If Tullie had killed somebody, he would have come and told me. He would never put that burden on his Nephew. That is not in his Character. He loves his Nephew Tony, dearly. As much as Tullie wouldn't want to go to the Penitentiary, if he actually did the crime and got caught, he would realize what he had done and sit his time in jail. He would never have his Nephew or anyone else accept that kind of responsibility for something he had done. The Lawrence Bailey(Tullie) story ran every day for six straight days on the nightly news. I was worried as fuck. I needed to know the details of what happened. Finally I got a call from Tullie. He,

Phat cheez, and Phat cheez's mother, Bonnie Kaye wanted me to go to SAPD Headquarters with them. Tullie is going to turn himself in. I thought, good. He didn't do anything. He can tell them what happened and clear his name. Tony will just have to be on the run then. When you take another human being's life, you must be prepared to be on the run, and live a life of obscurity, always looking over your shoulder.

That was his choice. If you have the heart to pull the trigger and then if you get caught, you gotta have the heart to do the time. When I saw Tullie in the parking lot, he looked nervous and as mad as the way he sounded on the phone six days ago. I said, "Before you go in there, tell me what happened." Tullie said, "Look, this geeker always comes into Wurzbach Manor in his Dooley truck. His name is Puff Daddy cause he puff a lot of crack. His real name is Dewayne or some shit. This nigga done stole from me a couple of times. Tony caught up to his ass, and we beat his ass one time. Then, this fool stole from us again, and Tony caught up to him, but he ran again, and Tony was tired of chasing him, and shot his ass." I said, "You didn't order no hit right? You didn't tell Tony to shoot this fool?" Tullie replied adamantly, "Hell naw nigga! I would have told you that shit! I'm not gonna shoot no sorry ass geeker. What I look like? We already beat his ass. Tony just fucked up! Nigga, I stayed wit Puff Daddy til the ambulance came." I believed Tullie completely, so did Phat cheez, and Phat cheez's mother, which is Tony's mother, Bonnie Kaye. I said, "Okay, go in there. look them in the eyes, and tell them you didn't do it. Tell them you stayed with that man until the ambulance arrived. Tell them you heard the shot, or shots obviously, because you went out there, and was with him almost the whole time. If they ask you, who was with you, or if they mention Tony by name, just say, I don't know where he is at. You don't know. You didn't see who shot that man. You heard shots, and came outside and there Puff Daddy was, and you stayed with him. You was the last person he saw before he took his last breath. If they ask why you eventually left, tell them you was scared because you thought the police might try to pin the murder on you, and that's exactly what y'all might try to do. Now be adamant. you didn't kill nobody, which is the truth."

Tullie did not respond. he just looked upset. Bonnie Kaye said, "Marcus, I'm gonna go in there with him." I said, "Okay, we'll be right here." About 30 minutes later, Bonnie Kaye came outside without Tullie. She walked right up to me and Phat Cheez and said, "They kept him. Marcus, Tullie didn't look right. He looked sick. I've never seen him look like that before." At that point, I knew they were gonna hold him until they found Tony, and get his story also. It was a very somber ride back to Kenwood. Nobody said a word until Bonnie Kaye said, "Marcus, I don't feel good about this situation at all." I replied, "Neither do I Bonnie Kaye, Neither do I."

A few days later, the worst case scenario you could think of happened. The police got Tony to say it was Tullie who pulled the trigger, so Tony could get less time. Everybody in their family knew this was a lie. All our homies knew this was a lie. I could not have imagined the heartache and disappointment running through Tullie, when he found out his own nephew would testify against him, stating that he had pulled the trigger. You have to understand, Tullie has been a big time dope dealer for the better part of a decade, As have I. They could never pin anything on us. So when this murder situation came around, it was a perfect opportunity for them to get Tullie off the streets for a long time. Tullie was a drug kingpin. They really don't want Tony. He is a small player in the grand scheme of things.

The detectives are no joke. I could just picture it. They probably threatened Tony with life in prison if he didn't tell on his uncle, a Drug KingPin. Tony probably was scared and they possibly coerced him into saying it was Tullie. Tullie will be the first to tell you he is not generally an innocent person and neither am I. Tullie will accept responsibility for anything he has done, but he didn't kill Dewayne Marquez! An Innocent man is in jail! Not innocent of the dirt that he's done prior to that incident, but innocent of murder, YES! I hope the Marquez family knows this! If it were my son, I would want the man or woman who actually made a conscious decision to pull the trigger and murder my son to do the most time for that crime. I wouldn't want my son's death to be involved in any kind of craziness like this: we could never get Person A (Tullie) on drug charges for 10 years, so let's get Person B (Tony) who actually pulled the trigger to turn on Person A(Tullie) so we can get him off the streets for a long time and Person B(Tony) who committed the murder, will get just a few years. Fuck that! You should live in truth, Not schemes, or possible coerced testimony!

As you can imagine, this destroyed a good family. Tony's mother has little communication with her siblings anymore because she sticks by her son. Tullie and Tony's family knows the truth, and that truth is that Victor Bailey (Tony) killed Dewayne Marquez. Lawrence K. Bailey was sentenced to 30 years in the Texas Department of Corrections for the murder of Dewayne Marquez. Victor Bailey (Tony) got a few years as an accomplice. It should have at least been the other way around. The beautiful thing in this was Tullie's heart for his family. He still loves his Nephew, as do I, and he has forgiven him.

For all the parties involved, including the deceased, one mistake and you can disappear forever, especially living this lifestyle we all lived. Did Dewayne Marquez deserve to die? No! But he was not some innocent victim that didn't know what he was doing. You take responsibility for your actions. You know when you go into a ghetto or housing project and steal dope from dope dealers and killers, anything can happen. This is to all of us involved in this cycle of shit. We all signed up for this. If you don't stop, the streets will eventually reach out from the grounds of hell, and snatch you up! In the ghetto when you come out of the womb and most of your family is selling crack or oncrack or incarcerated, what are you going to do? Most of the people I knew were products of their environment.

I got out of the game before the game got me. I am very fortunate. not everybody can do this. Some people, no matter what race they are have no other outlet. They're born in it. They are going to die in it. I left because I have a good family. others don't have that luxury. I love my children too much to keep doing what I was doing. I don't know if I could have seen my children visiting me only occasionally, in the penitentiary, for years. The hell with that! I was torn because on one hand I'm very happy to be home with my wife and kids, and I don't have to worry about when the feds or the police are going to come and take me away. on the other hand, I hurt every day for my homeboy. Part of me feels guilty because, had I not gotten out the game, I would have been there and Mr.Marquez would not have gotten shot because I would have had the gun, not Tony. We would have just beat his ass real good. I got home real late that night, and Ericka and the kids were asleep, so I had to wait and tell Ericka the bad news in the morning.

A few weeks later I started to bar-b-que one Saturday afternoon and while the meat was on the grill cooking, I took a quick break and sat on my couch. My three children ran up to me and attacked me. While I was playing with them, my eight-year old son Marquis stopped and said, "Hey Daddy. is Tullie coming over?" I replied, "No son. He is going to be gone for a while. He's gonna come back when you get bigger and stronger." Marquis replied, "Daddy are you gonna go with him?" I got a little emotional and hugged all three of my children simultaneously and said, "No son. I've got to stay here and watch you guys grow up. Daddy is not going anywhere." Marquis replied happily, "Okay Daddy. That's great!"

EPILOGUE

PRETTY MUCH FOR the better part of the ten years from 1991-2001, my crew and I had no opposition. It's not that we were the most feared organization in San Antonio, but if you ran into any of us you would know we don't play around. It's the fact that we didn't engage in any foolishness. I didn't allow it. There were plenty of times I used to reel us in, and say, no let's not do that. Tullie had a famous motto he uttered from time to time, "Don't start none and it won't be none, but if it comes your way, don't talk about it be about it." We all lived by that creed for 11 years, from 1991-2001. When me and my homies watched movies like Menace II Society and Belly, we used to think, "Hell Yeah nigga. That's us up on the screen, just smarter." I wrote this book because I'm tired of having all these thoughts roaming around in my head. I had to get them out, and make sure what Tullie, Vidal, my other homies, and I went through for eleven years meant something.

When I got out the game, I used to have nightmares from 2002-2005. Some of the nightmares would be about if I had not been there, and what would have happened to some of my homeboys? They might have reached the penitentiary sooner. Another nightmare would be about me getting shot. I'd wake up and think my stomach was on fire. I'm still amazed I never got shot. I don't have those nightmares anymore. It's funny how the human brain knows you're far removed in years from those situations. I have to give my wife, Ericka credit. She started telling me in 2005 to start writing everything down that I went through. I didn't take her up on it, until a few years later.

I still can't believe two things. One is, I don't have the AIDS virus. I have slept with over 400 women. That's not even comparable to two of my homeboys, Pierre and Vidal. In 2009, we were standing in front of the Player's Lounge, off Rittman Road, and Pierre and Vidal were talking about how many women they have slept with. Vidal and Pierre both admitted they have slept with more than 2,000 women, give or take 100. When I told them my number was 400 and something, they both laughed at my number and Vidal said, "That's right, Marcus sometimes tried to be the Family Man." I once watched Vidal have sex with six women in one day, two of them in a bathroom. My record is five in one day. Tullie, before he got locked up, was fast approaching 500 girls.

The other thing I can't believe is that I never went to the penitentiary. Every person I dealt with for an extended period of time, from 1991-2001, had at least one stint in The Pen. Most of them are either in the penitentiary right now or dead. I used to feel guilty about that. I did as many fucked up things as they did. Why am I not in the penitentiary, and they are? Finally, I know I caused a lot of pain on people during my time of craziness, so I am truly sorry from the bottom of my heart. I don't like all the things I've done to get where I am today. If I had to do it all over again, I would have joined the Air Force after Marquis was born, and with my intelligence and other skills would be thriving right now.

Other than that, I don't have any regrets. I wouldn't change a thing. I love the person who persevered through my journey. I love who I am today.

From 1973 to 1980, my childhood was crap. From 1981 to 1989, I got structure, discipline, love, and best of all my intelligence from my grandparents Joe and Gloria Valdespino. From 1990-2001, I basically strapped myself in with my homies, and went for a wild ride of terror, heartache, and fun. People would often ask me at family events: Why don't you smile? You never smile. Why do you always look so mean? Now you know.

POSTSCRIPT : WHAT HAPPENED TO SOME OF THE KEY PLAYERS IN MY STORY?

- Lawrence K. Bailey- Convicted of murder in 2000. Will be released in 2015.
- Vidal Sauls (Sugar Bear)- Convicted of gun and drug charges. Will be released in 2018.
- Joe L. Bailey (Phat Cheez)- Convicted of drug charges. Will be released in 2018.
- Adrian Hilliard (Mugsy)- Was shot at Santa's Place Bar, died of wounds, sustained by gunshots.
- Victor Bailey (Tony)- Has spent most of his adult life incarcerated. Still surviving in the streets.
- Devlin Jefferson (Baby Tyson)- Currently in Penitentiary.
- Omari Crawford (Murder 1)- Whereabouts unknown.
- Roy Crawford (Peanut)- Whereabouts unknown.
- Chris Kelly- Currently out of Penitentiary.
- Carlton Wilson- Currently out of Penitentiary and a productive member of society.
- Jamal Montgomery (Chubby)- Currently in Penitentiary.
- Lester Kyle (Puka)- Currently out of Penitentiary.

- Henry Toscano- Currently out of Penitentiary.
- Shawn Thorton - Currently out of Penitentiary.
- Charlie Pryor- Recently was shot but has made it through.
- Pierre Johnson- Probably having sex right now or about to have sex or just finished having sex. LOL.

ACKNOWLEDGMENTS

First, I would like to extend my devoted thanks to Ron Chepesiuk and his staff at Strategic Media Books. Ron took a chance on me and gave me the opportunity to start on a new career. A thanks to Patty Amick and Joe Mark Valdespino for giving me life. A special heartfelt thanks to my grandparents, who became my parents, Joe M. Valdespino and Gloria F. Valdespino, and for putting up with all my baggage.

A special thanks to all my siblings Greg Valdespino, Robert Valdespino, wife (Brenda Rolon), Vincent Valdespino, Anne Valdespino, Edward Valdespino, Adrienne Valdespino, Valerie Valdespino, Lorraine Valdespino, Joanne Valdespino, Penelope Valdespino. A very special thanks to my brother and best friend Martin Valdespino, who I could always lean on for anything. Thanks also to Martin's daughter, Anastacia Valdespino, and to the Canestaro Family.

A thanks to my friends John McClendon, who has listened to my crazy life stories since 2006, and to Myeshia Holt and children Sarai Love, Trinity Johnson, Jeremiah Johnson, and Matthew Johnson. Thanks to my friend Karl Muhammad (Britt) for showing me The Honorable Minister Louis Farrakhan. I became a better man as a result.

And finally, to my wife and children, for without them I would have had no desire to stop selling drugs and ended up in the penitentiary or died in the streets. They are wife Ericka Wilson, son Marquis Valdespino and daughters Shawnelle Valdespino, Valerie Valdespino and Destiny Adams.